AF573725

English Cookery New and Old

English Cookery New and Old

Susan Campbell

Published by Consumers' Association and
Hodder & Stoughton

English Cookery New and Old

Published by Consumers' Association,
14 Buckingham Street, London WC2N 6DS
and Hodder and Stoughton,
47 Bedford Square, London WC1B 3DP

ISBN 0 340 26630 9

Edited by Sarah Wright
Design by Tony Garrett
Cover drawing by Ken Cox

Typesetting by Tradespools Limited, Frome, Somerset
Printed by Hazell Watson & Viney, Aylesbury, Bucks

Also by Susan Campbell:

Poor Cook (with Caroline Conran) Macmillan, 1971
Family Cook (with Caroline Conran) Macmillan, 1972
Cheap Eats (a London restaurant guide) Penguin, 1975
Guide to Good Food Shops (Macmillan), 1979 and 1981
Cook's Companion (Macmillan), 1980

Contents

Acknowledgements

My acknowledgements go to:
Sarah Wright for her patient editing and her encouragement, and to other members of the Good Food Guide staff, Nora Carey for her research and assistance in trying out recipes, Julia Walker for her typing, Wendy Smith of the National Federation of Women's Institutes for her assistance with research and help with recipe books, Dick Margetts (Fisheries Research Laboratories), Mr H. Fleck and Mr C. Rookard (Clare College, Cambridge), the British Farm Produce Council, the Catering Manager (Trinity College, Cambridge), the Stilton Cheesemakers' Association, English Tourist Association (A Taste of England), the Fruit Department, R. H. S. Wisley, Mary Adams (British Turkey Federation), F. Marshall (Federated Deer Control Society), George Daniel (Colman's Mustard), Miss Lawrence (Silver Trout Farm, Romsey), Mr & Mrs Haslam (Miners' Arms, Priddy), Shirley Webster-Jones (Cheese Shop, Oulton Broad), Jordan Stern (Sunwheel Foods), Walter Coe, Mr & Mrs Lane, June Andrews, Charlotte Hancock, Roger and Brenda Cheshire, Renee Nash, Jane and Graham Young, Phyllis Pearn, Alice Gillett, Mrs Blackmoor, Mrs Dazzard, Vera McCauley, Mrs Alderson, Kit Calvert, Barbara Johnston, Norma Uttley, Mrs Porter, Peter Gott, Alan Goodland, Margaret Willmington, Mr & Mrs Lambert, Mrs Avison, Mrs Lunn, Mr & Mrs Stirton, Mrs Stoney (junior and senior), Helen Weatherall, the Everett family, Lionel Keedwell, Monica Martell, Mary Fitt, Felicity Kerr, Tim Denham-Smith, Stephen Marsh-Smith, Michael Paske, Derek and Moira Kelly, Jo Pattrick, Steve Hatt, Mr Harding, Philip Oakes, Patrick Rance. Illustrations supplied by J. H. Nelson & Sons (Bakewell), T. Appleton & Son (Ripon), Edis of Ely, H. E. Swarbrick Ltd. (Ormskirk), Ingles of Harrogate, The Granary (Truro), Rubber Stereos (Avon) Ltd, and J. W. Rigby & Sons (Gloucester).

Susan Campbell, July 1981

Introduction

Many cookery books on the subject of English food already exist, but in spite of this I began to collect the recipes for this book with the feeling that there was much more to be discovered. For one thing I wanted to find out how much of our traditional cooking still survived and how well we were assimilating new influences.

Underlying this was the knowledge, from my work on the first two editions of *The Guide To Good Food Shops*, that there were still many places in this country specialising in regional English food, some of them taking it so much for granted that they didn't even realise it *was* regional. You can go to Durham or Northumberland and find stotty cakes, to East Anglia for baked latchett and Suffolk rusks, to Gloucestershire for elvers and Oldbury tarts and to Devon for chudleighs and laverbread, and in spite of the relatively small size of this country it is most unlikely that these things will turn up anywhere else. But if you express interest or surprise at these local specialities the vendors are often amazed at you in their turn.

I knew, too, that our country is capable of producing some of the best raw materials for cookery on this earth. Fruit, fish, meat and vegetables can all be superlative (what happens to them on the way to the consumer, and what the consumer does with them in the kitchen is another story). Indeed some of our best products, notably beef and lamb, lobsters and other shellfish, game (in particular venison) and salmon, both fresh and smoked, are exported at such a pace that we are lucky to get even a sniff of some of them for ourselves. The plain truth is that foreigners are willing to pay more for such things than we are.

As for the present – modern, intensive farming and horticulture, plus the freezer, have made much that was seasonal in the past available all the year round, and much that was once grown only abroad can now be grown here – sweet-corn, green peppers and aubergines, for example. All the same, if I have kept imported food out of the recipes as much as possible, in an attempt to make the book properly English, I have not totally ignored foreign cookery, particularly in recipes where foreigners make better use of our native foods than we do. Nor have I been so nationalistic as to leave out basics such as rice, dried fruits, spices and flavourings that the English have imported for generations.

The book is divided into twenty menus, which might be described more accurately as recipe collections. Each 'menu' is designed for a different occasion of the sort that occurs in the 1980s. Some of them may be traditional, like St Valentine's Day or Christmas; others are new, like the barbecue or the wholefood menu. They are sometimes seasonal or regional as well and some are for breakfast, some for lunch or dinner and some for tea. It is obvious that you will have to pick and choose the dishes you most like the sound of from each collection, rather than cook the whole lot.

I have also had to adjust many of the more filling or extravagant traditional recipes to suit our contemporary way of life. I don't think most modern families have the great appetites that they had in England two hundred, one hundred or even fifty years ago. Some of us do still sweat and toil in the fields or down the mines, but more of us lead less energetic lives. Although electrical gadgets and food processors in particular have done much to lessen the work in the kitchen, we are no longer waited on by armies of cooks and skivvies. With this in mind I have tried to keep the recipes as simple and undemanding as possible, both for the cook's sake and for that of our digestions.

Susan Campbell

SPRING

Breakfast for a long day ahead
An Easter lunch in Gloucestershire
An early Spring picnic in the South-West
Dinner for Shrove Tuesday

Breakfast for a long day ahead

Barbara's good start to the day
Saffron or hot cross buns
Cheshire potato cakes
Wholemeal scones
Staffordshire oatcakes

Ways to cook eggs
Buttered eggs

Bloaters and kippers
Poached haddock
Fried or grilled herrings
Fried sprats
Dredgerman's breakfast (oysters and bacon)
Fish-cakes
Kedgeree
Bloater paste

Laverbread
Devon potato cakes, and bubble-and-squeak
Dock pudding or Easterledges pudding

Herb sausages and variations
Lambs' fries
Kidneys, grilled and devilled
Kidney toast
Black puddings

The modern breakfast is a modest affair with muesli, fruit juice and coffee and possibly, if you feel really hungry, a boiled egg, with toast and marmalade to follow.

It used to be a glorious feast and was, for those with servants, the only informal meal of the day. The sideboard would be laden with the sort of food that could be kept warm on hot-plates and needed no assistance in the serving of it; 'We can pick and choose what we fancy,' wrote Countess Morphy in 1936, '... in peace and quiet.'

Possibly we would all eat bigger breakfasts today if someone else had got up before us and left a choice of porridge, cereals, stewed fruit; bacon, sausages and eggs; tomatoes, mushrooms and kidneys; grilled herrings, kippers or bloaters; kedgeree; fried sprats or sole or plaice; cold ham, cold game or raised pies; potato cakes, scones, oatcakes and toast; marmalade and honey ...

Nor was this choice the prerogative of those with servants; before the war a working man could go to one of London's famous Dining Rooms, and find much the same menu for breakfast, all laid out on a side table with a white cloth. He could drink beer with it too, or else tea.

It is a good idea to have a cooked breakfast, especially if you have a long, energetic day ahead; anything from the following menu would do well. There is, too, a lot to be said for the way breakfast can dispose of left-overs, if they are made into fish-cakes or bubble-and-squeak. This is also a suitable menu for that hybrid meal that happens at weekends and on holidays and is called brunch.

Barbara's good start to the day

My friend Barbara, who lived in Derbyshire, was sent off to school each morning with this inside her: a raw egg beaten with the juice of an orange and a spoonful of brown sugar.

Saffron buns *(makes 12–18 buns)*

These are a plainer, East Anglian variation on the well-known hot cross buns. They are made in the same way but they are oval, and flavoured with saffron, cinnamon and lemon rather than with fruit. Saffron was grown extensively at Saffron Walden in Essex.

1	small packet of powdered saffron	1
285 ml	warm milk	just over ½ pt
15 g	fresh yeast (or half quantity of dried)	½ oz
75 g	sugar	3 oz
10 g	butter	¼ oz
600 g	flour	1¼ lb
	zest of one lemon	
	cinnamon	
	pinch of salt	

for the glaze

one 15 ml sp	sugar	1 tbsp
one 15 ml sp	milk	1 tbsp

Steep the saffron overnight in a little of the warmed milk.

Next day prepare the yeast by creaming it with a spoonful of the sugar and a little more warm milk. Rub the fat into the flour, add the rest of the sugar, the lemon zest, cinnamon and salt. When the yeast mixture is frothing, combine it with the saffron-flavoured milk and the remaining milk, warmed to just above blood heat, and add it to the flour. Knead it well and allow it to double in size. Knock it down, and form it into about 12–18 oval buns. Prove them on greased baking-sheets while the oven is heated to 200°C/400°F/gas 6.

Mark the buns with crosses, using a sharp blade. Bake them for 15–20 minutes, then brush them with the glaze. Return them to the oven for two minutes, to set the glaze.

To make fruited hot cross buns, add 100 g/4 oz currants, 25 g/1 oz candied peel and 1 egg to the above mixture, and make the buns round rather than oval. Bakers mark the cross with a runny paste made of 25 g/1 oz fat rubbed into 50 g/2 oz flour, mixed with 50 ml/2 fl oz water.

Cheshire potato cakes *(makes 24)*

These are more scone-like than the Devon potato cakes (page 18). Prepare them the day before and cook them in the morning. They are made with buttermilk or the whey from curd cheese (page 113).

500 g	warm boiled potatoes	1 lb
150 g	plain flour	6 oz
15 g	butter	½ oz
	pinch of salt	
	buttermilk or whey to mix	

Mash the potatoes and mix in the flour, butter and salt. Add enough buttermilk or whey to make a firm dough, working it in with a wooden spoon. Roll it out on a floured board to about 0.5 cm/¼ inch thick and cut it into rounds about 9 cm/3½ inches across.

Fry them in butter or bacon fat or on a greased griddle.

Wholemeal scones *(makes 12)*

These are quick to make if you are out of bread, and can be made with white flour as well.

50 g	lard or butter	2 oz
500 g	wholemeal flour	1 lb
	pinch of salt	
half 15 ml sp	cream of tartar	½ tbsp
half 5 ml sp	bicarbonate of soda	½ tsp
1	beaten egg	1
250 ml	buttermilk or sour milk	½ pt (scant)

Preheat the oven to 200°C/400°F/gas 6.

Rub the fat into the flour. Mix in the salt, cream of tartar and bicarbonate of soda. Add the egg and enough buttermilk or sour milk to make a soft dough. Roll it out lightly and cut small rounds about 6.5 cm/2½ inches across and 2.5 cm/1 inch thick.

Put them on a baking-sheet and bake them for 20–30 minutes.

Eat them split open with butter and honey or marmalade (page 251).

Staffordshire oatcakes *(makes 12)*

These are not the hard, dry, crisp, biscuit-like oatcakes made in the North of England (page 145); they are a Midland version, soft and floppy, more like pancakes, and made with a batter of oatmeal and yeast. You find them on sale in great heaps, in bakers' shops, and in butchers' shops too.

In the Potteries there are, or were until recently, many bakeries with huge iron hot plates or bakestones, big enough to cook a dozen oatcakes at a time. They are eaten for breakfast and are delicious with anything fried. You can cut them into pieces, or use them as an envelope for bits of bacon, or roll things up in them. At the Victoria Theatre, Stoke-on-Trent, they are sold with a variety of fillings, rather like Greek pittas or Breton crêpes (chicken and chutney is especially recommended).

250 g	fine oatmeal	8 oz
250 g	plain flour	8 oz
two 5 ml sp	salt	2 tsp
425 ml	milk	¾ pt
425 ml	water	¾ pt
15 g	fresh yeast (or half quantity of dried)	½ oz
	lard for frying	

Combine the oatmeal, flour and salt in a large bowl.

Warm the milk and water together to blood heat. Cream the yeast with a little of the warm liquid. When it is frothing, stir it into the flour and oatmeal mixture with the remaining liquid (the mixture will be very runny).

Cover the bowl with a tea towel and leave the mixture to rise for about one hour, or until it has doubled in bulk.

Make the oatcakes like pancakes, using a large frying-pan or a moderately hot griddle. Fry each side in lard for about three to four minutes or until they are golden. Keep the cooked oatcakes warm in a folded cloth.

To reheat the oatcakes, pile them on one plate, cover them with another and put them in a moderately warm oven – they will come out all hot and steamy.

They will keep for up to a week in a cool place, well wrapped in a tea towel. Keep the tea towel damp if you are eating them the same day.

Ways to cook eggs

Eggs can be boiled, fried, scrambled or poached for breakfast; all these ways of cooking them are too well known to be described here.

Scrambled eggs lend themselves well to variations – the addition of a little cream towards the end of their cooking, or a few flakes of cooked, left-over fish such as salmon or smoked haddock, is very tasty. So are strips of crisp fried bacon, pieces of smoked salmon, grated cheese or asparagus tips, mixed in just as the eggs are thickening.

Boiled eggs are good eaten with cold ham, thin slices of very mild cheese, radishes and watercress.

Eggs can also be baked in cocottes over a bed of chopped ham or a puree of smoked fish mixed with a little cream.

Buttered eggs

Metric	Ingredient	Imperial
6	fresh eggs	6
25 g	butter	1 oz
	salt, pepper	
	breadcrumbs	

Preheat the oven to 190°C/375°F/gas 5.

Use some of the butter to grease a small, flat, fire-proof dish. Break the whole eggs into it and season them. Cover them lightly with a few breadcrumbs and dot with the rest of the butter. Bake the eggs until they are just set, then finish the dish under the grill to brown the crumbs.

Smoked fish

For bloaters, see page 163; for kippers, see page 110.

Poached smoked haddock

The best haddock for serving in a piece is filleted before smoking. Choose a nice fat fillet; it will have been dyed yellow but this doesn't affect the flavour – it is merely cosmetic. What is important is that is should smell of smoke; if it doesn't it is probably only dyed and salted. Smoked cod is equally good and is smoked in fillets like haddock. Smoked haddock on the bone, looking like a little honey-coloured kite, is the kind to buy for dishes in which the fish is to be flaked after cooking (see the kedgeree overleaf) – it is better flavoured than the fillets and is not usually dyed.

To poach smoked haddock or cod for breakfast cook it gently in unsalted water for ten to fifteen minutes, drain it well and serve it with a poached egg on top. Leave the skin on or it may fall apart during cooking.

Fried or grilled herrings and fried sprats

A Battersea fishmonger recommends a preliminary salting before you cook herrings. He cuts off their heads so that the innards can be pulled out at the same time. He washes them, then lays them on a bed of salt with another thick layer covering them, and leaves them for an hour. They are then washed, scored on either side with a knife, and either grilled or fried. They can also be filleted, coated in fine oatmeal, brushed with melted butter, fried, and served with mustard.

Sprats should be left whole, but washed and dried, then coated with flour or fine oatmeal. They can be fried without fat if you sprinkle the bottom of a heavy, heated frying-pan with fairly coarse salt. The salt stops them burning and the heat brings out their own oil, which cooks them. Serve them with lemon wedges.

A dredgerman's breakfast

This recipe comes from a Whitstable oyster merchant. Whitstable oysters are dredged up in the Thames Estuary and the dredgermen are supposed to hand them all over, but it isn't unheard of for them to smuggle a few ashore in the roomy pockets of their oilskins.

For breakfast they fry bacon rashers until the fat runs, then add some shelled oysters and cook them very gently, until they have just turned opaque. Oysters shrink a lot when they are cooked, and they must not cook too long or they become tough. Eat them straight away.

Fish-cakes

Without a doubt, the remains of the fish pie on page 149 make the best fish-cakes. Mash the fish, sauce, eggs and potatoes together – the mixture should be stiff. Form it into little cakes, flour them, dip them in beaten egg and then in breadcrumbs and fry them in lard till they are crisp and golden on both sides, and heated through.

To make fish-cakes from left-over fish and boiled or mashed potatoes, flake the fish, removing all skin and bones. Mash the potatoes with a little milk. Mix the fish and potato together with enough beaten egg to bind them and season the mixture with salt and pepper. Form it into cakes and proceed as above. Some cooks like to add a few herbs and sautéed, chopped onions to the mixture.

Kedgeree *(for 4–6)*

Kedgeree is said to be an Anglicised version of an Indian rice dish called 'kicheree'. The strongest hint of India in our kedgeree is a touch of curry powder and the accompaniment of chutney. Most recipes advise mixing the cooked rice with the cooked fish and some hard-boiled eggs, but I like to incorporate a creamy sauce as well. Make kedgeree the day before as it reheats well.

750 g	smoked haddock on the bone	1½ lb
575 ml	milk and water mixed	1 pt
375 g	long grain rice	12 oz
50 g	flour	2 oz
50 g	butter	2 oz
half 5 ml sp	curry powder	½ tsp
	freshly ground black pepper	
3	hard-boiled eggs	3

Poach the haddock gently in the milk and water for about ten minutes, or until it can be taken easily from the bones. Remove the skin as well and flake the fish. Keep the poaching liquid for the sauce.

Partly cook the rice by boiling it in salted water for about ten minutes. Drain it and keep it warm.

Make a béchamel with the flour, butter, curry powder and fish liquor, adding black pepper to taste and more milk if necessary, in order to make a fairly runny sauce (see page 254).

Mix it with the fish, the rice and the cut up hard-boiled eggs. Put it into the top half of a double-boiler and steam it for 20–30 minutes. Serve it with knobs of butter on each helping, and a sweet mango chutney.

AUTHOR'S NOTE: Left-over salmon is superb in kedgeree.

Bloater paste *(for 4)*

This paste can also be made with kipper, smoked trout, smoked mackerel or even smoked salmon. Only bloaters and kippers need the preliminary dousing with boiling water.

1	bloater	1
50 g	softened butter	2 oz
	salt, pepper	
	cayenne	
	lemon juice	

Pour boiling water over the fish (best done in a jug) and leave it for ten minutes. Drain off the water and carefully remove all skin and bones.

Mash or liquidise the fish with the softened butter, salt, pepper, cayenne and enough lemon juice to taste.

Pack it either into individual pots or into one big one and decorate the top with fork marks.

If you leave enough space at the top of its pot you can pour clarified butter (page 264) over it, which will help it to keep for some time in the refrigerator.

Serve it well chilled with toast or with hot, plain Yorkshire tea-cakes (page 113).

Laverbread

This is the only seaweed (apart from caragheen moss) found on British shores that is considered good enough to eat. Its Latin name is *Porphyra leucostica* or *P. umbilicatus*. It grows on the northern shores of Devon and Somerset, as well as in Wales on the other side of the Bristol Channel. The Welsh are much more appreciative of it than the English, but it can be bought, freshly cooked, in Bristol, Ilfracombe and Barnstaple and I have seen it on sale at a butcher's in Bideford, as well as frozen in Harrods. Some places sell it in tins. Dried Japanese *kombu* is similar.

If you find it growing on a beach the preparation to make it edible is laborious. First it must be washed free of sand, then steeped in fresh water with a little bicarbonate of soda, then boiled for hours until it becomes as tender as spinach. It goes from a filmy purple cellophane to a black mush, but it tastes rather pleasant, sweetish with undertones of seafood. It is also often sold as a sloppy mess, but it becomes much easier to handle once it is mixed with oatmeal. This is the best way to eat it for breakfast: mix the prepared laverbread with enough fine oatmeal to enable you to form it into patties, then fry them in bacon fat. The patties are delicious with eggs and bacon – very filling and nutritious.

Laverbread can also be made into a traditional West Country sauce (page 258) for roast lamb, and makes a good salad too, if seasoned with oil, vinegar, salt, pepper and a little sugar.

Devon potato cakes and bubble-and-squeak

Not long ago every Devon farmhouse kitchen had a special implement for making these potato cakes; it was a crank-shaped cutter called a potato chopper. It was like a long palette-knife with the blade set on its side, so that you could chop the potato as it cooked in the frying-pan. These choppers are now museum pieces, but the potato cakes are still made.

To make the potato cakes: Roughly mash some left-over boiled potato and season it with salt and pepper, then fry it in some good bacon fat. (If you had a potato chopper you would chop whole potatoes as they fried.) Let it go crisp and brown on the underside, then turn it over and fry the other side. Serve it with the bacon rashers that provided the fat.

Devonshire stew or bubble-and-squeak: Another good breakfast dish is Devonshire stew, a mixture of cold cooked potatoes, cabbage and onions all fried together and better known in the rest of England as bubble-and-squeak. You need two parts of left-over boiled potato to one of left-over cabbage and one of left-over boiled onion. Chop all the ingredients and mix them together, with salt and pepper. Fry the mixture in good beef dripping or butter, until they go crisp and brown underneath.

Dock pudding or Easterledges pudding *(for 6)*

I had great trouble deciding which was the best recipe to give here, as there are so many versions of this dish. The main ingredient is bistort, sweet dock or snakeweed (*Polygonum bistorta*) which is also known as persecaria, and astrologia (hence the name of Easterledges). The name 'dock pudding' is misleading because it would not be at all nice made with the common or field dock. My research was further hampered by my being in the wrong part of England (the South, where the plant doesn't grow) at the right time for the pudding (which is springtime). The natives of the Calder Valley, near Halifax in Yorkshire, have a World Champion Dock Pudding Competition early in April to raise funds for charity. The organiser, Mrs Uttley, actually sent me some of her pudding and also gave me the recipe printed here.

She says: 'The plant is only suitable for this pudding from the middle of March to April or early May. It is best when young as the leaves have a bitter taste when they are large, so really there are only about four weeks when the pudding can be made. The plant is common here in the Calder Valley, and it is also found (and the pudding made) in Wigton (Cumbria); the Yorkshire Dales; Fulwood, near Preston; Arnside, and on the Isle of Man. . . . It is considered a great springtime tonic, especially good for cleansing the blood.'

Mrs Uttley always freezes some so that the family can have it for breakfast on Christmas morning. She adds, '. . . when it's in season we almost live off it. The recipe varies from family to family but it is basically the same, although I don't know many people who put in eggs. Some add a handful of nettles and some do not mince or chop it, but I like mine to have a fine texture.'

1.5 kg	bistort leaves	3 lb
4	chopped large onions	4
75 g	fine oatmeal	3 oz
100 g	butter	4 oz
	salt, pepper	
3	beaten eggs	3

Strip the stems from the leaves, wash them and cook them in a little boiling salted water with the onions. When they are tender put them through a mincer or chop them up in the pan until they are very fine, then add the oatmeal and simmer it for 15 minutes more. Drain off any excess liquid, add the butter, and salt and pepper to taste. Add the eggs and cook it a little longer, then serve it as it is.

It can also be left to go cold. To reheat it, make it into patties, and fry it in bacon fat; have it with bacon and lots of bread and butter.

Author's note: Some people use pearl barley instead of oatmeal, soaking it overnight, with the leaves in a muslin bag, before cooking it. Others add all sorts of green leaves – cabbage, broccoli, gooseberry, redcurrant, raspberry and dandelion. I made a passable southern version of this delicious pudding with a mixture of sorrel and nettles, following Mrs Uttley's recipe.

Herb sausages *(for 8–10)*

1 kg	lean pork	2 lb
500 g	pork back fat	1 lb
250 g	fresh breadcrumbs soaked in water	8 oz
two 5 ml sp	salt	2 tsp
half 5 ml sp	pepper	$\frac{1}{2}$ tsp
one 5 ml sp	grated whole nutmeg	1 tsp
6	finely chopped sage leaves	6
one 15 ml sp each	finely chopped fresh thyme, savory and marjoram	1 tbsp each

Trim and roughly cube the meat and fat. Pass the pieces through the medium blade of a mincer. Alternatively chop the meat in batches in a food processor. Squeeze excess water from the breadcrumbs. Put the minced meat in a large mixing bowl and add the remaining ingredients.

If you can't get hold of proper casings, the sausage meat can be shaped into patties and sautéed or grilled plain, or wrapped in a piece of caul fat before cooking.

If you have got a sausage-making attachment on the mincer, fill the casing with that or use a forcing bag fitted with a large nozzle, or attach the casing to the neck of a funnel and push the mixture through the funnel with a pestle.

To cook the sausages, prick them all over with a fork, put them in a large frying-pan and add enough water to measure 0.5 cm/¼ inch deep. Bring the water to the boil over a moderate heat, simmer the sausages, covered, for ten minutes. Remove the cover and cook them, uncovered, until the water has evaporated and the sausages are golden brown – about ten more minutes.

AUTHOR'S NOTE: Most butchers will provide natural pig, lamb and ox casings or they can be ordered from a wholesaler in bulk, usually in salted form. The salted casings will keep for several months in the refrigerator or freezer.

Other kinds of English sausage

Oxford sausages are made with equal quantities of pork, beef suet and veal with a small proportion of breadcrumbs. They are seasoned with salt, grated lemon rind, pepper, nutmeg, sage and thyme. They are not put into skins but are rolled into sausage shapes and floured before frying.

Cumberland sausages are made of coarsely minced pork, four parts of lean meat to two parts of belly and one of back fat, seasoned with sage, rosemary and thyme as well as salt, pepper, cayenne, nutmeg and ginger. Their distinguishing feature is that they are made in one continuous strip, rather than in links, and this is sold coiled up like a rope. The best way to cook it is not to fry it but to grill it or bake it in the oven. In Cumberland they like apple slices or apple sauce with their sausage.

Beef sausages are made with two parts of lean beef to one of beef suet with a small proportion of breadcrumbs. They are seasoned only with salt and pepper and fried in beef dripping. They are usually made longer and thinner than pork sausages.

Tomato sausages are made of very finely minced pork or beef which has been flavoured with tomato puree. They are particularly popular in the Midlands.

Lambs' fries *(for 4)*

Lambs' fries is the polite name for lambs' testicles, which are removed from the creatures at an early age so that they will fatten up into good 'sheep meat'. Their availability depends on demand; butchers in Camden Town in London have them because Greek people like them. I have also seen them on sale in the North. They have a mild, delicate flavour and a soft texture. Another name for them is 'Mountain Oysters'.

500 g	lambs' fries	1 lb
	seasoned flour	
1	finely chopped small onion	1
50 g	butter	2 oz
	lemon juice	
	chopped parsley	

Prepare the fries by making a shallow cut on the rounded side of the fries and peeling the skin off. Next soak them in cold water until all traces of blood have disappeared. Put them in a pan of cold water, bring it to the boil and let them simmer for thirty seconds; drain them and pat them dry with paper.

Cut the fries into thin slices and coat them in the seasoned flour. Sauté the onion in the butter until it is golden. Add the fries and cook them gently for about three minutes on both sides. The slices should be well browned.

Add a squeeze of lemon juice and serve them sprinkled with parsley.

Three ways to prepare kidneys for breakfast

The kidneys must be lambs' kidneys; they should be prepared for cooking by removing the external fat (if it is still attached) and by peeling off the covering of skin. They should then be split lengthways, but not quite divided in two, and opened out flat, still joined by their fatty core. Run a fine skewer across them so that they stay flat.

For plain grilled kidneys: prepare them as above, then brush them over with melted butter or oil. Season them with salt and pepper and grill them on both sides. A couple of blanched oysters can be served on top of each kidney.

For devilled kidneys: skin, split and skewer them, then make light cuts in them and rub in a mixture of freshly made mustard, salt and pepper. Grill them on both sides. Serve both plain and devilled kidneys on rounds of fried bread.

For kidney toast: poach some whole, unskinned kidneys for only a few minutes, drain and dry them, then skin them and take out the cores. Chop them very finely, or pound them with a pestle and mortar, then very briefly fry the mixture in a little melted butter and season it with lemon juice, salt and pepper. Mix it well and spread it on hot buttered toast. If this has to be done in advance, warm it before serving, in a hot oven.

Accompaniments to kidneys might be grilled mushrooms, fried or grilled rashers of bacon, fried or scrambled eggs, grilled or fried halves of tomatoes, grilled or fried sausages. Don't forget to provide a pot of freshly made English mustard.

Black puddings

These are very much liked in the North, where every butcher sells them, hanging in shining black bunches from the ceiling. They are made of pig's blood which has to be used as soon as the pig is killed – it must be stirred continuously to stop it setting. Milk and boiled pearl barley are added, sometimes with grated raw onion. Salt and pepper and sage or mint are the seasonings. The mixture is poured into large casings, tied in small fat loops and boiled until the puddings are firm. This is how you buy them.

To heat them up, either boil them again for a little while, or split them open lengthways and grill them, or slice and fry them.

Traditional accompaniments are bacon, fried eggs, fried apple rings, Staffordshire oatcakes (see page 13) and, for a main meal, mashed potatoes. Serve mustard with them.

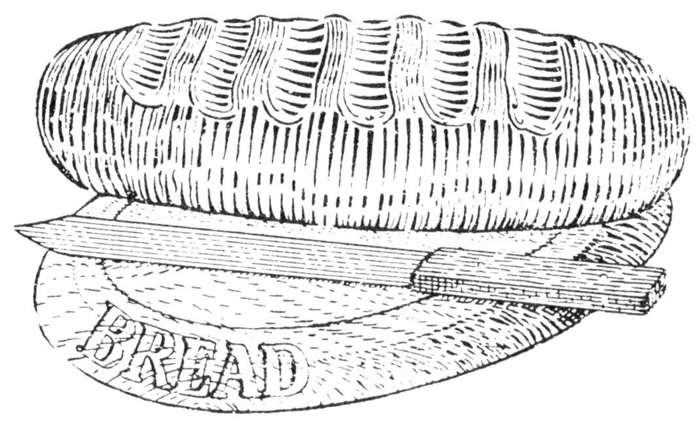

An Easter lunch in Gloucestershire

Decorated Easter eggs for egg mayonnaise
Elvers
Trout with fennel
Snails

Pork in cider
Escalopes of pork with cream and cider
Roast lamb

Jacket potatoes with snail butter
Seakale
Spring salad

Rhubarb tansy with Easter cakes
Rhubarb pasties with rhubarb puree
Oldbury tarts

Gloucestershire cheese
Cheese and ale

Cabbage bread

Easter in Gloucestershire coincides with the arrival of swarms of elvers up the Severn, pressing inland away from the sea and towards fresh water. Even more intensity is shown by swarms of motorists rushing (or attempting to) in the opposite direction.

And, as everywhere else, Easter means new growth in the garden, a desire for fresh, clean tastes and, with any luck, weather good enough to hide Easter eggs outside. If you have children, they can have egg mayonnaise, and eat the decorated eggs that they have been hunting for, instead of elvers and snails which may not be quite to their tastes.

Oldbury tarts are a bit premature for Easter, but they are so successful with frozen gooseberries, I think they can be allowed here.

Decorated Easter eggs

The simplest way to dye eggs is also one of the prettiest: wrap the eggs in onion skins and then sew or tie them in a piece of plain cloth. Put the wrapped eggs in a pan of cold water, bring it to the boil and simmer for ten minutes, when the eggs should be both hard-boiled and patterned in one go. (If you like, fix gorse blossom inside the onion skin and see what happens.)

Any pieces of material dyed with non-fast colours can be used instead of onion skins. You can also boil eggs in coffee to turn them dark brown, or paint them with commercial dyes after they have been boiled.

Either hide them in the garden and send the children out to hunt for them before lunch, or heap them in a pretty bowl, with moss as a bed and with flowers among them. Have a bowl of mayonnaise (page 254) alongside and let people peel and slice their own eggs.

Elvers

Between late February and mid-May, at fortnightly intervals on the ebbing spring tides, the elver-catchers will be out with their huge, bath-shaped, long-poled nets, scooping masses of these tiny, transparent, shoelace-thick creatures from the shallow edges of the tidal part of the River Severn. They have swum on the Gulf Stream all the way from their spawning ground in the Sargasso Sea; they will spend up to nine years as adults in fresh water before returning.

The Severn is one of the less polluted rivers in Europe; if you happen to be in the district when the tides are right you may be lucky enough to find someone to sell you live elvers. (Gloucester market sometimes has them, but they are usually dead.) Take a pillowcase to put them in and a shallow tray to put the pillowcase on, as elvers are best cooked alive. They suffocate quite quickly in a bucket or a plastic bag, so the pillowcase is an ideal receptacle, confining their wrigglings and providing air at the same time. Don't be alarmed if they lack moisture, as a quite dehydrated-looking elver revives again in fresh water. Most of them are exported, by air, from the villages along the Severn Estuary in mesh trays to Spain, Germany and France, not for eating, but for restocking Western European rivers. They can be frozen satisfactorily, but it is best to give them a preliminary clean to get rid of the 'vomp' or slime. You need to do this anyway before you can cook them.

To clean elvers, put them in a sieve and wash them well in running water. Let them drain for five minutes (covered to prevent escape), then pour them onto a tea towel. Rub them really hard with another scrumpled tea towel. This gets rid of the vomp and, as it goes, the elvers all roll into a ball. This is the moment to cook them in any of the following ways, or to freeze them.

English ways of cooking elvers

In spring, elvers are found in several other West Country rivers and in some East Anglian rivers in huge swarms, and the recipes are almost all the same. Allow 100 g/4 oz of elvers per person unless you are going in for an elver-eating competition.

The most usual way to eat them is fried in bacon fat, with a mixture of well-seasoned beaten egg poured over them as soon as they have become opaque. The dish is stirred while it cooks and is ready as soon as the egg has set. Bacon rashers, salt, pepper, and vinegar (if you must, in which case let it be cider vinegar), are the traditional accompaniments. This recipe comes from the landlord of the Durrell Arms, Framilode. He serves the elvers with toast or brown bread and butter. One eel-catcher from the same village likes his elvers fried in bacon fat till crisp, 'almost burnt'. He then adds salt and pepper, vinegar and sometimes soya sauce.

In North Devon they make elver cake. Elvers are boiled with green herbs such as parsley, chopped fennel leaves and chervil, and onion juice. When the elvers are cold they set to a jelly 'smelling like pork'. It is turned out and cut like a cake.

None of these recipes seems to me to do credit to these delicious little creatures, and if I am ever lucky enough to find them I prefer them cooked as they are in Spain or Italy, with olive oil. They are served very hot in individual earthenware dishes, with wooden forks to stop you burning your mouth.

English elvers done in a Spanish way *(for 6)*

750 g	elvers	$1\frac{1}{2}$ lb
	olive oil	
	hot chilli pepper	
	garlic	

Put the serving dishes to heat while you cook the elvers. Heat the oil in a frying pan, using an amount that will just cover the elvers. First sizzle a little chopped chilli and some slivers of garlic, then throw in the elvers. Serve them as soon as they are opaque, with lots of bread to mop up the oil.

Trout with fennel *(for 3–6)*

Trout is now available all the year round, and what is more, it is becoming increasingly so. As we eat so few (the average consumption of trout in this country is said to be no more than one per person every four years), this can be no bad thing. Most of it, whether fresh, frozen or smoked, is farmed rather than wild or game fish. There are two kinds: the native brown trout (which is the same species as the white-fleshed wild trout) and the rainbow trout (which is pink-fleshed and a North American immigrant, imported in the 19th century).

Some people claim that wild brown trout taste far better than farmed rainbow trout; this may well be so because flavour and quality depend very much on diet, but a well-fed farm trout should be indistinguishable from a wild one.

The best way to eat trout is indisputably as fresh as possible. If you don't have a fisherman in the family most trout farms welcome callers. They will sell you fish, straight out of the water, killing and gutting them for you there and then. Some, particularly those situated on rivers already populated by brown trout, have both species on sale, in which case, as both have been eating the same food, both may have pink flesh and taste much the same.

The fennel to cook them with grows wild along many riversides and can be easily cultivated in the garden. In spring the white parts of the leaves are very tender. (This is the native English fennel, not the sweet bulbous Italian kind.)

3	large trout of about 375 g/12 oz each	3
	salt and pepper	
	a few young fennel stems	
50 g	butter	2 oz
125 ml	double cream	$\frac{1}{4}$ pt

Preheat the oven to 180°C/350°F/gas 4.

Fillet the trout and season them well.

Chop up the white parts of the fennel stems, keeping the feathery green parts for later, and sauté them lightly in a little of the butter.

Grease a gratin dish with the rest of the butter, put the fennel stems in it and lay the trout fillets, skin side down, on top. Pour the cream over everything, and scatter the green fennel on that. Bake the fillets for 20 to 25 minutes.

Serve one fillet to each person if this dish is your first course, two each if it is the main course.

AUTHOR'S NOTE: A dash of Pernod, either sprinkled onto the fillets or mixed in with the cream, gives this dish a little fillip.

Snails

Why is it almost impossible to persuade people to eat free, fresh common or garden snails (*Helix aspersa*)? It is no trouble at all to get them to consume expensive foreign ones (*Helix pomatia*) which are quite likely to be tinned and imported from Taiwan. The only advantage possessed by the latter is that they are bigger.

Parts of the Cotswolds and chalky hills like the North Downs and the Chilterns still harbour colonies of *Helix pomatia*, which are said to have been brought to England by the Romans. However they are now a protected species, so even if you do find any, leave them be (I hear that they have been seen in Surrey 'as big as tennis balls'). Meanwhile *Helix aspersa* thrives lustily everywhere south of Yorkshire, east of Herefordshire and all around the coast of Wales. The biggest are about as large as a small walnut and you need at least a dozen per person; they make a nice start to a meal and they are, moreover, traditional in many places.

Great quantities of these 'wallfish' were collected in Gloucestershire in the 19th century, and sent to Bristol to be eaten by the tobacco workers and glass-blowers there: they were thought to be good for the chest (sympathetic magic because of their mucus). There is no record of how they cooked them, but Mrs Haslam, who serves them at the Miners' Arms, Priddy, in Somerset, says roadmen used to cook them on shovels over their braziers. She also told me how to prepare them.

First they must be fed on leaves that are not harmful to people. They may have been eating ivy or insecticides, so keep them in captivity for two weeks to be on the safe side, feeding them with cabbage, lettuce or, best of all, vine leaves.

Wash the snails well, then kill them by plunging them into boiling brine (25 g/1 oz salt to 500 ml/1 pint water). It will foam up so use a deep pan. Cook them for five minutes, then rinse them and give them another five minutes in plain boiling water. Wash them once more, and take them out of their shells with a sharp skewer. Remove their tightly curled-up intestines.

Meanwhile make a court-bouillon of water with a little cider or red wine, and a few slices of onion, and herbs such as parsley, thyme, fennel and bay leaves. Add a little salt and a few peppercorns. Poach the snails in the court-bouillon for about an hour, when they should be tender.

They can then be pushed back into their shells (which have been washed and cleaned in boiling water meanwhile). The shells can be sealed either with the classic snail butter (page 101), butter mashed with chopped mint, or butter with a mixture of green herbs plus a little cream or Cheddar cheese. Add cayenne and black pepper to all of these.

Either put them in little dishes designed for snails or cut holes for them with an apple corer in soft thick slices of bread. Cook them under the grill until the butter is heated through. Serve them very hot, using the slightly toasted bread to mop up the juices.

Pork in cider *(for 6)*

The country between the Severn and the Wye is rich, red-earthed land. It is full of cider-apple orchards and hilly fields of grazing cattle and sheep, and is the home of Hereford beef and of three almost extinct Gloucester specialities – Gloucester Old Spot pigs, Gloucester cattle and the cheeses made from their milk: Double and Single Gloucester. Charles and Monica Martell who farm at Dymock have revived the breed of cattle and make the authentic cheeses (see page 241), as well as breeding Old Spot pigs. (The long jaws of these pigs were once the traditional source of Bath Chaps – see page 41.)

I went to see Mrs Martell one balmy, sunny April day. Her Old Spot sows, each a creamy white with one or two hand-sized black spots, were grubbing about in the orchard. Their piglets, gambolling under the apple blossom with the sun making their ears transparently pink, were a pretty sight. She gave me this recipe, which combines the fruits of her labours – pork, cider and cheese.

1 kg	slices of pork (see Author's note)	2 lb
	oil, oil and butter, or pork dripping for frying	
500 g	peeled and chopped onions	1 lb
100 g	sliced mushrooms	4 oz
	salt, pepper	
275 ml	cider	½ pt
	dried sage	
2	large peeled and sliced cooking apples	2

for the topping

100 g	grated Double Gloucester cheese	4 oz
100 g	brown breadcrumbs	4 oz
50 g	butter	2 oz

Brown the pork slices (trimmed of their rinds) in a frying-pan, using a little pork dripping, oil, or oil and butter mixed. Put them aside and brown the onions, then the mushrooms. Season the meat and vegetables with salt and pepper.

While you are cooking the meat and vegetables, boil the cider fast to reduce it by half.

Grease a cast-iron or earthenware casserole and put a layer of half the onions and mushrooms in it. Follow with half the pork, the rest of the mushrooms and onions and then the rest of the pork. Sprinkle the meat with the crumbled sage, then put the apples in a thick layer on top of that. Pour over the reduced cider, cover the pot and bake at 190°C/375°F/gas 5 for 1½–2 hours, when the meat should be tender and the apples reduced to a mush.

Mix the cheese and breadcrumbs and put them in a thick layer on top of the stew. Dot the top with the butter and return it to the oven, or put it under the grill, until it is brown and crunchy on top.

Potatoes baked in their jackets, split open and spread with garlic butter (page 101), and a Spring salad (page 31) go well with this dish.

Author's note: You could use Cheddar or any other hard cheese instead of Double Gloucester. Cut the pork from the leg, loin or 'oyster' (the meat that lies over the shoulder blade). In this recipe dried sage is more satisfactory than fresh as it can be crumbled very finely.

Escalopes of pork with a cream and cider sauce

If the pork and cider casserole seems too filling, serve this lighter dish.

Take one escalope of pork per person. Coat the slices with seasoned flour to which you have added a sprinkling of dry, powdered sage and fry them in butter until they are cooked. Keep them warm while you make a sauce by deglazing the pan with cider. Simmer until the cider is reduced by half, then add an equal amount of cream. Stir it well, and serve the meat with the sauce poured over it.

Roast lamb

Spring lamb, once the traditional Easter delicacy of every sheep-rearing country (at least in the Northern Hemisphere) meant really young milk-fed lamb born earlier the same year. Nowadays, 'lamb' is available all the year round but it's hardly, if ever, even three months old and only half of what we eat is English. Modern farming has also made mutton virtually unobtainable; the nearest thing to it today is a castrated male lamb, over one year old but still nothing like as tasty as old-fashioned mutton, which was usually four-year-old ewe's meat.

The best cuts to roast are, in order of both size and cost: the saddle (for large parties), the leg (for average to large-sized dinners), the rack or best end (for small dinners), the shoulder (for small and less formal dinners). Note that a saddle, split down the middle, makes two loins, and that two racks or best ends will make a guard of honour or a crown. The same preparation and accompaniments, however, apply to all these cuts.

Push slivers of garlic into any crevices you can find, or make a few with the point of a sharp knife. Press a few sprigs of rosemary in as well (but take them out before you serve the meat as they are rather spiky). Rub the whole surface with oil or butter and salt it a little. Squeeze lemon juice all over the skin.

Calculate about 20 minutes to the half-kilo/pound, and add an extra 20 minutes for large joints. Cook the meat at 190°C/375°F/gas 5. Baste it often during the cooking, and let it rest for a while in a warm place before carving it – this helps the meat to 'set'.

Deglaze the roasting pan after pouring off the surplus fat. Add stock, reduce it if necessary, and strain it into a gravy boat. This makes a thin gravy. Children seem to prefer thick gravy. Make it by leaving a little fat in the pan. Add a spoonful of flour, stirring in as much of the sediment as you can. Add stock slowly, stirring it all the time to avoid lumps. Taste for seasoning, and strain it into a sauce boat when it is to your liking.

Serve the lamb with roast potatoes (page 141), leek puree (page 140), broccoli or Brussels sprouts and chestnuts (page 184) in winter, and new, mint-covered potatoes, young turnips, broad beans, green peas or French beans in summer. Also provide either redcurrant or rowan jelly (see pages 249 and 250) or a sharp, minted crab-apple jelly (page 248). Runny, vinegary English mint sauce would be all right if it didn't get across the plate into the vegetables. Another, much nicer traditional sauce liked by people on both sides of the Bristol Channel is laverbread sauce (page 258).

Jacket potatoes with garlic or snail butter

Bake large, floury potatoes (old ones of the Golden Wonder, King Edward, or Majestic varieties) in their jackets at the same time as a casserole, in a moderate oven.

Split them open and spread them with the garlic or snail butter described on page 101, or with a herb butter, or a mixture of grated cheese, chives, parsley and thick cream.

Seakale

Crambe maritima is the ancestor of our cultivated cabbage and a wild plant that grows at various places on the coasts of the southern half of England; it also grows well in vegetable gardens. It should not be confused with seakale beet, which is a popular name given to Swiss chard, a spinach-like member of the beet family.

Seakale is rarely seen in its natural state, for it gets trampled on, or eaten by cows, or picked for its honey-scented flowers, but I do know of one Hampshire beach where it has its stalks blanched in the old-fashioned way, with shingle heaped up in a great mound over its dormant leaf buds. If this is done early in January you can have the first stems on All Fools' Day. In gardens it can be blanched under tall pots, like rhubarb. It makes as good a first course as asparagus, and it ought to be grown more.

Cut off any earthy stumps and tiny leaf tips. Cook the succulent white stems in boiling salted water for ten to twelve minutes. Drain them well and serve them with melted butter or a hollandaise sauce (page 256). It needs a knife and fork to eat it with rather than fingers.

Spring salad

Around Easter most shop salads are still grown in heated glasshouses, or are imported from abroad. This makes them very expensive.

The answer is to look in the hedges, or in your own garden where you could be growing a spring salad of blanched salsify leaves. They have an 'asparagus' flavour and are rich in iron. You might also consider growing autumn-sown lettuce, spring onions and lamb's lettuce (mâche). Other possibilities are sorrel and blanched dandelion (remove the stem and spine before eating), alexanders buds, and watercress – but do be sure that it *is* watercress and that the water is not polluted.

Mix everything together with a fairly sweet vinaigrette (page 255), using cider vinegar.

Rhubarb tansy *(for 6)*

English vegetable plots in spring are full of upturned pots, drums and boxes – all forcing certain suitable plants to make an effort to penetrate the dark and grow towards warmth and light. After a time stems and leaves emerge, taller, paler, sweeter and more tender than their fellows growing slowly in the cold, open air. The tallest tubs may be covering sea-kale or more likely rhubarb, to enable it to become the earliest fruit of the year. The first puddings made from it taste almost as good as champagne; it's no coincidence that one of the best varieties has the same name.

Omelettes and purees of fruit cooked with eggs and cream used to be flavoured with a bitter, wormwood-like herb called tansy; it was traditionally eaten at Easter in case the eating of Lenten fish had engendered worms. That danger and the taste of tansy are nowadays things of the past, but this sort of pudding is still called a tansy. It can be made with purees of other local fruits – blackcurrant, apple, gooseberry and damson, as well as rhubarb.

1 kg	trimmed rhubarb	2 lb
250 g	butter	8 oz
250 g	granulated sugar	8 oz
4	separated eggs	4
2	lemons or oranges	2
275 ml	double cream	½ pt
	sugar for sprinkling	
	sponge fingers	

Slice the rhubarb very finely. Melt the butter in a saucepan (enamelled if you have one) and cook the fruit with half the sugar until it forms a thickish puree. Allow it to cool, standing the pan in a basin of cold water if you are in a hurry.

Beat half the remaining sugar into the egg yolks.

Remove the zest from the fruit with a potato peeler, and blanch it in hot water for a minute or two. Squeeze out the juice from the fruit and reserve it.

Whisk the egg whites to a soft foam and lightly whip the cream with the last of the sugar and the orange zest.

Combine the fruit, egg yolks, cream and egg whites in that order, then cook the mixture gently till it thickens a bit more.

Turn it into a shallow dish, sprinkle it with a little more sugar and the lemon or orange juice. Serve it cold with sponge fingers or Easter cakes (see next recipe).

Easter cakes *(makes 24)*

These are more of a biscuit than a cake and are nice to eat on their own or with the tansy.

125 g	caster sugar	4 oz
250 g	butter	8 oz
2	egg yolks	2
300 g	plain flour	10 oz
50 g	currants	2 oz
	a little nutmeg	
two 5 ml sp	brandy	2 tsp

for the glaze

egg white
sugar

Beat the caster sugar with the butter to a creamy consistency. Add the egg yolks, sifted flour, currants, nutmeg and brandy. Mix well and leave the resulting paste to stand a while in a cool place (all night is not too long).

Preheat the oven to 180°C/350°F/gas 4. Roll the paste out to 0.3 cm/⅛ inch thick. Cut it into 6.5 cm/2½ inch circles with a fluted cutter.

Bake the biscuits watchfully for ten minutes, then brush the tops with a glaze made of egg white beaten with a little sugar and return them to the oven for a further ten minutes to cook the glaze.

Author's note: The brandy sometimes has saffron steeped in it for extra flavour. Another variation uses half wholemeal and half white flour.

Rhubarb pasties *(makes 12)*

500 g	rough-puff pastry (page 266)	1 lb
250 g (approx.)	rhubarb	8 oz (approx.)
	sugar (see below)	
1	lightly beaten egg white	1

Preheat the oven to 220°C/425°F/gas 7.

Roll the pastry out to about 0.5 cm/¼ inch thick. Cut it into rectangles measuring approximately 13 cm/5 inches long and 10 cm/4 inches wide. Place a piece of rhubarb, about 8 cm/3 inches long, on each rectangle and sprinkle one 15 ml sp/1 tbsp of sugar over the rhubarb.

To make the package, fold over the long side of the pastry and crimp the loose edges together.

Slash the top of each pasty in two or three places to allow the steam to escape during the cooking. Brush the tops with the beaten egg white and sprinkle on a little sugar.

Cook the pasties on a greased baking-sheet for 15 minutes or until they are golden brown. Transfer them to a wire rack.

You can serve the pasties almost immediately or when they have cooled, with fresh cream and rhubarb puree.

Rhubarb puree

500 g	rhubarb	1 lb
100 ml	water	4 fl oz
250 g	sugar	8 oz

Roughly chop the rhubarb into 2.5 cm/1 inch pieces and put them in a small pan. Add the water and sugar to the rhubarb and cook over a medium heat, stirring occasionally, until the fruit becomes a very soft puree (about 15 minutes).

Serve it hot or cold with fruit pies.

Oldbury tarts *(makes about 15)*

These are not really tarts, but little raised pies made with a hot water crust. They have a filling of very sticky, juicy gooseberries and you need to eat them with a spoon.

The gooseberries should be small and hard – those hairy, green ones that grow wild in the hedges all over Gloucestershire and especially around Oldbury-on-Severn are ideal. So are unsweetened gooseberries straight from the freezer – their coldness helps to keep the pastry firm.

Lots of local people still make Oldbury tarts for Whitsun, when the gooseberries are in season. The lady who gave me this recipe learnt it from her mother, who, having come from Bristol (all of ten miles away), had to live many years in the village before anyone would give her the recipe, or show her how to make them.

750 g	hot water crust (see below)	1½ lb
500 g	gooseberries	1 lb
150 g	soft brown sugar	6 oz
50 g	caster sugar	2 oz

Make a hot water crust following the recipe on page 267, but use half butter and half lard instead of all lard. Form two thirds of the dough into walnut-sized pieces (about 15) leaving the rest for the lids. Roll each ball into a thin saucer-sized circle. Roll the same number of balls from the lesser amount into cup-sized circles.

Put four pleats into each of the larger circles to make them stand up like shallow pots – the sides will be about 2.5 cm/1 inch high. Fill each 'pot' with topped and tailed gooseberries.

Mix the sugars together in a basin and put one 15 ml sp/1 tbsp into each pie. (The white sugar is supposed to stop the juice boiling over.)

Place the cup-sized lids over the filling and pinch the edges of the top and the bottom pastry together, flattening and thinning the pastry. Make 21 little pleats (the traditional number) so that the rims stand straight up all round the top. Make three holes in the lids. Put the tarts in the fridge to cool while you heat the oven to 200°C/400°F/gas 6.

Bake them for about 40 minutes. The rims should be brown, and the juice just beginning to bubble out of the top. Test the berries for tenderness by pushing in a sharp needle; remove the pies as soon as they are done, and eat them while they are still hot, with cream.

AUTHOR'S NOTE: Some cooks put a drop of water or beaten egg and a sprinkling of white sugar on the lids to glaze them, just before they go into the oven. These pies are also very good made with blackcurrants.

Gloucestershire cheese

For Single and Double Gloucester, see page 241.

Cheese and ale *(for 6)*

This makes a fine savoury lunch or supper dish. It is also a good way of using up any hard cheese that has become *too* hard.

375 g	hard cheese (Double Gloucester or Cheddar)	12 oz
three–four 5 ml sp	freshly made English mustard	3–4 tsp
425 ml	strong ale	$\frac{3}{4}$ pt
6–12	slices of toast	6–12

Preheat the oven to 200°C/400°F/gas 6, or light the grill. Slice the cheese thinly and put it into an oven-proof dish in layers with the mustard. Cover it with a little of the beer.

Cook it for five to ten minutes until the cheese has melted and become like a fondue. Heat the rest of the beer and pour it over the slices of toast, one or two to each plate. Spoon the cheese mixture over the toasts. Serve it at once with more beer (mulled in cold weather) and pickled onions (page 245).

AUTHOR'S NOTE: Don't overcook the cheese or it will become grainy.

Cabbage bread *(makes 8 rolls or 1 loaf)*

I owe thanks to the 'Taste of England' campaign and to Carol Wright for alerting me to the pretty custom of wrapping bread dough in cabbage leaves before baking it.

The baker she mentions – Mr Harding of Stroud – will make a

cabbage loaf, large or small, if warned in time and if the customers bring him the outside leaves of the biggest cabbage they can find.

The practice seems to be local to this town, and Mr Harding appears to be the last of the many bakers who once did it.

The rolls are easier to make than large loaves.

25 g	fresh yeast (or half quantity of dried)	1 oz
one 5 ml sp	sugar	1 tsp
275 ml	lukewarm water	½ pt
500 g	strong white bread flour	1 lb
one 5 ml sp	salt	1 tsp
8	large cabbage leaves	8

Make the bread dough in the usual way: cream the yeast in a cup with the sugar, add a little of the water and put it in a warm place to start 'working'. Warm the flour and mix it with the salt. Add the yeast when it is covered with froth (after about ten minutes) plus the rest of the water. Mix well and knead the dough until it becomes soft and elastic. Leave it to rise to twice the size, which will take one or two hours in a warm place.

Divide the dough into eight pieces and shape each into a cylindrical roll. Dust them well with flour.

Trim the thick stem part of each cabbage leaf on the outside so that it lies flat and is no longer ridged. You need only trim off 4–5 cm/1½–2 inches.

Roll up one piece of dough in each leaf. Arrange it so that the top of the leaf tucks under the flattened stem, with the weight of the dough keeping it in place. The leaves should not fit too tightly round the dough.

Put the rolls carefully on a baking-sheet, spacing them so that they are not touching. Heat the oven to 240°C/475°F/gas 9.

When the rolls have proved (risen by about 0.5 cm/¼ inch) put them in the oven. As they cook the cabbage leaves will soften, allowing the dough to rise and become imprinted with the veins. The bread will then firm up and the leaves will start to burn. Don't worry about the smell – this is all as it should be. Leave the rolls as they are, to cook for 40–45 minutes. By this time the leaves will be quite black and will rub off easily. The rolls inside will have a lovely crisp, shiny golden crust, patterned rather like curved scallop shells and tasting faintly of Marmite. The crumb inside will be quite soft and damp.

AUTHOR'S NOTE: For a bloomer you may need two leaves – one on top and one beneath. Large loaves take about an hour to cook.

An early spring picnic in the South West

Cheddar cheese soup
Mulligatawny soup

The perfect Cornish pasty and variations
Bath chaps
Beef cake

Plum bread
Apple cream cake
Porridge pastry

Dorset cheeses
Cheddar cheese

The weather is icy, but even so, the English are gluttons for outdoor life. It is the end of the hunting season; point-to-points have begun, and hikers are putting dubbin on their hob-nailed boots.

This menu includes a few of the traditional foods that were once eaten winter or summer, at work, in the fields or down the mines. They are portable and sustaining things to keep you going till you get home again. Pasties and turnovers are pocket-sized and pocket-shaped; meat pies (page 60) would do too, but they are really designed for the sideboard. First of all, though, ward off the chill by drinking one of these soups from a thermos flask.

Cheddar cheese soup *(for 6–8)*

three 15 ml sp	butter	3 tbsp
1	finely chopped small onion	1
1	finely chopped stick of celery	1
three 15 ml sp	flour	3 tbsp
1 litre	chicken stock (page 263)	2 pt
275 ml	double cream	½ pt
250 g	grated Cheddar cheese	8 oz
	salt	
	cayenne	
	grated nutmeg	

Melt the butter in a large saucepan. Add the onion and celery and cook them until they are soft but not brown. Stir in the flour and when it starts to foam, stir in the stock. Bring the mixture to the boil and simmer for about 15 minutes, stirring occasionally.

Add the cream and the cheese in several batches, stirring to melt each batch before adding more. Add the salt, cayenne and grated nutmeg to taste.

Make some coquilles (page 76) or cabbage bread rolls (page 35) to go with this soup.

Mulligatawny soup *(for 6)*

This is a relic of the British Raj, and very suitable for drinking at point-to-points – hot and slightly curried. It is a corruption of two Tamil words *milagu* (pepper) and *tannir* (water). It can be made thick, in which case all the ingredients are pureed, or clear, in which case the soup is strained before serving. It can be based on almost any meat – lamb, oxtail, chicken and rabbit are favourites.

1 kg	chopped-up neck of lamb or mutton (or chicken, oxtail or rabbit)	2 lb
2	peeled and chopped onions	2
2	peeled and chopped carrots	2
1	small peeled and chopped turnip	1
2	peeled and chopped apples	2
two 15 ml sp	flour	2 tbsp
one 15 ml sp	curry powder or paste	1 tbsp
2 litres	water	4 pt
	bunch of herbs	
	salt, pepper	
	lemon juice	
	chopped cooked ham or chicken	

Trim the fat from the meat and render it down in a large pan. When it has given up quite a lot of its fat remove the crisp remains and sauté the meat, followed by the vegetables and apples. Sprinkle in the flour and the curry powder or paste and add the warmed water and the herbs.

Cook the soup for about two hours, skimming it at first. At the end of this time strain the soup and check the seasoning. Pick the meat from the bones if you are going to puree it. Add the lemon juice just before serving. Otherwise serve the strained soup, the fat removed from the top, with the lemon juice added at the last minute. Add cooked chopped ham or chicken as a garnish. Boiled rice used to be handed round with the soup.

The perfect Cornish pasty

Shop pasties made with flaky pastry and filled with gristly minced meat and an overseasoned mixture of onion and potato are very much despised by Cornish pasty experts, most of whom will only eat home-made ones. All the same, cooking methods and fillings vary – it seems that one can put almost anything that comes to hand in them (see next page).

The lady who gave me this recipe was cook to a rather grand house near Bodmin. She herself came from near Penzance. Since every Cornish cook swears that hers and only hers is the right way to make a pasty, I don't dare claim that this is right and all others are wrong, but it certainly makes the best pasty that I've eaten so far. This makes three smallish pasties. Make 375 g/12 oz of shortcrust pastry (page 264) using plain flour, margarine and lard.

Keep the pasties hot by wrapping them in several layers of paper with a towel wrapped round the outside.

for the filling

150 g	beef skirt	6 oz
1	onion and swede (optional)	1
1	large potato	1
	butter	
	salt, pepper	
	flour, milk, beaten egg	

Preheat the oven to 230°C/450°F/gas 8. Flour the meat before slicing it very finely (this helps to make the filling homogenous and creamy). Chop the onion finely, putting a little or a lot into each pasty, depending on how much people like it. Slice the swede and the potato into thin flakes on the side of a grater. (If the pasties are for the freezer, slice the potato thicker and blanch it first or it will go black.)

Roll the pastry out to small plate-sized circles. Just off-centre put first a layer of potato, then the onion, then the swede, then the meat, then and *only then*, salt and pepper. Then add more potato and two knobs of butter. (This is rather an unorthodox addition but it makes the pasties quite luxurious.)

Dampen the edges of the pastry and pull them together, making a good, firm wide join just off-centre. Pick the pasty up by the join (using both hands) and gently tap it down on the board to settle the filling a little. Crimp the join so that a neat, rope-like seam lies well to one side of the pasty, but clear of the bottom. Cut three slits in the top and brush it with milk or beaten egg. Lay the pasties on a greased baking-sheet or 'sheath'.

Cook them for 15 minutes, then lower the temperature to 200°C/400°F/gas 6 for the next 15 minutes, and to 180°C/350°F/gas 4 for the last fifteen minutes. Any leaking of the delicious juices that the pasty creates inside itself is a disgrace to the pasty-maker.

AUTHOR'S NOTE: Mark those without onion, or without swede or whatever, in a different way, so that each person gets a pasty filled as he or she likes. Drink scrumpy with them.

Cornish pasty fillings

Almost anything can go into a pasty as long as it is moist, and cut small enough for the pasty to be eaten without a knife and fork. However, having said that, there are still some things that are better than others, notably the following. (Cook all the pasties as indicated in the preceding recipe, unless it says otherwise.)

Potato and cream: to every 250 g/8 oz raw, new, sliced potatoes, add 75 g/3 oz clotted cream with salt and pepper. Or instead of potatoes use young swede (which the Cornish, like Americans, call rutabaga) or turnip. (A tiddy oggy is a pasty with nothing but potato inside.)

Bacon: use streaky bacon, cut up, instead of meat.

Lamb and apple: use lamb and parsley instead of steak and keep that at one end. Put chopped, sweetened apple at the other end, and mark it, for pudding. There is a similar pasty, made with suet crust, from the Midlands, called a Bedfordshire clanger.

Fish: use any filleted fish, chopped up, with parsley and dabs of butter, salt and pepper. Bake the pasty for 30 minutes.

Herbs: mix finely chopped fresh green herbs with a beaten egg and some chopped streaky bacon and spring onion (no potato, no butter). When the pasty is cooked, cut a little hole in the top, open it and pour some cream in. Put it back into the oven to heat through.

Bacon and egg: inside the pasty make a nest of chopped bacon and break a whole egg into it, with a knob of butter and seasoning. Seal the pasty carefully and bake it for ten minutes in a hot oven (220°C/425°F/gas 7), then reduce it to 180°F/350°F/gas 4 for 20 minutes.

Priddy oggies: these are named after the Somerset town of Priddy and are another recipe from the Miners' Arms in Priddy (page 27). Slivers of lean pork are mixed with a little chopped bacon, grated Cheddar cheese and chopped parsley, and a touch of sage as well as the usual seasoning. This filling is baked in an egg-glazed pasty for ten minutes only, then the whole pasty is deep-fried for another ten minutes.

Blackberry and apple: mix thinly sliced apples with blackberries and brown sugar. Cut a little hole in the pasty when it is cooked so that cream can be poured into it. Bake the pasty for 30 minutes.

Sour sauce or sorrel: (also liked in Lancashire). Roughly chop fresh sorrel and mix it with brown sugar. Pile it high as it shrinks a lot. Bake the pasty for 30 minutes and serve it with more sugar and cream.

Bath chaps

These are sold by good grocers all over the West Country. The best pigs for this little ham, made from the cheek, are Gloucester Old Spots, as they have long jaws (see page 28). However, as these are now a rare breed you will have to make do with any large pig's head. Ask the butcher to cut the jaw bone from the head for you (half a jaw makes one chap). Make a brine of 50 g/2 oz salt to each 575 ml/1 pt of water, and add a pinch of saltpetre to keep the meat pink. Also add 50 g/2 oz sugar to each 575 ml/1 pt of brine, with a few flavourings such as juniper berries, garlic cloves, bay leaves, peppercorns, thyme and nutmeg. Boil it all together, then leave it to cool. Strain it, and it is ready for the chaps. Leave them in it, for two or three days, weighted down so that they stay submerged, then rinse them and simmer them in plain water for four hours.

Take them out of the water, remove all the bones and take off the skin. Remove the snout too. Roll the meat into a cone shape and press it in an oval dish (a small casserole is suitable). When it is cold, coat the fat in toasted breadcrumbs. Eat it sliced across with mustardy pickles (page 247, for instance), with salad or in sandwiches.

Beef cake *(for 6–8)*

This book does not have much in the way of pâtés, as these are not essentially English, but this spiced beef cake, designed to be eaten hot and equally good cold, is an old-fashioned and quite traditional meat loaf.

400 g	fairly finely minced lean beef	14 oz
50 g	shredded suet	2 oz
225 g	minced bacon	8 oz
1	minced, medium-sized onion	1
100 g	minced mushrooms	4 oz
two 5 ml sp	mixed powdered mace, cloves, cayenne, allspice, pepper	2 tsp
two 5 ml sp	salt	2 tsp
75 ml	red wine, port or sherry	3 fl oz

Mix all the ingredients together and leave them for the flavours to amalgamate for an hour or two. Preheat the oven to 160°C/325°F/gas 3. Pack the mixture into a terrine, either round, rectangular or oval, so that it fills it well. Bake it, uncovered, in a bain-marie for two hours. If you intend to eat it hot, cook it with a weight on top or it will be impossible to slice. Serve it with hot gravy, made from the juices that have come from the meat, fat removed, with a little water and flour for thickening. If you intend to eat it cold, let it cool with a light weight on top, in its own liquor, which should set to a jelly.

AUTHOR'S NOTE: This can also be made with venison and veal.

Plum bread

This is traditional to Lincolnshire and it makes an excellent cake for picnics and high teas.

125 g	butter	4 oz
125 g	demerara sugar	4 oz
2	eggs	2
one 15 ml sp	brandy	1 tbsp
200 g	self-raising flour	7 oz
	pinch of salt	
125 g	chopped prunes	4 oz
125 g	sultanas	4 oz
125 g	currants	4 oz
50 g	chopped, candied peel (optional)	2 oz

Preheat the oven to 150°C/300°F/gas 2.

Beat the butter and sugar together until the mixture is light and fluffy. Stir in the eggs, one at a time; add the brandy.

Sift the flour and salt together and toss the fruit in a few spoonfuls of it. Fold the flour and fruit into the creamed mixture and turn the batter into a well-greased 25 × 10 cm/10 × 4 inch tin.

Bake it for 1½ hours or until an inserted skewer comes away clean. Cool the cake in the tin before turning it out.

Apple cream cake

1	thinly sliced cooking or dessert apple	1
150 g	butter	6 oz
250 g	sugar	8 oz
2	eggs	2
275 ml	double cream	½ pt
one 5 ml sp	vanilla essence	1 tsp
250 g	plain flour	8 oz
one 5 ml sp	bicarbonate of soda	1 tsp
one 5 ml sp	baking powder	1 tsp

for the topping

50 g	sugar	2 oz
one 5 ml sp	cinnamon	1 tsp
125 g	chopped walnuts	5 oz

Preheat the oven to 180°C/350°F/gas 4.

Sauté the apple slices in two 15 ml sp/2 tbsp of the butter until they are soft, then set them aside to cool.

Cream the rest of the butter with the sugar until it is light and fluffy. Beat in the eggs, one at a time, then stir in the cream and the vanilla. Sift the dry ingredients together and fold them into the creamed mixture. Put half of the mixture into a well-greased 25 × 10 cm/10 × 4 inch tin and layer the apple slices on top.

Combine the topping ingredients and sprinkle half of the mixture over the apples. Place the remaining cake mixture over the apples and sprinkle the other half of the topping over it. Bake the cake for 45 minutes or until an inserted skewer comes away clean. Allow the cake to cool in the tin before turning it out.

Porridge pastry

The farmer's wife who makes this says: 'It fills them up at hay-time.' The pastry is rather fragile, so pack it carefully.

300 g	shortcrust pastry (page 264)	10 oz
500 g	raspberry jam	1 lb
50 g	butter	2 oz
50 g	sugar	2 oz
100 g	porridge oats	4 oz

Preheat the oven to 220°C/425°F/gas 7.

Butter a 27.5 × 17.5 cm/11 × 7 inch Swiss roll tin and line it with the pastry. Spread the jam over the bottom. Melt the butter and stir in the sugar and the oats. Sprinkle this mixture over the jam and bake it for 25 minutes or until the edges of the pastry are nice and brown. Cool the pastry and cut it into squares.

Dorset and Cheddar cheeses

For these cheeses, see pages 241 and 243.

Dinner for Shrove Tuesday

Mussel and saffron soup
Tomato soup

Roast chicken stuffed in the modern way
Dorchester duck (stuffed shoulder of lamb)

Broccoli with Maltese sauce
Broccoli sautéed with cheese
Brussels sprouts with cream
Jerusalem artichokes

Traditional pancakes with variations
Apple pancakes
Curd cheese pancakes

Catholic countries may have more of a feast and more fun before the fasting and sobriety that ought to accompany Lent, but in England the only surviving Shrove Tuesday tradition is pancake-making and, in some places, scrimmaging for them or racing down the village street with them. Most English families insist on having the pancakes cooked just before they are to be eaten, with only lemon juice and sugar sprinkled on them by way of embellishment. This is fine if the rest of the meal has been cooked beforehand, leaving the top of the stove clear for two or three frying-pans so that the pancakes can be cooked as fast as they are eaten.

If the kitchen is too small to eat in, or if you prefer to have everything ready and waiting before you sit down to dinner, you can make filled pancakes that are heated up without spoiling just before serving.

Mussel and saffron soup *(for 6)*

1 kg	mussels	2 lb
1	small packet of saffron	1
1	glass of white wine or cider	1
125 ml	water	¼ pt
1	finely chopped medium-sized onion	1
50 g	butter	2 oz
two 15 ml sp	flour	2 tbsp
125 ml	cream	¼ pt
	chopped parsley	

Wash the mussels very well, using a scrubbing brush to remove any mud. Scrape off any barnacles and pull out the 'beards'. Discard any that float or have cracked shells. Leave them in a basin of cold water until you are ready to cook them: this helps to make their own sea-water juices a little less salty. Steep the saffron in the wine or cider. Drain the mussels and put them in a large pan with the measured water, over a high heat. Cover it and steam the mussels until they are all open. If you shake the pan vigorously once or twice during the short time that this should take, the mussels at the top will open as quickly as those at the bottom. Tip the mussels into a colander over a bowl. Remove any empty half-shells and any that haven't opened. Strain the liquor through a cloth into another bowl.

In a smaller pan sauté the onion in the butter until it softens. Stir in the flour and let it cook for a moment. Add the saffron-flavoured wine; stir well and then add the strained mussel liquor. This should make a smooth, lemon-coloured, creamy base for the soup. Add the cream and heat the soup almost to boiling point. Add the mussels and the shells of those that are still attached and continue to heat the soup, but do not cook the mussels.

Seasoning is unnecessary but sprinkle on parsley before serving the soup.

AUTHOR'S NOTE: I like to leave a few shells in the soup because they look so pretty against the yellow of the broth.

Tomato soup *(for 4–6)*

The beauty of this soup is that although it is made from tinned tomatoes, it doesn't taste in the least like tinned soup. The cream and egg yolks should not be stinted as they give a luxurious finish to it. If you want to make the soup in the late summer, when fresh tomatoes are plentiful and cheap, you will need approximately 1.20 kg/2½ lb of fresh tomatoes in place of the tinned ones.

100 g	chopped bacon	4 oz
one 15 ml sp	oil	1 tbsp
3	chopped medium-sized onions	3
1	chopped clove of garlic	1
3	chopped sticks of celery	3
three 396 g tins	tomatoes	three 14 oz tins
575 ml	chicken stock (page 263), or veal or beef stock	1 pt
1	small potato, cooked and mashed	1
	salt, pepper	
3	egg yolks	3
125 ml	single cream	¼ pt
	chopped parsley	

Fry the bacon in the oil until it is lightly browned. Add the onions, garlic and celery and cook them for about ten minutes until they are soft. Add the tomatoes and stock and cook, covered, for about one hour.

Puree the soup, then return it to the pan and stir in the potato, having first mixed it with a small amount of the soup in a bowl. Taste it for seasoning.

Leave the soup at this point if you are cooking well ahead of time.

Beat the yolks and cream together and stir them into the soup just before serving. Scatter plenty of parsley on each helping.

Roast chicken stuffed in the modern way *(for 4)*

The influence of France's *nouvelle cuisine* is as welcome to English cooking as it is to French. Its intention is to lighten the burden of rich, heavy food on our overworked digestions, and to allow fresh, uncluttered and original flavours to be tasted by our tired palates. It is inventive and bold too; this method of putting all the stuffing underneath the skin of the breast and thighs rather than into the cavity of the chicken has the double advantage of making the skin very crisp and the flesh deliciously tasty and moist. The stuffing used here is a traditional English one; other stuffings using finely chopped and sautéed vegetables such as mushrooms, celery and courgettes are worth trying, with a moist curd cheese (page 113) instead of breadcrumbs.

one 1.5 or 2 kg	chicken with its giblets	one 3 or 4 lb
1	finely chopped medium-sized onion	1
100 g	butter	4 oz
1	beaten egg	1
	fresh breadcrumbs	
one 15 ml sp	fresh thyme (or half quantity of dried)	1 tbsp
one 15 ml sp	crumbled dry sage	1 tbsp
1	clove of garlic, pounded to a paste	1
	salt, pepper	

Finely chop the liver, heart and gizzard of the bird.

Sauté the onion in half the butter until it is soft and golden, then add the chopped giblets and cook for two or three minutes more. Put the contents of the pan into a mixing bowl to cool, then add the egg and enough breadcrumbs to take up the moisture. Add the herbs and garlic and season the stuffing well.

Preheat the oven to 230°C/450°F/gas 8. If the chicken is trussed, untie it. Starting at the neck end, gently loosen the skin over the breast with your fingers, being careful not to break it. Work your way right along the breast to the other end as well as around the meat of the thighs, breaking any connective tissues between the meat and the skin.

Work the stuffing, a little at a time, beneath all the loosened skin, distributing it evenly by massaging it along from outside.

When all the stuffing is disposed of, retruss the chicken: tie the legs to the parson's nose and fold the pinions of the wings under the shoulders. Tuck the flap of neck skin beneath them. The chicken can be prepared a few hours in advance up to this point.

Rub the bird all over with the rest of the butter. Sprinkle it with salt and roast it for ten minutes before reducing the temperature to 180°C/350°F/gas 4. Cook it, basting often, for another 45–50 minutes, or until the thigh, when pricked, yields pale brown juices.

Serve the chicken with broccoli and Maltese sauce (see next page) or Brussels sprouts and cream (page 50); pass bread sauce (page 259) and gravy as well.

Dorchester duck *(for 6)*

This is a recipe not for duck but for a boned, stuffed shoulder of lamb, but it is tied in such a way that it looks like a duck. *You must make sure that the butcher leaves the shank bone intact* as this represents the 'duck's' head and neck. The butcher should take out the blade bone, and the middle bone of the three so that it leaves a 'tunnel' for the stuffing.

Dorchester is the capital town of Dorset, an area so famous for its spring lamb that it is now virtually unobtainable in that county in ordinary butcher's shops, since it is all sent to London or abroad where people are more willing to pay a high price for it. Coincidentally, this recipe is an adaptation from another Dorchester – the hotel in Park Lane – where chef Anton Mosimann stuffs a pastry-encased leg of lamb with herbs and lambs' kidneys and sweetbreads.

2.5 kg	shoulder of lamb	$4\frac{1}{2}$ lb
3	lambs' kidneys	3
	butter for frying	
	salt, pepper	
1	crushed clove of garlic	1
	large bunch of fresh green herbs such as parsley, thyme, sage and sorrel	
	dripping	

Bone the shoulder carefully as indicated above. The shank bone must remain intact and the outside should not be cut through at all. Trim off any excess fat.

Skin the kidneys. Cut them in half and trim out the fatty parts. Sauté them lightly on both sides in a little butter. Set them aside, sprinkled with a little salt and pepper and the crushed garlic.

Trim the stems from the herbs and chop them finely.

Open out the lamb and put half the herbs along the parts where the bones were, then lay the kidneys end to end on top of them. Cover the kidneys with the rest of the herbs.

Fold the meat carefully over the stuffing and, with a trussing needle and a long piece of string, sew it up in the shape of a duck, with the 'elbow' part of the shank bone representing the point of the breast bone. Start sewing at the 'tail end', where the curved top edge of the blade bone once lay. Spread a little dripping over it, and season it.

Weigh the 'bird' before roasting it, propped up on its bones. Calculate 20 minutes to the half-kilo/pound, starting with 20 minutes at 230°C/450°F/gas 8, and reduce the heat to 190°C/375°F/gas 5 for the rest of the time, basting often.

Remove the string before serving and prop the 'duck' with roast potatoes if it shows signs of keeling over.

Carve it like a loaf of bread, from the 'tail end'.

AUTHOR'S NOTE: The festive but slightly ludicrous aspect of this dish makes it very popular with children; however, not all of them like kidneys, so you could use the stuffing given for the chicken in this same menu.

Broccoli with Maltese sauce

Cook 1 kg/2 lb broccoli until it is only just tender. Drain it well and put it in a warmed serving dish with a covering of Maltese sauce (page 256).

Broccoli sautéed with cheese

After cooking 1 kg/2 lb broccoli in boiling salted water, drain it well and sauté it in plenty of butter. When it is well coated with the butter, mix in a spoonful or two of grated cheese. Serve it at once.

Brussels sprouts with cream

Prepare and cook 1 kg/2 lb sprouts in the usual way in boiling salted water until they are just tender. Drain them, then return them to the pan and toss them in enough thick cream to coat them well. Serve at once.

Jerusalem artichokes

Although I have not yet met anyone who is able to digest artichokes of this kind (the root variety) without having the most appalling wind some three or four hours later, it doesn't prevent me serving them to good friends. Artichokes can be boiled, then pureed with cream; sliced and sautéed with garlic and parsley; grated raw and added to salads; or steam-roasted in butter, in a single layer in a covered pan. Cooked like this they are a delicious alternative to potatoes with any roast. They may also be par-boiled and finished under the roast.

Traditional pancakes *(for 4)*

The longer a batter stands, the better it will be, so this is one thing you should prepare in advance. Give it anyway at least an hour to stand. This quantity should make 16 pancakes 18 cm/7 inches in diameter.

125 g	plain flour	5 oz
one 5 ml sp	salt	1 tsp
250 ml	milk	8 fl oz
3	eggs	3
one 15 ml sp	melted butter or flavourless oil	1 tbsp
	oil, butter or lard for frying	

for serving

sliced lemons
sugar

Sift the flour and salt into a bowl, make a well in the centre and add half the milk. Carefully mix it with the flour, using a batter whisk or a wooden spoon. In order to avoid a lumpy batter allow the flour to fall little by little from the sides of the well into the milk.

Mix in the eggs, one at a time, and then the rest of the milk with the melted butter or oil. You should have a perfectly smooth batter the consistency of thin cream. If it is lumpy put it through a strainer; if it is too thick add more milk.

Leave the batter to stand until you are ready to make the pancakes and stir it before you do so.

If you have a proper crêpe pan, use that; otherwise use a well-seasoned iron pan or a pan with a non-stick lining.

Heat a little oil, butter or lard in the pan. When it is hot pour about 50 ml/2 fl oz of batter into the pan and tilt it so that it flows evenly all over. (It is a great help if you can find a coffee cup or ladle that holds precisely the right amount of batter for the subsequent pancakes.) Cook over a fairly high heat. Shake the pan and lift the edge of the pancake to see if the underside is cooked. At this point show-offs will toss the pancake to turn it. More cautious cooks may prefer to turn it with a fish slice or fork. Cook the other side, more briefly.

Slide the pancake onto a hot plate, sprinkle with lemon juice, dredge it with caster sugar and roll it up. Have sugar and sliced lemons on the table so that everyone can add more sugar and squeeze more juice over their own pancakes.

Keep going till all the batter is used up, and make sure that you get some pancakes yourself.

Variations on pancake batter

The batter given above can be varied in many ways. In the first place, if it is to be used for savoury fillings, make it with less milk. Otherwise:

Add one 5 ml sp (a teaspoon) of *granulated sugar*, in order to make it browner and sweeter.
Wholemeal flour can be used instead of plain flour for a wheatier flavour.
Instead of all milk use: *all beer*, or *half water and half milk* for a lighter pancake; *half yoghourt and half milk; half soured cream and half milk*; *half orange juice and half water* – all for different textures and flavours.
Separate the eggs, beating in the yolks first, then add the stiffly whipped whites just before cooking. This makes light, almost soufflé pancakes.
Flavour the batter with a spoonful or two of *rum or brandy.*
Add more liquid and less egg for a more economical batter.

Apple pancakes *(for 4)*

Make twelve pancakes, using three-quarters of the batter given above, with a little rum in the mixture.

	for the filling	
500 g	cooking apples, peeled, cored and sliced	1 lb
	sugar to taste	
	grated lemon rind	
	grated nutmeg	
25 g	butter	1 oz

to finish

100 ml	rum	4 fl oz
	caster sugar	
	sweetened, whipped cream (optional)	

Cook the apples till they become a puree, then add sugar, lemon rind and nutmeg to taste, with the butter. Cook it some more until it is really thick.

Fill each pancake with a little of the puree. Roll them up and sprinkle them with a splash of the rum and caster sugar. Put them in a gratin dish under the grill to glaze the sugar.

Bring them to the table and warm the rum in a ladle over a burner. Ignite the rum as soon as it is hot enough and pour it, flaming, over the pancakes. You could serve sweetened whipped cream as well.

Curd cheese pancakes (blintzes) *(for 4)*

These are Jewish in origin, but the filling is almost identical to that in the curd tart (page 115).

Make eight pancakes (18 cm/7 inches), using half the quantity of batter on page 50. If you like, substitute beer for the milk. Cook them on one side only, then turn them over, cooked side upwards, to cool on a tea-towel.

for the filling

500 g	creamy curd cheese (page 113)	1 lb
1	large beaten egg	1
two 15 ml sp	vanilla sugar (page 268)	2 tbsp
100 g	raisins	4 oz
	pinch of salt	

to finish

butter

icing sugar

Mix all the ingredients for the filling together and put one eighth of the filling on one side of each pancake. Fold the edge over the filling, then fold in the sides, and roll it all up to make a neat bundle. Do this in advance and keep the pancakes very cool till you need them.

Just before serving, fry the blintzes in butter on all sides in a large frying-pan. Serve them very hot, liberally dredged with icing sugar.

SUMMER

A picnic lunch for a sporting occasion
An elegant English tea
A picnic for a Summer night
A May Week dinner

A picnic lunch for a sporting occasion

Green pea soup with shrimps
English clam chowder
Cold cucumber soup

Salt duck
Ginger chicken pieces
Raised veal, pork and chicken pie

Pitta bread (with salad fillings)

Fresh fruit

Doughnuts

All too often in England picnics take place in settings and on days which are dictated not so much by the landscape and the weather as by the sporting calendar. Rain stops play at tennis and cricket matches, but gymkhanas, regattas and agricultural shows continue regardless. All the more reason then, as the cold, wet and shivering spectators huddle in the lee of a car boot parked on a marshy waste, to cheer the participants and themselves with a good warming lunch. Not that you can count on the weather to be nasty, or the country to be windswept and sodden. It may be a scorching day, with blue skies and larks singing; it's best to be prepared for both possibilities.

The soups can be heated just before you leave home and kept hot in wide-necked thermos flasks. The next course is designed to be eaten without plates, knives or forks, as is the fruit – provide peaches, plums, apples, pears or bananas. It is therefore even possible to eat the whole picnic in a small dinghy, on your pony or up a tree if you want to get away from the rest of the family.

Green pea soup with shrimps *(for 8)*

By late summer, garden peas are becoming rather bullet-like, which makes them and their pods ideal for soups and purees. At the same time the shallow water at the edge of the beach is lovely and warm for paddling, shrimping and prawning. All around the coasts of Norfolk, Hampshire and the Isle of Wight, if the shore below high-tide mark is sandy and covered with a certain fine, hair-like green seaweed, there is a likelihood that you will find shrimps and prawns. (Morecambe Bay, in Lancashire, is an even richer shrimping ground.)

If you do find your own shrimps, cook them in boiling salty water (as salty as the sea) until they change colour. If not, all good fishmongers nearby sell local (and imported) shrimps in summer.

	for the stock	
	a ham bone or well-soaked knuckle of bacon	
2	peeled and sliced carrots	2
2	peeled and sliced onions	2
3 litres	water or light chicken stock	$6\frac{1}{2}$ pt
	pea-pods and shrimp shells (see soup, next page)	

	for the soup	
1 kg	fresh peas	2 lb
1.5 kg	shrimps in their shells	3 lb
	chopped fresh herbs (such as chervil, tarragon, summer savory or mint)	
	white wine or sherry	

Pod the peas and shell the shrimps.

Simmer the ingredients for the stock for an hour or so, without seasoning, as the ham bone or bacon may be salty enough. Strain the stock and measure 2.4 litres/ 4 pt into a saucepan.

Add the peas and cook them until they are tender. Sieve, puree or liquidise the soup and taste for seasoning. Add the shrimps and the chopped herbs. Stir in a little wine or sherry to taste, and serve the soup when it is heated through.

This amount fills one mug per person, if you are on a picnic. If you decide to have it in soup plates at home, serve croûtons and a whirl of cream in each helping.

English clams

Before puzzled readers reach for their pens to complain that there are no such things as English clams, let me assure them that there are and that they live and breed and are doing very well in Southampton Water. They are, in fact, exactly the same as American quahogs. They were first noticed after the war, just off the shore at Fawley. Here the water coolers of the oil refinery take cold water in and pump hot water out, raising the sea-water to around 70°F. No one knows exactly how they got there, but the notion that stewards on ocean-going liners were tossing their surplus New England clams overboard seems quite plausible.

Clams are now breeding in similar situations all round the British coastline, and being fattened, cleaned and marketed like our own native mollusc, the oyster. They are much cheaper than oysters, stay alive out of water longer, are less vulnerable to disease, and taste almost as good, some say better. But there is still no great demand here for the English clam. As a result, most of them are exported, like our lobsters, salmon, venison . . .

It is certainly easier to buy clams in London than in any of the fish shops within a mile of their breeding grounds. They keep well in a cool place for up to three weeks without needing any water, and can also be frozen as they are, in their shells. Discard any clams that have opened when you come to use them.

English clam chowder *(for 8)*

If you are having salted duck for this picnic, use the fat from that in place of the first ingredient. If you are having chicken, make the stock for this soup from its carcase (the stock from the duck may be too salty).

500 g	very fat belly of salt pork or bacon, or the fat from salt duck	8 oz
24	medium-sized clams *or* the contents of two 300 g/10 oz tins	24
1	sliced onion	1
500 g	peeled and cubed potatoes	1 lb
one heaped 15 ml sp	flour	1 heaped tbsp
1 litre	juice from the clams made up to the right amount with chicken stock (page 263) or water	2 pt
500 ml	milk	1 pt
25 g	butter	1 oz

Cut the pork, bacon or duck fat into small pieces and render down the fat in a heavy frying-pan.

Open the clams by steaming them in a little water in a closed saucepan over a high heat. As soon as they are open stop cooking them. Strain the liquor for the soup and mince or chop the clams quite finely. (If you are using tinned clams reserve the liquor. The clams may be small enough to need no further attention.)

As soon as the renderings in the frying-pan are crisp, take them out; they are to be served with the soup. Fry the onion in the remaining fat until it is soft and lightly coloured.

Put the onion slices into a saucepan with the potatoes and clams and sprinkle them with the flour. Do not season the soup as the clams and their liquor are already salty. Add the stock and clam liquor and cook until the potatoes are tender.

At this point mash the potatoes down a little, then add the milk. Heat the chowder through and taste it for seasoning. Stir in the butter.

If the chowder is for a picnic, put it, very hot, into thermos flasks, with the crisp pork, bacon or duck fat pieces in another container to sprinkle on as you serve it. You will need mugs, teaspoons to scoop up the clams, and rolls to eat with it.

Author's note: Cockles (page 100) are a very good substitute for clams. Sweet-corn (which grows prolifically and commercially on the Isle of Wight) can also be put in a chowder. Cook it first, then scrape the cooked corn into it.

Cold cucumber soup *(for 4–6)*

Just in case the weather is warm, here is a pale green soup that is delicious chilled. If it is really cold when you put it in the thermos, it will stay that way. Otherwise put it in a preserving jar and wrap it well in layers of wet newspaper.

50 g	butter	2 oz
1	peeled and chopped medium-sized onion	1
2–3	peeled and chopped medium-sized potatoes	2–3
1.5 litres	chicken stock	3 pt
1	large cucumber (or 2 small ones)	1
	salt, pepper	
1	small bunch of watercress *or*	1
1	large tomato	1
125 ml	sour cream or plain yoghourt	$\frac{1}{4}$ pt

Melt the butter in a large saucepan and soften the onion in it without letting it colour. Add the potatoes and stock and simmer for ten minutes.

Peel the cucumbers only if the skin tastes bitter, otherwise leave it on as it makes the soup a pretty colour. Leave about a quarter of the cucumber to be diced finely for the garnish and put the rest, roughly chopped, into the soup. Cook it for another ten minutes, when both potatoes and cucumber should be tender.

Puree the soup, either through a sieve or in a liquidiser or food processor, and adjust the seasoning; chill it.

Make a garnish with a combination of the cucumber and either the finely chopped watercress, or the tomato, peeled, de-seeded and cut into small dice. Stir it into the soup with the cream or yoghourt before serving, or before you pack it for the picnic.

Salt duck *(for 8)*

This recipe is Welsh in origin. It has the effect of making duck taste rather like ham, and it is definitely better eaten cold than hot. Salt was once 'won' from the sea-water all along the flat, low-lying coastline of Hampshire (hence the numerous places called Salterns). The only place in England that processes sea salt commercially now is Maldon in Essex.

Lady Llanover, who first published this recipe in 1867, recommends poaching it in a panful of water that is itself standing in a pan of boiling water, a sort of bain-marie, but I suspect this may have been because she had no other way of keeping the duck at the merest whisper of a simmer. In fact, a modern cooker, while probably too small to accommodate such a contraption, will at least ensure that the duck cooks *as slowly as possible*.

Start salting the duck four days in advance of the picnic.

1	large (or two small) duck(s)	1
100 g	coarse sea salt or Maldon salt	4 oz
	bunch of herbs (optional)	
1	onion (optional)	1

Rub the duck very well all over with the salt, and make sure plenty goes inside too. (If the salt is too coarse you may have to crush it down a bit.) Put the duck in a cool place in a china dish. Turn it over a few times during the next three days and baste it with the brine that forms round it.

The day before the picnic rinse the salt off in cold water and wrap the duck in a muslin cloth.

Cover it with cold water and add a bunch of herbs and an onion, if you like. Let it reach boiling point very slowly, and simmer it for about two hours from this moment, depending on its size.

Take the duck out of the water to cool. You will be pleased to find that it has not shrunk nearly as much as a roast duck, but the fat and skin, it must be admitted, are not so attractive. Trim them off as you carve the duck into fine slices.

Use it either for a salad, or, if you are having a picnic, for filled pittas (page 62) or brown bread sandwiches.

A salad that goes well with this duck is composed of watercress and slices of orange (page 226). Picnickers may like to eat slices of melon instead, or try pickled samphire (page 246).

AUTHOR'S NOTE: The duck fat should most certainly not be thrown away. Render it down, keeping the fat that runs out for sautéed potatoes and the crisp, salty little 'scratchins' that remain as a garnish for soup (see the clam chowder on page 57) or as appetisers with drinks. The stock may be rather salty; if so, use it with caution.

Ginger chicken pieces *(for 8)*

Skilful cutting will make eight pieces from one large chicken: two drumsticks, two thighs, two wings with a fair slice of breast attached, and the remaining breast cut across into two pieces. Use the back, giblets and skin to make stock for soup. Start the day before, as the chicken needs several hours to marinate.

8	large skinned chicken pieces	8
two 15 ml sp	grated fresh ginger (or half as much powdered)	2 tbsp
2	peeled, crushed cloves of garlic	2
	juice of a large lemon	
two 15 ml sp	oil	2 tbsp
50 g	seasoned flour	2 oz
1 or 2	beaten eggs	1 or 2
	dry breadcrumbs	
	oil for frying	

Prick the skinned chicken pieces all over with a skewer, and soak them overnight in a marinade made from the ginger, garlic, lemon juice and oil. Turn them once or twice.

Next day shake as much marinade

from the pieces as you can and coat them in the flour, then the egg, then the breadcrumbs.

Fry them in fairly deep oil (about 1 cm/½ inch), then let them drain and cool before packing them up for the picnic.

AUTHOR'S NOTE: These are, of course, also very good hot. Pass lemon wedges with them.

Raised veal, pork and chicken pie

The best raised meat pies (pork pies in particular) are made in Yorkshire and the Midlands; the shops there make them so well that no-one would dream of making their own at home. In the South, however, a home-made meat pie may well turn out better than a shop one. Also, with home-made ones you can vary the fillings to suit yourself and decorate the top with appropriate symbols, initials, or whatever.

This recipe will give you one 1.375 kg/2¾ lb pie, or about one dozen little 100 g/4 oz pies.

You need a special hinged boat-shaped or rectangular pie tin with a capacity of about 1 litre/2 pints. Otherwise use a well-greased loaf tin or a cake tin with a removable base.

Make the jelly well in advance because it takes a long time.

to make the stock for the jelly

1	calf's foot (or 2 pig's trotters)	1
1	veal knuckle	1
2	large carrots	2
1	unpeeled, medium-sized onion, stuck with a few cloves	1
	bunch of herbs	
	water to cover the bones	

Simmer all the ingredients together for at least four hours, partially covered, skimming off all the floating particles as they appear.

Strain the stock through a cloth and skim off the fat when it is set. You will now be able to see the strength of the jelly: if it is not strong enough reduce the stock by fast boiling, but don't season it before you have done so. The jelly must be very firm.

	for the filling	
150 g	lean veal	6 oz
325 g	lean pork	10 oz
250 g	pork fat	8 oz
one 15 ml sp	salt	1 tbsp
one 15 ml sp	fresh thyme	1 tbsp
half 5 ml sp	ground allspice	½ tsp
1	crushed clove of garlic	1
1	beaten egg	1
three 15 ml sp	port or cognac	3 tbsp
100 g	chicken breast meat	4 oz

Mince half the quantity of veal, pork and pork fat very finely. Chop the remainder into small cubes. Mix all the meat together with the rest of the ingredients, excluding the chicken which will be used at a later stage. Cover the mixture and leave it to mellow for at least six hours, preferably overnight.

Next day if you are dubious about the seasoning, sauté a small spoonful of the mixture for a minute or two, then taste it. Seasoning should be stronger than usual, as when the pie is cooked and cold it seems much milder.

For the pastry:
Use either 500 g/1 lb hot-water crust (page 267) or a shortcrust enriched with two egg yolks (page 265).

To line a boat-shaped tin:
Grease the tin. Roll the dough fairly thickly (about 2 cm/¾ inch thick), reserving enough to make two lids for the top. Make a rectangle to fit the base and sides of the tin. Dampen the short sides. Fold the rectangle in half lengthways and press the damp sides together at each end. You can now lift and position the pastry inside the tin. Pat the dough well into the corners, being very careful not to allow it to crack – it should stretch a bit. Trim off the excess, leaving an overhang (pinched fairly thin) of about 2.5 cm/1 inch.

Make *two* covers for the top, of exactly the same size and shape (use a paper pattern to do this). These two lids should each be 0.5 cm/¼ inch thick. The lining can be made an hour or so in advance.

To fill a large pie:
Put half the filling into the pastry-lined mould and then a layer of the chicken breast, cut into strips. (See also the Author's note for alternative fillings.) Fill up the mould with the rest of the filling, not packing it too tightly as it expands at first during cooking, and might burst the lining.

Put one of the lids on and fold the overhanging pastry lining over it. Brush the top with water and press the second lid in place. Decorate the top with appropriate patterns, using water to attach the decorations.

Cut two steam holes through the pastry top, making sure they are big enough to insert a small funnel when the pie is cooked. Keep them open with a tube of foil or paper while the pie bakes.

To make small pies:
Roll out the required number of circles about 1 cm/½ inch thick. Shape the pies round a well-floured pot or jam jar or use an old fashioned wooden pie mould. Make sure the pastry is kept very cool. Fill the pies at once, putting a well-sealed lid on top with a hole for the jelly to go in eventually. Support the sides by tying on a band of grease-proof paper.

To cook the pie(s):
Preheat the oven to 200°C/400°F/gas 6.

Glaze the top with beaten egg mixed with a pinch of salt. Bake the pie for 20 minutes. Lower the heat to 160°C/325°F/gas 3 and continue baking for another two hours. (Small pies need only a little over an hour.) If the pie appears to be getting too brown, cover the top with a piece of grease-proof paper or foil.

When it is cooked, let it cool for about one hour before removing the pie form or tin. Chill the pie for at least six hours before filling the space between the meat and the crust with jelly (though there's an equally strong school of thought that says put in the jelly as soon as the pie leaves the oven). Let the jelly set for two or three hours before you cut the pie.

AUTHOR'S NOTE: Instead of, or as well as, the chicken breasts in the middle of the pie, you could have strips of cooked ham or tongue or whole hard-boiled eggs, whole pickled walnuts (page 246) or even chicken livers.

Other raised meat pies can be made with:

all pork (Yorkshire and the Midlands); veal and ham; mutton, mushroom and onion (Cumbria); game; beef, suet and a whole hard-boiled egg (Devon); rabbit or hare; venison with redcurrant jelly (page 249) instead of meat jelly. If you make more than one sort of pie for the same occasion, let the decoration be a clue to the contents. It was always the custom, in markets and pie-shops, to give mutton pies a garnish of mint sprigs and pork pies a sprig of sage, to tell one from the other.

Pitta bread *(for 8)*

There is nothing traditional or English about pitta bread, nor would you have expected to find it in grocers' shops and supermarkets in towns all over the land, ten or even five years ago. But it makes an ideal pouch, not just for Greek-Cypriot kebabs and mezes, but also for all sorts of English salads and savoury foods. In one English family at least the filled pitta has replaced sandwiches, pies and pasties in the school lunch-box as well as in the picnic basket. It is, of course, ideal for barbecues too (page 121).

Pittas are as easy to make as ordinary bread and they use the same dough. The secret of success is to bake them on pre-heated earthenware tiles (the unglazed kind used on roofs). They transmit the heat to the dough better than a tin sheet. The aim is to create a pocket of steam inside, which, when the pitta is cooked, remains a pocket to be filled.

To make eight pittas, use the same quantity of dough as that given on page 35 for cabbage bread. Let the dough rise once, then knead it again.

Shape the pittas by dividing the dough into eight equal pieces. Make each piece into a neat ball. Let them rest for a few minutes, then roll them into ovals about 0.5 cm/¼ inch thick. Cover them with a cloth and leave them to prove until they are twice as thick.

Preheat the oven with as many tiles in it as will fit, to a temperature of 230°C/450°F/gas 8. Bake the pittas on the hot tiles (or tin tray) for ten minutes. Let the cooked pittas cool a little before splitting and filling them. If you are not using them at once, keep them soft by wrapping them in a cloth. If you want to use them after they have cooled completely, warm them a little in a toaster or under the grill to make them easier to split open.

Good fillings for pittas:
First, peanut butter, spread inside, is better than ordinary butter.

Then a selection of:
sticks or slices of cucumber; shredded raw cabbage, carrot or lettuce; slivers of cold meat such as ham, beef, chicken, duck; slices of tomato, onion or hard-boiled egg; mustard and cress, spring onions, grated cheese; grilled skewers of meat (page 126) or hot hamburgers; tinned sardines or tunny fish, roughly broken up (but leave out the peanut butter).

Author's note: You can sprinkle a salad dressing or mayonnaise in as well if you like, but don't let the contents become soggy. Have everything sliced, cut, or grated small enough to make it easy to eat. Pittas can also be made with wholemeal flour, and will freeze well.

Doughnuts *(makes 8)*

These are supposed to be traditional to the Isle of Wight; I had been making them for sailing club picnics for years on the other side of the Solent before I discovered this, so they now seem even more appropriate. If you want to keep them warm, which is how they taste best, half-fill a cardboard box with hay or straw, line it with a cloth and then some grease-proof paper, put the hot doughnuts in that, cover them with more paper and another cloth and then more hay or straw. Shut the box and the doughnuts will stay warm for hours.

25 g	sugar	1 oz
15 g	fresh yeast (or half quantity of dried)	½ oz
125 ml	warm milk	¼ pt
250 g	plain flour	8 oz
	pinch of salt	
1	egg	1
25 g	melted butter or margarine	1 oz
	fat or oil for deep-frying	
50 g	caster sugar	2 oz

Cream the sugar and the yeast, then add the milk, flour, salt, egg and melted butter or margarine. Knead to a dough and leave it to prove until it has doubled in bulk. Knead again, and divide the dough into eight pieces. Roll them into balls, flatten them, and put them on a greased baking-sheet to prove.

Heat the fat or oil hot enough to brown a crumb of bread within a minute. Drop as many doughnuts as you have room for into the fat. After a time they will turn over of their own accord but if they don't, help them on their way with a slotted spoon. Cook the doughnuts until they are golden all over. Take them out of the fat and roll them in the sugar.

Author's note: If you want to make ring doughnuts, either use a special doughnut cutter or use one large cutter with a smaller one to make the hole in the middle. For jam or cream doughnuts, it is much simpler to slice them open after they are cooked and put the jam or cream in then.

An elegant English tea

Potted shrimps and potted crab

Sandwiches

Kentish huffkins
Sally Lunns

Fruit tartlets
Choux buns with cream and caramel
Hazelnut meringues
Brandy-snaps

Walnut cake
Sponge cake
Victoria sponge cake
Cherry cake

In contrast to the other teas in this book, this one is rather restrained, mainly because it is not, and never was, designed as a main meal – there has been lunch beforehand, and there will be dinner later.

It is the aristocratic kind of tea that used to be served every day, with special cakes for an occasion such as a birthday, or a tennis party, or the visit of a local dignitary, perhaps the Vicar. It could be taken in the garden if the weather is warm enough; if not, the tea table should be laid indoors, with the best linen cloth, a silver tea service, buttered toast kept warm in a lidded silver dish, the best china and a bowl full of roses in the centre. Naturally there is a choice of Indian or China tea, with milk or lemon, and most of the participants should be ladies, gossiping.

Elegant afternoon tea came into vogue in the 18th century. Cakes, scones and biscuits are now rarely home-made in the South – it's easier to buy them. You might even think the art had died out, unless you have the good fortune to visit a local fête, or a garden party, or a market stall, where those great upholders of English cake and jam making, the ladies of the Women's Institute, are selling their wares. The speed with which they sell out shows that home-made cakes are still among England's favourite foods. If you want this occasion to be extra festive, include either the tea cream or the Sussex cream from the midsummer night's menu (pages 83 and 84).

Potted shrimps and potted crab

To 500 g/1 lb of shelled and chopped shrimps or shelled and mashed crab-meat, add 150 g/6 oz of melted butter. Stir it all together until the butter is absorbed, and season it to taste with salt, cayenne, ground ginger and powdered mace. Pack the mixture tightly into small pots leaving a little room at the top.

Melt 50 g/2 oz of clarified butter (page 264) and pour this over the shrimp or crab. Let it solidify so that the butter on top forms an airtight seal. Serve the paste next day with thin slices of warm toast, either as an appetiser or as a start to tea.

Sandwiches and their fillings

The sandwiches for an elegant tea party should be as dainty as possible – forget about the two-inch doorsteps which you've made for school lunches, hikes and sporting picnics – these sandwiches will consist of two mouthfuls each and no more. Nor will there be much to chew – the crusts are all removed, of course. The bread (as close-grained and as fresh as possible) must also be cut very thin, so have a good sharp knife, or ask the baker if he has a slicing machine which can be set to fine.

Sandwiches take much longer to make than they do to eat, so it is a good idea to make them a few hours in advance – they will keep quite fresh wrapped in plastic film or in a damp cloth. Platefuls of sandwiches can be kept in the fridge if they are covered first with grease-proof paper and then with a damp cloth. It helps if the butter is soft before you start to spread it, but if the fillings are very moist, put the already buttered bread in the freezer for a little while before you spread the fillings – the hardened butter will then stop the fillings seeping through. It also helps to speed things up (and economise on butter) if you spread one side with butter only and the other with the filling (if it is not too soggy) before fixing the two together.

Don't make too many sandwiches or people will never get round to eating anything else. If you have a great many different fillings either cut each kind in a different shape – fingers, triangles, half-moons or rounds of white as well as brown bread – or label them with little flags.

SANDWICH FILLINGS

Apart from the classic favourites such as lemon-juiced and black-peppered slivers of *smoked salmon* in brown bread, thinly sliced seasoned *cucumber* in white or brown bread, and any home-made, stoneless red *jam* with white bread, these are a few other suggestions.

Egg: chopped hard-boiled egg mashed to a paste with softened butter, salt, pepper and cayenne. (This can also be mixed with mashed sardine.)

Mustard and cress (or one without the other): chopped finely, then mixed with softened butter or cream cheese and salt.

Watercress or nasturtium leaves: treated as above (they are related species).

Chicken, ham or turkey and mayonnaise: finely chopped and seasoned chicken, ham or turkey moistened with a little mayonnaise or cream cheese. You might also add a layer of shredded lettuce or watercress.

ROLLED SANDWICHES

These are whole slices of crustless buttered bread rolled round a filling.

They may need fastening with a tooth-pick at first, which can be removed after chilling and before serving. The best fillings are cream cheese flavoured with chopped herbs or chopped nuts, tiny sprays of watercress and (best of all) cooked asparagus tips. The bread for these sandwiches needs to be about 6.5 cm/2½ inches square.

PIN-WHEEL SANDWICHES

These look like miniature slices of Swiss roll and should be made with a filling that contrasts well with the colour of the bread. Cut slices lengthways from a loaf of bread and cut off the crusts. Spread each slice with the filling. Roll it up from the short end and chill the roll before cutting it across into little pin-wheels. Fillings for white bread could be jam, pâté or a creamed fish paste (see the bloater paste on page 17). For brown bread, choose cream cheese, egg or cress (see above).

Kentish huffkins *(makes 10–12)*

These are soft, oval rolls with a dent in the middle. Bakers in East Kent appear to have forgotten how to make them; if they're made at all these days, they're made at home.

25 g	fresh yeast (or half quantity of dried)	1 oz
two 15 ml sp	granulated sugar	2 tbsp
225 ml	warm water	8 fl oz
100 g	lard or shortening	4 oz
two 5 ml sp	salt	2 tsp
225 ml	scalded milk	8 fl oz
500 g	plain flour	1 lb
	beaten egg	

Cream the yeast with a little of the sugar and a little of the water, and leave it to become frothy. Cream the fat, the salt, and the rest of the sugar in a bowl and add the hot milk and water. Stir it in until the fat has melted and the mixture has become lukewarm. Add the yeast mixture. Gradually incorporate the flour with your hands until you have a soft dough. Knead it a little, then leave it to rise in a covered bowl in a warm place for about an hour.

When the dough has doubled in size, knock it down again, then roll or pat it out on a floured board to about 2.5 cm/1 inch thick. Cut out rounds about 6.5 cm/3½ inches across and pull them into oval shapes (or, if you have one, use an oval cutter 11.5 cm/4½ inches long). Make a dent in the centre with your thumb. Put them on a greased baking-sheet and leave them to prove while the oven heats up to 220°C/425°F/gas 7. Glaze them with the beaten egg.

Bake the huffkins for 15–20 minutes until they are golden. Wrap them in a cloth when you take them out of the oven to keep the crusts soft. Eat them with butter and jam.

Sally Lunns *(makes 2 large or 4 small buns)*

These are the southern English equivalent of a plain Yorkshire tea-cake – but here they are slightly lighter and are given a glaze to make them golden and shiny, a feature which lends strength to the theory that their name is really a corruption of the French *soleil lune* (meaning a sun and moon cake), rather than the name of the lady of Bath who sold these buns in the streets there in the 18th century. They should be split open and served, still hot, with clotted or whipped cream inside them. Some recipes give cream or milk and butter in the ingredients for the dough too; if you use good, well-flavoured rich cream it will give the buns a better flavour than the milk and butter. The size can be anything between 10 cm/ 4 inches and 15 cm/6 inches across, and 6 cm/2½ inches to 8 cm/3 inches high. Sally Lunns are delicious in wedges with strawberries or fresh peaches and cream.

500 g	plain flour	1 lb
one 5 ml sp	salt	1 tsp
25 g	fresh yeast (or half quantity of dried)	1 oz
25 g	sugar	1 oz
125 ml	warm milk *and*	¼ pt
100 g	melted butter *or*	4 oz
250 ml	warm, single cream (instead of the milk and butter)	½ pt
2	eggs (one of them beaten)	2

Sift the flour and salt. Add the yeast, creamed with the sugar, and mix in the milk with the butter stirred into it, or the warmed cream. Add the beaten egg. This will make a rather soft dough.

Leave it to rise in a warm place for half an hour, or until it has doubled in size. Knock it back and divide it among the round, greased tins. Preheat the oven to 200°C/400°F/gas 6 while the buns prove.

Separate the yolk from the white of the other egg and brush the buns with the yolk. Bake them for 15 to 20 minutes.

Split them open and fill them with cream that has been whipped, sweetened and mixed with the whipped, left-over egg white.

English cakes

The oldest recipes for cakes in England are almost all forms of enriched, sweetened, fruited and sometimes spiced yeast doughs, like bread with a few extras thrown in. These are still with us, in the shape of plum bread (page 43), saffron cake (page 216) or Ripon spice cake (page 187). They were usually made for special occasions and feast days, and baked in tin or wooden hoops, after the bread had been in the oven. Other, smaller cakes were made for fairs, and were called fairings. These are still made too: see Cornish fairings (page 218) and brandy-snaps (page 71). People also made scones and cakes on griddles (pages 116 and 144).

The invention of ovens with controllable temperatures and the use of aluminium as well as tin for cake-tins has made cake-making easier and more reliable at home. As soon as cooks found they could get the temperature exactly right, they could use eggs instead of yeast to make their cakes rise, and with the invention of baking powder and self-raising flour, eggs and yeast became alternatives rather than essentials. Also, as sugar became cheaper, cakes got sweeter.

The sort of cakes that were eaten by farmers and farm-workers were robust and filling, like the cakes given in the high-tea menus. Ladies sipping tea in their tea-gowns would have lighter, more delicate cakes and biscuits, often with rich cream or chocolate fillings, like the ones here.

Fruit tartlets *(makes 12)*

375 g	rich shortcrust pastry (page 265)	12 oz
	pastry cream (page 268) made with about 275 ml/½ pt of milk	
250–500 g	cooked or raw fruit (see below)	8–16 oz
	light-coloured fruit jelly	

Preheat the oven to 220°C/425°F/gas 7. Grease twelve 8 cm/3¼ inch tartlet tins.

Roll out the pastry and line the tins. Chill the pastry for about an hour.

Spread a layer of pastry cream on each tartlet and bake them for 15 minutes before or after arranging the fruit in them (depending upon the choice of fruit).

Finish the tartlets by glazing them with the heated jelly (preferably when they are cold), or glaze the tartlets with a reduction of the sugar syrup in which the fruit was cooked.

Cherry tartlets

Add 250 g/8 oz of fresh, pitted cherries before cooking the tartlets. Glaze them with a red fruit jelly.

Bilberry tartlets

Cook 500 g/1 lb of bilberries in a light sugar syrup, drain them, and reduce the syrup by fast boiling until it is very thick. Bake the tartlets with a layer of pastry cream and allow them to cool. Cover each tartlet with a layer of bilberries and glaze them with the reduced syrup.

Pear or apricot tartlets

Cook 250 g/8 oz of pear slices in a light sugar syrup until they are tender; drain them and reduce the syrup as before, until it is very thick. Bake the tartlets with a layer of pastry cream (page 269) and allow them to cool. Arrange the pear slices on each tartlet. Glaze them with the reduced syrup.

AUTHOR'S NOTE: The tartlet shells can also be filled with pastry cream and fruit *after* the pastry has been cooked.

Choux buns with cream and caramel *(makes 16)*

choux pastry made with 100 g/4 oz of flour (page 267)

350 g	sugar	11 oz
100 ml	water	4 fl oz
1	beaten egg	1
575 ml	double cream	1 pt
one 5 ml sp	vanilla essence	1 tsp

Preheat the oven to 200°C/400°F/gas 6.

Put the pastry into a pastry bag fitted with a wide nozzle (approx. 1 cm/½ inch), and pipe 5 cm/2 inch mounds well apart on a well-greased baking-sheet. Brush the buns with the beaten egg and bake them for 25–30 minutes or until they are firm and golden-brown. Transfer them to a rack to cool. (They can be kept overnight in an airtight container, or they can be frozen, but they are best eaten within a few hours of baking.)

For the caramel, dissolve four large spoonfuls of the sugar in the water and then boil the mixture until it develops a nice golden colour. Plunge the base of the pan in a bowl of warm water to prevent the caramel from cooking more. Dip the top of each bun into the caramel and set them aside to allow it to harden.

Whip the cream with the remaining sugar and the vanilla just until it forms soft peaks. Pipe it from a pastry bag fitted with a small nozzle (approx. 0.5 cm/¼ inch) into the base of each bun in order to fill it with cream.

AUTHOR'S NOTE: Instead of caramel you could make a coffee icing by heating a mixture of icing sugar, water and instant coffee powder.

Hazelnut meringues *(makes 12)*

150 g	shelled hazelnuts	6 oz
4	egg whites	4
100 g	caster sugar	4 oz

Preheat the oven to 180°C/350°F/gas 4.

Spread the hazelnuts on a baking-sheet and toast them for 12–15 minutes or until they have browned. Transfer them to a cloth and rub them with another cloth to remove their skins. Grind the nuts to a powder in a food processor or liquidiser. Turn the oven down to 160°C/325°F/

gas 3. Beat the egg whites until they hold stiff peaks. Beat in two large spoonfuls of the sugar and continue beating until the whites are glossy. Fold in the remaining sugar and the ground nuts.

Spoon the mixture into a piping-bag fitted with a large nozzle and pipe it out in uniform circles onto a lined and greased baking-sheet. Alternatively, drop the mixture from a large spoon onto the baking-sheet.

Bake the meringues for 30–40 minutes or until the tops are very crisp. Transfer them immediately to a wire rack to cool. Serve them plain or sandwiched together with cream.

Brandy-snaps *(makes 25)*

These, like many other sweet, sticky, spicy things (gingerbread men, toffee apples, Cornish fairings) were traditionally sold at fairs. These brandy-snaps are associated in particular with Nottingham Goose Fair.

100 g	butter	4 oz
100 g	sugar	4 oz
six 15 ml sp	black treacle or golden syrup	6 tbsp
one 5 ml sp	powdered ginger	1 tsp
100 g	sifted plain flour	4 oz
575 ml	brandy-flavoured whipped cream	1 pt

Preheat the oven to 150°C/300°F/gas 2.

Heat the butter, sugar and treacle together and stir them well. Add the ginger. Take the mixture off the heat and add the flour, a little at a time, beating well between additions.

Drop blobs of the mixture from a small spoon onto a greased baking-sheet. Leave plenty of space for the blobs to spread out into thin wafers as they cook. Bake them, a few at a time, for about 12 minutes.

Take them out of the oven and let them cool for about two minutes, then roll them carefully round the greased handle of a wooden spoon. As they cool you can remove them. Alternatively, shape them into cones round a cream horn mould.

Fill them with brandy-flavoured whipped cream just before you serve them.

AUTHOR'S NOTE: If they start to set before you've rolled them up, you can soften them again by returning the tray to the oven for a few moments.

Walnut cake

A walnut tree is a bonus in any large garden – tall and shady and, in a good year, a provider first of green walnuts for pickling in June or July (page 246) and then of ripe walnuts, for cracking by the fire, eating with port, adding to sauces (see page 138), putting in bread (see page 108), or storing till next year when they will still be good enough to make one of the most English tea-time treats, walnut cake. (Store the walnuts in sand to keep them fresh.)

4	separated eggs	4
200 g	caster sugar or vanilla sugar (page 268)	7 oz
125 ml	double cream	¼ pt
one 5 ml sp	vanilla essence (optional)	1 tsp
90 g	sifted, plain flour	3½ oz
200 g	ground walnuts	7 oz

for decoration

sweetened, whipped cream
ground walnuts
icing sugar

Preheat the oven to 180°C/350°F/gas 4.

Beat the egg yolks with 150 g/6 oz of the sugar until they are light and creamy. Stir in the cream and the vanilla essence (if you are not using vanilla sugar).

Whip the egg whites with the remainder of the sugar until they are firm. Combine the flour and walnuts and add this to the yolk mixture, alternating with spoonfuls of the egg white. Fold all the ingredients together, but only just enough to distribute the ingredients evenly.

Put the mixture into a well buttered and floured 20 cm/8 inch cake tin and bake it for 45–50 minutes, or until a cake-tester comes out clean. Turn it out of the tin when it is cool.

To decorate the cake, slice it in half horizontally, and spread a mixture of sweetened whipped cream and ground walnuts on the lower half. Replace the top half and scatter icing sugar over it, or make a soft glacé icing (see opposite) and stick walnut halves all round the top.

Sponge cake *(weighs 500 g/1 lb)*

4	eggs	4
125 g	sugar	5 oz
125 g	plain flour	5 oz
50 g	melted and cooled unsalted butter (optional)	2 oz
half 5 ml sp	vanilla *or* the grated rind of one lemon or orange (optional)	½ tsp
	sweetened whipped cream or jam	
	icing sugar	

Preheat the oven to 180°C/350°F/gas 4.

Put the eggs in a large bowl and whisk them till they are well broken up. Gradually add the sugar, beating constantly. Put the bowl over a pan of simmering water and continue to whisk the mixture until it is thick enough to leave the track of a figure of eight with the whisk. (If you do this by hand it is much easier to do the whisking standing on a low stool at the side of the stove – it takes about 15 minutes. Alternatively, use an electric whisk – this takes ten minutes.)

Remove the bowl from the heat and add the flavouring, if any. Continue to beat as the mixture cools.

Sift the flour over the now foamy egg mixture, stopping three times while you blend in the flour with your bare hand. Keep it as airy as possible while blending it as well as you can. Add the butter, if you are using it, with the last sifting.

Pour the mixture into a well-buttered and floured 20 cm/8 inch cake tin and bake it for 20–25 minutes, or until the cake is springy to touch, with the edges shrinking from the sides of the tin. Leave it to cool for five minutes before taking it out of the tin. Cover a wire rack with a cloth before turning the cake onto it if you wish to have a completely smooth surface. Leave it to cool completely before slicing the cake in two horizontally, and spread the lower half with sweetened whipped cream, or raspberry preserve (page 250), or even both. (Put the jam on the other half.) Sandwich the two halves together and sift icing sugar over the top.

AUTHOR'S NOTE: The addition of butter gives the cake a richer flavour and slightly firmer texture, but without it the cake is much more ethereal. This cake is very popular as a birthday cake for small children, many of whom appear to be unimpressed by the more traditional kind made with dried fruit and covered with hard icing.

Cherry cake

100 g	butter	4 oz
100 g	sugar	4 oz
2	separated eggs	2
100 g	halved glacé cherries	4 oz
100 g	plain flour	4 oz
50 g	ground almonds	2 oz
one 5 ml sp	baking powder	1 tsp

Preheat the oven to 180°C/350°F/gas 4.

Cream the butter and sugar together until the mixture is light and fluffy. Beat in the egg yolks, one at a time. To prevent the cherries from sinking to the bottom of the mixture, toss them in a spoonful of the flour, and incorporate them and the almonds into the mixture.

Sift the flour and baking powder together and beat the egg whites until they are stiff. Fold the flour and whites alternately into the mixture and turn it into either two small or one large well-greased and lined loaf tins. Bake it for approximately 45 minutes (an hour for one large cake) or until an inserted skewer comes away clean.

AUTHOR'S NOTE: If you like, give the cake a coat of icing. Wait till it is cold, then make a quick frosting by beating one egg white with a pinch of salt, 150 g/6 oz of caster sugar, two 15 ml sp/2 tbsp of water and a pinch of cream of tartar. Beat the mixture in a bowl set over a pan of simmering water until it thickens, whitens and forms peaks. Pour it over the cake and smooth it quickly with a warmed palette knife over the top and sides. Put six glacé cherries round the top and one in the middle. This icing can also be used for the walnut cake (page 71) in which case decorate the cake with walnut halves.

Victoria sponge cake

This is known as a Victoria sponge (or Victoria sandwich), to differentiate it from the other kind of sponge (page 72). It is more substantial and keeps better.

150 g	margarine or butter	6 oz
150 g	caster sugar	6 oz
3	large beaten eggs	3
150 g	sifted plain flour	6 oz
one 5 ml sp	baking powder	1 tsp

for the filling

butter cream or Vienna cream (see below)

Preheat the oven to 190°C/375°F/gas 5. Grease two 20.5 cm/8 inch sandwich tins and line the base with greased greaseproof paper.

Cream the butter and sugar together until the mixture becomes light and fluffy. Add the eggs a little at a time, beating them in well to make sure the mixture doesn't curdle.

Sieve the flour with the baking powder and fold it into the creamed mixture in batches.

Pour the mixture equally into the two tins and level off the tops. Bake them on the same shelf for 20 minutes. Cool them on wire racks after they have rested in their tins for five minutes.

Make sandwich fillings with a butter cream mixture or a Vienna cream. *To make a butter cream* mix 125 g/5 oz of creamed and softened unsalted butter with 250 g/10 oz of sifted icing sugar, adding one or two 15 ml sp/1–2 tbsp of warm milk or water and some vanilla essence.

To flavour it with orange or lemon, leave out the vanilla and substitute the grated rind and juice of the fruit. To flavour it with coffee, add a few spoonfuls of strong coffee. To flavour it with chocolate, mix in 25–40 g/1–1½ oz of melted chocolate.

To make a Vienna cream beat 100 g/4 oz of unsalted butter and 100 g/4 oz of icing sugar until the mixture is white, then add the yolk of an egg, with flavourings as above.

For special occasions coat the top and sides of the cake with the butter or Vienna cream, as well as putting it between the two layers of cake. For ordinary tea parties, just dust the top of the cake with icing sugar and sandwich them together with jam.

A picnic for a summer night

Courgette strips
Trout and mushroom paste with Norwich coquilles
Squid stuffed with squid
Watercress cream soup

Cold lobster soufflé

Fillet of beef
Stuffed duck with green salad

Cucumber salad with yoghourt

Frosted redcurrants
Meringue nests
Tea cream
Sussex cream

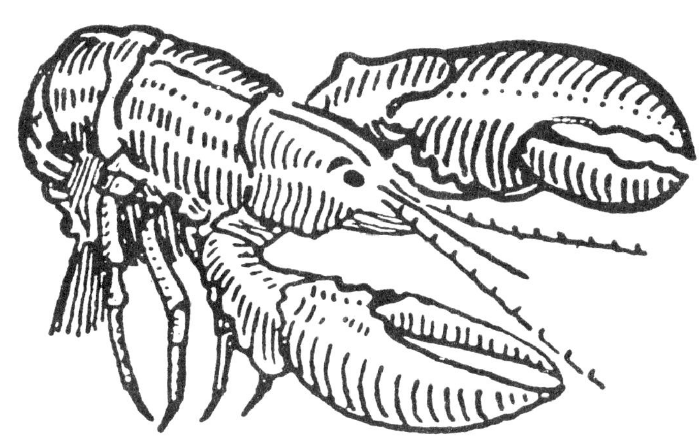

This slightly extravagant menu is for a very grand, midsummer night picnic, the sort you can take to Glyndebourne.

Everyone is in evening dress; the setting is a beautiful garden, there is the scent of flowers that have been open to the sun all day, and now the night is musky, with not the slightest hint of rain.

It is considerably easier to serve this sort of food in your own garden (especially as the house is a close retreat if it *does* rain); the kitchen is nearby and nothing needs packing up if you stay at home. But with freezing bags, tightly closing polythene boxes and insulated picnic bags this sort of meal could be transported anywhere, to emerge several warm hours later as cool, crisp and fresh as it was when you packed it.

Courgette strips

These are crisp and nutty, nice to eat with drinks before the meal begins and a very good way of using up a glut of courgettes. Freshly picked courgettes are best. Peel them in strips, leaving bands of skin lengthways, or leave them unpeeled. Then cut them into thin strips, about 1 cm/½ inch wide. Sprinkle them with lemon juice and salt. Eat them raw.

Trout and mushroom paste *(for 6)*

1–2	trout (total weight about 750 g/1½ lb)	1–2
100 g	butter	4 oz
50 g	finely chopped mushrooms	2 oz
	salt, pepper	
	anchovy essence	
	clarified butter (page 264)	

Clean the trout but leave them whole. Put a little of the butter into the stomach cavity, wrap the fish in buttered foil or grease-proof paper and steam them for half an hour.

Meanwhile, sauté the mushrooms in the rest of the butter. When the fish are cooked, drain them, carefully reserving any juice that has formed, and skin and bone them. Mash the flesh well and mix it with the mushrooms and cooking liquor. Add salt, pepper and anchovy essence to taste and mix everything very well.

Pack it firmly into a pot and cover it with clarified butter. Refrigerate it and eat it cold as a first course spread on the coquilles (see next recipe) or toast (if you are at home) or with a little salad.

Norwich coquilles *(makes 20)*

These plain buns are baked in scallop shells (rather like Aberfrau cakes, in Wales). The pattern of the shell imprints itself on the underside of the bun. They were once made during Lent. Use small, well-indented curved scallop shells; if you can't get them use shell-patterned bun tins. (The very reason that these tins are patterned in such a way is because at one time scallop shells were always used to bake tarts, little cakes and buns.)

50 g	sugar	2 oz
25 g	fresh yeast (or half quantity of dried)	1 oz
275 ml	warm water	$\frac{1}{2}$ pt
500 g	plain strong bread flour	1 lb
50 g	butter	2 oz
1	egg	1
half 5 ml sp	salt	$\frac{1}{2}$ tsp

Cream the yeast with the sugar and stir in the water. Rub the flour and butter together; add the egg and the salt. When the liquid has a froth on top mix in the flour and knead the resulting dough well.

Leave it in a warm place to rise, and when it has doubled in size knock it down again, then divide it into 20 pieces. Roll each piece into a smooth ball and put it in a greased and floured scallop shell, slightly flattening the top. Leave the balls to prove while the oven heats up to 200°C/400°F/gas 6. Bake them for 20 minutes, or until the underneaths as well as the tops are brown. Arrange them so that the patterned sides show.

Squid stuffed with squid *(for 4–6)*

Channel fishing boats often catch squid and cuttlefish; they used to be sold for their ink and their flat, internal, calcareous shells. They are in fact molluscs but their shells are inside rather than outside. The ink made sepia ink (the Italian for squid is *seppia*) and the cuttlefish bones were given to cage birds to peck, but few people in England ever actually ate the fish. Even quite recently English fishing boats would exchange their catches of squid with French fishermen for more acceptable fish.

Today, travel abroad has broadened our range of taste, but lacking any traditional English recipes for our own native squid we have to use foreign ones. This, from Spain, makes a good cold start to a meal, or you can eat it (as in Spain) as a *tapas* with drinks.

2	large squid weighing 150 g/6 oz *and*	2
2	small squid weighing 75 g/3 oz	2
60 ml	olive oil	2½ fl oz
4	finely chopped spring onions	4
three 15 ml sp	finely chopped parsley	3 tbsp
1	finely chopped clove of garlic	1
25 g	breadcrumbs	1 oz
	salt, pepper	
1	lemon	1

for garnishing

slices of white, red or black radish

Prepare the squid by pulling off their heads and removing the transparent bone inside each body. Wash the bodies well and peel off the thin brown skin that covers them. Take the triangular fins from the sides of the bodies and peel them too. Cut the tentacles from the head and remove the little 'beak' that forms the mouth. Chop the fins and tentacles very finely and sauté them in a little oil. Add the spring onions, parsley, garlic and breadcrumbs and season the mixture with salt and pepper. Add a little grated lemon rind and a squeeze of lemon juice. This is the stuffing.

Put some of the stuffing into the larger squid, then push each of the smaller squid into the bodies of the larger ones, and fill them with the rest of the stuffing. Close the tops with tooth-picks.

Preheat the oven to 180°C/350°F/gas 4. Put the stuffed squid into a casserole with the olive oil and lemon juice and add water to cover. Put the lid on and bake them for two hours, when they should be very soft. Let them cool in the liquid, then take them out and slice them into thin rings. Serve them on a flat dish, with slices of white, red or black radish between each stuffed squid ring.

Watercress cream soup *(for 8–10)*

50 g	butter	2 oz
1	sliced onion	1
2	thinly sliced sticks of celery	2
2	diced medium-sized potatoes	2
1½ litres	chicken stock (page 263)	3 pt
150 g	watercress leaves	6 oz
575 ml	single cream	1 pt
	salt	
	white pepper	

Melt the butter in a deep saucepan. Add the onion and celery and cook them until they are soft. Add the potatoes and the stock, and simmer until the potatoes are completely soft. Add the watercress and continue cooking for a few minutes until the watercress wilts.

Puree the mixture in a food processor or liquidiser and return it to the saucepan. Stir in the cream. Season to taste and heat the soup through before serving, or chill it and put it in a thermos for the picnic.

Lobsters

Like crabs, these are caught in abundance around our coasts, but they command far higher prices. As a result, they find their way to the markets abroad, like so many of our other best foods.

They are at their best and most plentiful in the summer. Lobsters are not sold smaller than 700 g/ $1\frac{1}{4}$ lb. If you are buying one ready-cooked, ascertain that it has been only recently cooked and, what is more, cooked alive. The meat deteriorates very fast once the animal is dead, and even if cooked alive, it becomes dry and tasteless if it is not eaten soon after cooking. Make sure too that the lobster has both its claws, as they contain a lot of meat.

A lobster is dark blue in life, and very nippy; if you can face cooking it yourself make sure its claws are bound up. The official way to deal with a live lobster or crab is to put it into a large pan with plenty of cold, salted water. Put the lid on and weight it down. Bring the water slowly to the boil and close your ears to the scrabbling noises. Time the cooking to allow 15 minutes from when the water boils for the first 500 g/ 1 lb and ten minutes for each subsequent 500 g/ 1 lb. Take it out of the water to cool (it is now bright red), and if it is to be displayed in its shell, make it shiny with a rubbing of oil. Cool crabs upside down after cooking, to keep their meat moist.

To extract the meat, use nutcrackers or a hammer on the claws, skewers or picks on the legs, and use poultry shears or a sharp knife for halving the body. There is some meat in the head. If the lobster is female, you may find some bright red coral under the tail, which should be reserved for decoration or for making a sauce. Remove all the parts which are grey and are not edible.

If you can afford it, serve lobster just as it is, with mayonnaise (page 254) and a plain green salad. If not, spread one expensive animal among several people by making the following dish.

Cold lobster soufflé *(for 4–6)*

1	freshly boiled 750 g/1½ lb lobster	1
125 ml	single cream	¼ pt
two 5 ml sp	brandy	2 tsp
	salt, pepper	
15 g	gelatine	½ oz
25 g	butter	1 oz
575 ml	milk and water, mixed	1 pt
	bay leaf	
one 5 ml sp	tomato puree	1 tsp
2	egg whites	2

for garnishing

paprika
lettuce leaves, tomatoes
hard-boiled eggs
mayonnaise (page 254)

Take the meat out of the lobster, reserving any coral for decoration. Liquidise or mince the meat finely and mix it with the cream and brandy, seasoning it well. Put the gelatine in a cup of water to soften it.

Crush the shells as finely as you can (using a hammer, with the shells confined in a wrapping of paper). Sauté them in the butter, then stew them, covered, in the milk and water mixture with the bay leaf and other seasoning for ¾–1 hour. Strain it – it will have reduced to about 275 ml/½ pt. Melt the gelatine in its cup in a bain-marie, then stir it into the liquor and heat it gently over the bain-marie to make sure that it dissolves properly. Add the tomato puree. Fold it into the lobster and cream mixture and taste for seasoning.

Beat the egg whites with a pinch of salt to a fairly stiff foam and fold them into the mixture. Put it all either into a soufflé dish which holds it comfortably (700 ml/1½ pt, and best for transporting it to a picnic) or, if you are eating at home, into one that you can heighten with an oiled collar of paper, to be removed once the soufflé has set. If it is to be left in its dish, decorate the top with the coral, cut into pieces, or a dusting of paprika.

Turn it out at the picnic onto a bed of lettuce leaves and decorate it with slices of tomato and hard-boiled egg. Serve it with mayonnaise.

AUTHOR'S NOTE: This soufflé can also be made with 250 g/8 oz of minced chicken, crab or salmon; use chicken stock (page 263), crab-shell stock or salmon fumet (page 263) for the liquor.

Fillet of beef

Allow 125/150 g (5/6 oz) of meat per person. Preheat the oven to 220°C/425°F/gas 7. Remove the surplus fat and skin from the centre cut of a piece of fillet weighing at least 2·5 kg/5 lb. Rub the surface of the meat with a generous amount of olive oil and sprinkle it with salt and pepper.

Place it on a rack in a shallow roasting pan and roast it for about 35 minutes or until it has reached an internal temperature of 50°C/125°F for a rare piece, or 60°C/140°F for medium-rare. Allow the roast to stand for 15 minutes before carving it. The meat may be served hot, or eaten cold with a strong horseradish sauce (page 258) and pitta bread (page 62).

AUTHOR'S NOTE: If you intend to slice your meat in advance and package it for a picnic, let it cool first.

Stuffed duck *(for 8–10)*

This is troublesome to make, but well worth it. To outward appearances it is a cold duck, decorated or not as you wish; it is in fact boneless and stuffed with a rich mixture of liver, veal, duck and chicken.

Start work on the preparations two days before it is to be eaten. All the duck should be boned except for the lower legs and wings. If you don't know how to do this ask the butcher. (It is in fact quite easy if you have a strong, sharp knife and lots of patience.) Reserve the liver for the stuffing and keep the bones for the stock.

1	boned duck (2.5 kg/5 lb original weight)	1
	salt, pepper	
four 15 ml sp	brandy	4 tbsp
four 15 ml sp	white wine	4 tbsp
750 ml	stock made from the duck and chicken bones and giblets, a pig's foot, a bunch of herbs, a carrot and an onion	$1\frac{1}{2}$ pt

To bone the duck it may be necessary to cut right through the skin down the back. If so, spread the duck out, skin side down, and salt and pepper the inside, giving it a sprinkling of the brandy and wine as well. Leave it to rest while you prepare the stuffing.

for the stuffing

1	duck liver	1
250 g	pig or chicken livers	8 oz
	oil and butter for frying	
100 g	rindless bacon rashers	4 oz
275 g	pie veal	12 oz
1	small roasting chicken (or the breasts of a large one)	1
1 or 2	whole chicken livers	1 or 2
250 g	cooked ham or tongue in one piece	8 oz
2	crushed cloves of garlic	2
	marjoram, thyme, parsley	
	salt, pepper	
	a few skinned pistachio nuts	

Sauté the duck liver and the 250 g/8 oz of pig or chicken livers in a little oil and butter, just enough to colour it, then mince it with the bacon and veal, plus any pieces of the chicken that are too small to make into nice long strips.

Marinate the whole chicken livers and the best pieces of the chicken, cut into strips, in the rest of the brandy and wine. Cut the ham or tongue into strips 0.5 cm/ ¼ inch square and 10 cm/4 inches long.

Mix the minced meats with the garlic, herbs and seasoning, and add the pistachios. Add a little of the cooled stock to moisten the mixture. Test the stuffing for seasoning by frying a very little piece of it, then tasting it. Put the liquid from the marinated chicken into the mixture.

Heat the oven to 160°C/325°F/gas 3. Stuff the duck with alternating layers of minced meat, chicken livers, chicken and the ham or tongue, laying the strips lengthways so that they look pretty when the bird is sliced across. Make the stuffing into a bolster-shape and carefully sew the duck up and around it, matching the edges. Tie two broad tapes round it at each end to stop it spreading out flat. Put the bird seam side down on a piece of foil so that you can easily lift it in and out of a casserole. Put it into a casserole, baking tin or fish kettle which just fits it and surround it with the cooled stock. Cover the duck with foil and cook it for one and a half hours, then remove this foil, turn up the heat to 190°C/375°F/gas 5 and cook it for another half hour, when it should become quite brown. It will also have returned to more or less its original shape. Take the duck out of the pan and allow it to cool before you undo its tapes and threads.

For a picnic the duck can be taken just as it is, garnished with lettuce leaves and sliced as you want it. For a party at home, it can be decorated with strips of blanched green spring onion leaves, cucumber skin, slices of pimento or orange, and so on, and then glazed with the jellied stock.

Serve it with a green salad. Keep the vinaigrette (page 255) in a separate container and mix it in at the last minute.

Cucumber salad with yoghourt

This is a favourite salad in the Middle East and India. Shred the cucumber coarsely, or cube it fairly finely, then salt it. Rinse and drain it and mix it with yoghourt, to which you can add a crushed clove of garlic, a little cayenne and some finely chopped mint.

Frosted redcurrants

This can be done for July picnics, when redcurrants are in season. Choose bunches with big currants, not too squashy and over-ripe or it will not work. Boil 250 g/8 oz of sugar with 575 ml/1 pt of water to make a thin syrup. Cool it to lukewarm, then dip each bunch of redcurrants into it. Shake them and roll them at once in caster sugar. Lay them on grease-proof paper, in the sun (if there is any) to dry, or in a warm, airy place.

Meringue nests *(makes 24)*

6	egg whites	6
quarter 5 ml sp	salt	$\frac{1}{4}$ tsp
375 g	caster sugar	12 oz

Preheat the oven to 200°C/400°F/gas 6.

Begin to beat the egg whites with the salt, if possible in a copper bowl. When the whites hold soft peaks, gradually beat in the sugar, and continue whisking until the whites are very stiff.

Spoon the meringue in mounds onto parchment paper on baking-sheets, and with the back of a spoon make nest-shapes – they should be about 7.5 cm/3 inches across. Put the meringue nests into the preheated oven and immediately turn off the heat. Do not open the oven door for at least 12 hours.

Remove the nests from the sheets and fill them before serving, or store them in airtight tins.

AUTHOR'S NOTE: The nests can be filled with a base of either ice-cream, whipped cream, or pastry cream (page 268) and topped with fresh fruit. Strawberry ice-cream (page 93) and freshly sliced strawberries are one possibility, but for a picnic stick to whipped cream and fresh soft fruit, and assemble the nests when you arrive.

Tea cream *(for 6)*

This is a delicate thick cream from a collection of old Sussex recipes. It should be eaten with a teaspoon from a wine glass. It is poured in the glasses as soon as it is cooked and is therefore only suitable for eating at home. It also needs to be served very cold.

575 ml	double cream	1 pt
one 5 ml sp	crushed coriander seeds	1 tsp
	the thin peel from a whole lemon	
75 g	caster sugar	3 oz
125 ml	strong, cold China tea	$\frac{1}{4}$ pt
6	egg whites	6

for decoration

ratafias or macaroons

Simmer the cream with the coriander, lemon peel and sugar for about ten minutes. Add the tea.

Whisk the egg whites fairly stiffly and strain the cream and tea onto them, whisking as you do so. Continue whisking the mixture in a saucepan over a gentle heat until it becomes thick (about 15 minutes). Pour it into six small wine glasses. The foam will set at the top and the rest will stay creamy. Pass ratafias or macaroons with it.

Sussex cream *(for 6–8)*

This is another Sussex recipe. It can be carried in its bowl and turned out at the last moment. It is a custardy, orange-and-almond-flavoured jelly, and similar to an old English flummery.

25 g	powdered gelatine	1 oz
575 ml	milk	1 pt
4	egg yolks	4
	grated rind of an orange	
125 g	sugar	5 oz
100 g	finely crushed macaroons	4 oz
125 ml	single cream	$\frac{1}{4}$ pt
three 15 ml sp	sherry	3 tbsp
	a few halved glacé cherries or other glacé fruits	

Soak the gelatine in a cupful of the milk. Bring the rest to the boil.

Beat the egg yolks in a basin and pour the hot milk onto them, as if you were making custard. Add the orange rind, sugar and macaroons and stir the mixture over a double-boiler until it thickens. Heat the cup of gelatine until it melts. Add the sherry, the cream and the gelatine and make sure this mixes in completely. (Heat the mixture over a double-boiler to be quite certain.)

Strain the custard through a sieve. Arrange the cherries or glacé fruits at the bottom of a prettily shaped 1 litre/2 pt wetted mould. Pour in the jelly and turn it out when it is set.

A May Week dinner

Asparagus
Tomato consommé
A fish terrine

Turkey breast with potatoes and cream
Spring stew of veal

Early summer vegetables

Strawberries and cream
Strawberry ice-cream or strawberry fool
Elderflower sorbet
Grassy Corner

Like Welsh rarebits, which are neither Welsh nor rabbits, and wedding breakfasts which are not breakfasts at all, but lunches, teas or dinners, Cambridge May Week is not held in May, but in the first two weeks of June. Like Oxford Commems, May Balls are occasions of great feasting and jollity, with dancing and champagne lasting all night till dawn. They celebrate the end of the academic year and the graduation of students and add a little more gilding to the most golden years of their youth.

It is nice to have a celebratory dinner too. If the idea of eating at a restaurant or in College, or at the Ball itself is unappealing, this menu is designed to help you feed as many people as possible quite festively; if you prepare as much as you can in advance it even allows the Cinderella in the kitchen to go to the Ball as well.

The land around Cambridge is rich, and largely horticultural. From it come asparagus, turkeys and strawberries – all the best things for a May Week dinner.

Asparagus

Every morning from early May to the end of June the asparagus fields of Cambridgeshire, Suffolk and Lincolnshire are filled with bent-backed figures – women cutting asparagus long before their children have even got to school, so that the spears can be graded, packed and put on a train by midday. From here it goes all over England, to be eaten as fresh as possible. If you live nearby you may have the advantage of being able to buy odd or unshapely spears very cheaply at the farm gate, with the added advantage of even greater freshness.

It is an expensive crop to grow, because you must wait for three years before cutting it, and once established it stays there for up to fifteen years, to the exclusion of anything else. However, in one season an acre can yield as much as two tons of asparagus, so it may be said to earn its keep.

The kind mostly grown here is green and tender all the way down. Michael Paske who grows and sends many tons of asparagus every year from this area, recommends cooking it like this: put the washed and lightly scraped asparagus in a single layer in a baking tin, tie it loosely together and support the heads with a pillow of foil. Pour boiling salted water over the stems and simmer them on top of the cooker, uncovered, until the bases of the stems feel soft. If it has been frozen it can be cooked in the oven straight from the freezer, arranged in a baking tin in the same way without the water, dotted with butter and covered with foil.

Asparagus is sold in 1 kg/2 lb or half kg/1 lb bundles. Half a kilo/ 1 lb is a modest amount for four people.

The best way to eat it is undoubtedly with melted butter and nothing else, but if you want a change, try it with a hollandaise sauce (page 256) or dipped into softly boiled egg yolks (one egg per person).

Tomato consommé *(for 10–12)*

This is a beautiful, clear, light red, jellied consommé, made with a base of chicken stock (page 263). To colour and clarify it for this recipe, proceed as follows:

3 litres	chicken stock	5–6 pt
6	egg whites	6
375 g	chopped lean beef	12 oz
4	chopped carrots	4
4	chopped celery sticks	4
4	chopped leeks	4
8	pulped tomatoes	8
	salt, pepper	
100 ml	dry sherry	4 fl oz
	peeled, de-seeded tomatoes (optional)	

Put the stock into a large pan and heat it to lukewarm. In a large bowl mix the egg whites, chopped meat and vegetables.

Pour the stock into this bowl, whisking at the same time. Return the mixture to the pan and bring it slowly to the boil, still whisking continuously. In about ten minutes the mixture will turn milky white. When this filter has become quite firm make a 'chimney' in it to allow the steam to escape.

Without allowing it to boil, leave the pan to simmer for 30 minutes to one hour, in which time the meat and the vegetables should have given their flavour to the soup. (The egg tends to reduce the original flavour somewhat.) Strain it by putting a damp cloth over a bowl, and carefully ladling the soup into it. It should then be completely clear. If it is not, strain it again. Taste for seasoning and add the sherry.

Allow the consommé to cool. It should set to a light jelly. Spoon it into individual bowls (white china or plain glass show off the colour nicely) and garnish each one with strips of peeled, de-seeded tomatoes if you like.

AUTHOR'S NOTE: If the chicken stock is clear and strong enough to begin with it will not need clarifying, but you should cook it with the tomatoes for about ten minutes to colour and flavour it before straining it through a cloth as above.

Alternative flavours and garnishes for a plain chicken consommé

Oysters or clams: Put two or three small, raw oysters or clams in each bowl. (This is an economical way to add a luxurious touch to the first course.)

Herbs: Simmer a bunch of fresh herbs such as parsley, thyme, marjoram and tarragon with the consommé for about 20 minutes, then take it out and serve the soup with a garnish of chopped chives or chervil.

Vegetables: Cut carrots, celery, turnips and leeks into thin shreds or small dice, as appropriate. Blanch them and add them to the soup.

Eggs: For each person, poach a small hen's egg or, even prettier, a couple of quail's eggs in the soup. Serve them with the soup. (A large poached egg on a slice of toast with hot consommé poured over it is a remarkably nourishing meal in itself.)

Peas and chicken (Princess): Add cooked green peas and diced cooked chicken to the soup.

Lemon and parsley: Add lemon juice to taste to the hot consommé, then let it cool and jellify. Serve it broken up with a thin slice of lemon and a sprig of parsley in each bowl.

A fish terrine *(for 10)*

Fish terrines are rather in vogue these days. They are just as easy to make as the more familiar meat pâtés, and much more delicate. They can look extremely pretty too.

This one contains two different mousselines or purees, one an opaque white, the other pink, interspersed with strata of green, orange and translucent white. It is served hot with a cream sauce, made from the bones of the fish.

for the white mousseline

750 g	skinned fillets of white fish (such as sole, whiting, pike or cod)	$1\frac{1}{2}$ lb
2	lightly beaten egg whites	2
	finely grated and blanched rind of a lemon	
	salt, pepper	
425 ml	double cream	$\frac{3}{4}$ pt

Make a puree of the raw fish, either in a food processor or with an old-fashioned pestle and mortar. Blend in the egg whites. Pass the mixture through a sieve or food mill to make sure you have a really smooth, fibre-free puree. Add the lemon rind and seasoning to taste. Cover, and refrigerate the mixture for about an hour.

When it is well chilled, add the cream (which should be equally cold) a little at a time, beating each addition vigorously with a wooden spoon. Make sure that the fish absorbs it before adding more. The mixture should remain very firm.

for the pink mousseline

250 g	smoked salmon scraps	8 oz
2	lightly beaten egg whites	2
125 ml	double cream	$\frac{1}{4}$ pt
two 15 ml sp	lemon juice	2 tbsp
	cayenne pepper	

Make a puree of the salmon adding the ingredients in the same way as for the previous mousseline, making sure that it remains very firm.

to assemble the terrine

	the white and pink mousselines	
	salt, pepper	
250 g	blanched and dried spinach leaves, stripped of stems	8 oz
6	large scallops	6
	any roe from the white fish	
	parsley or watercress	

Preheat the oven to 190°C/375°F/gas 5.

Generously butter an 850 ml/$1\frac{1}{2}$ pt terrine. Test the seasoning of the two mousselines, either by tasting them raw or by cooking a spoonful in boiling water, then tasting, and add a little salt or pepper if necessary.

Spread half the white mousseline on the bottom of the terrine, and half the spinach over it in a thin layer. Spread half the pink mousseline over that and then arrange any roes on top of that, to either side. Cut the white parts of the scallops across if they are very large, and line them down the centre. Arrange the corals of the scallops on either side of the white parts.

Cover this with the remaining salmon, spinach and white fish, in layers, in that order.

Cover the terrine with aluminium foil if it has no lid of its own. Put it in a bain-marie and cook it in the oven for 35 minutes, or until the pâté feels firm.

Turn it out onto a long dish. Blot up any juice that may ooze from it and garnish it with sprigs of parsley or watercress. Serve it hot in slices with a cream sauce (page 260).

AUTHOR'S NOTE: You could take this recipe as a starting point for even more decorative-looking terrines; the white puree could be divided into three: one part stained yellow with saffron, another made red with tomato puree. Speckled effects can be obtained with chopped watercress or parsley. You could also use thin strips of carrot, string beans or mushrooms to enliven the pattern (blanch firm vegetables before arranging them).

Turkeys

Turkey rearing has always been traditional in East Anglia; it is now a thriving industry creating a national all-the-year-round appetite to consume all the turkey meat, which costs half as much as red meat.

Turkey farming suits the arable farms of East Anglia because turkeys are mostly fed on grain. Three hundred years ago Norfolk turkeys would be walked to London in time for Christmas, taking three months to get there and eating on their way at farms along the route. (Fortunately in 1724 someone invented a four-storey carriage so that they were able to do the journey in crates, in only 60 hours. After 1890 they were sent by train.) Old-fashioned turkeys were bronze or black; today the customer prefers white ones as the feather stubs show up less on the plucked bird. Indeed it is only the occasional trail of white feathers dotting the hedges of lanes to and from the 'processing stations' that gives any evidence of the huge flocks of turkeys being reared in these parts.

The best turkeys have been reared in open-sided sheds to give them a good 'finish', which includes some fat on their breasts at maturity. They have a good flavour and are allowed to hang a while after being killed. They are then 'dry-plucked' by hand. The pluckers are skilled local ladies on piece-work; the best can pluck eight birds an hour and a champion plucker takes only three minutes per bird.

After dry-plucking, the bird is either blast-frozen or sold fresh. Birds thus reared, hung with the guts in and plucked, but with the head and feet still on may be officially described as 'traditional farm fresh'.

Cheaper birds are often killed before reaching maturity and 'wet-plucked' – scalded before plucking by rubber flails – then 'wet-frozen' – a process that can add up to 15 per cent of water to their weight.

If you buy a frozen turkey, of either kind, let it *thaw in the fridge* as slowly as possible: four to five days is not too long for a 16-pounder.

Turkey pieces can be bought at very advantageous prices from the packing plants of turkey farms. They are also becoming increasingly available fresh and frozen along with 'burgers' and rolled and stuffed fillets at many butchers and supermarkets. These pieces cut from huge 18–27 kg/40–60 pound birds are rapidly becoming a cheaper alternative to beef, pork or lamb. A leg from a really large turkey could easily weigh the same as a leg of lamb, and escalopes or fillets from the breast make an excellent alternative to veal.

Turkey breast with potatoes and cream *(for 8)*

This is an admirable way of cooking turkey escalopes (or fillets as they are sometimes called). Two of the other ingredients, main-crop potatoes and onions, are also grown widely in Cambridgeshire.

1.5 kg	raw turkey slices (from the breast)	3 lb
75 g	butter	3 oz
three 15 ml sp	cooking oil	3 tbsp
100 ml	chicken stock (page 263) or turkey stock	4 fl oz
	salt, pepper	
1 kg	finely sliced onions	2 lb
1 kg	thinly sliced potatoes	2 lb
750 ml	milk	1½ pt
	grated nutmeg	
1	peeled clove of garlic	1
one 5 ml sp	mixed herbs (thyme, marjoram, savory and powdered bay leaf)	1 tsp
100 ml	thick cream	4 fl oz
	chopped parsley	

The turkey should be cut into about sixteen 1 cm/⅜ inch thick slices. Quickly sauté each one in a mixture of half the butter and half the oil, in a heavy iron pan, cooking them just enough to turn them from pink to creamy white. Set them aside as they are done.

Deglaze the pan with half the stock, pour it over the turkey and season the slices. Heat the oven to 200°/400°F/gas 6.

Heat the rest of the butter and oil in the pan. Cook the onions in it, very gently, covered, stirring from time to time until they are soft and golden (about 20 minutes). Season them lightly and if they have made a lot of juice, leave the lid off for the last five minutes.

At the same time, cook the potatoes in the milk with a little salt and nutmeg, until they are just done. They will also need to be stirred from time to time.

Rub a large gratin dish with the garlic. Put in a neat layer of half the onions and then the turkey. Add the rest of the onions and sprinkle the herbs over them. Pour over the rest of the stock and any accumulated meat juices. Lastly put the potatoes in a layer to cover everything, with the milk which by now will have thickened considerably. The dish can be prepared this far in advance. Keep it cool.

Just before it goes in the oven dribble the cream over the top. Bake it for about 15 to 20 minutes, finishing it under the grill to brown the surface.

Serve it sprinkled with parsley.

Well buttered and minted green peas, broad beans, and baby carrots, would go well with this dish.

Spring stew of veal *(for 4–6)*

This recipe comes from Eliza Acton. Her excellent *Modern Cookery* first appeared in 1845, some sixteen years before Mrs Beeton, but (although her equal) she is still, inexplicably, by far the less well-known of the two.

1 kg	trimmed, cubed veal from the neck or shoulder	2 lb
	salt, pepper, flour	
	butter and oil for frying	
1	large cucumber, quartered lengthways	1
1	coarsely chopped soft lettuce	1
100 g	gooseberries	4 oz
275 ml	water	½ pt
	bunch of spring onions (optional)	

Season the meat and coat the pieces with flour. Sauté them in a mixture of oil and butter until they are pale golden, then transfer them to a casserole.

Cut the cucumber, unpeeled, into neat 2.5 cm/1 inch pieces, trimming them to the shape of olives if you want to give the dish an elegant touch. Sauté them in the same pan that was used for the meat and put them in the casserole too. Sauté the lettuce and the gooseberries, adding more butter if necessary. Cook them long enough for the juices to come out and evaporate. Add them to the meat.

Deglaze the pan with the water and when it boils pour it into the casserole.

Cover the casserole and cook it on a very low heat for 45 minutes to one hour. Taste for seasoning (the gooseberries will have given it a nice sharp tang) and, just before serving, stir in the finely chopped spring onions, if you like. Alternatively, the spring onions can be cooked with the other vegetables at the beginning.

Serve this stew with new potatoes and the young summer vegetables suggested for the previous turkey recipe.

Strawberries and cream

Parties like this would be nothing without strawberries and cream – two essentially English products which are at their very best at this time of the year. Although they grow wild all over Europe (and I'm very fond of a dish of wild strawberries sprinkled with caster sugar and soaked in a little white wine), the English were the first to cultivate them as long ago as the 15th century; it may be this head-start over other countries that gives

English strawberries a far better flavour than all others; on the other hand, it may be the climate.

There are some 14,000 acres devoted to commercial strawberry growing in England (25 per cent of these are on farms inviting you to 'pick your own'). The south-facing, sheltered valleys of Devon and Cornwall grow the earliest strawberries, southern Hampshire follows, and the second crop comes mostly from Kent, Cambridgeshire, Norfolk and Lincolnshire – often from the same farms that grow asparagus.

As for how to eat them, nothing beats serving them plain, with cream and sugar, each of the three ingredients to be passed around the table in huge bowls.

Second best is *strawberry ice-cream*. To make this, follow the recipe for vanilla ice-cream on page 268, adding 850 ml/ 1½ pt of sieved, sweetened fresh strawberry puree to the mixture. If you have no way of freezing this, serve it unfrozen as a *strawberry fool*.

Ice-cream and sorbet-making

In order to make traditional ice-creams and sorbets, you can either use specially made equipment (sorbetières or ice-cream churns) or the ice tray of an ordinary refrigerator or a freezer. Use the coldest part of the freezer or set the refrigerator to its coldest setting well in advance. The main thing is to incorporate air during the freezing process so that the result is a light and foamy mass rather than a solid brick of ice. In the sorbetière or churn this is achieved by the use of paddles, but if you have neither, it must be done by periodically beating or whisking the mixture as it freezes.

If you have a modern food processor you can make the most excellent sorbets by freezing all the mixture including the egg white, unwhipped, until it is fairly firm, then whizzing it in the processor to a frothy mush and re-freezing it.

Elderflower sorbet *(for 5–6)*

In early June the hedges appear to be covered in flecks of creamy foam; these are elderflowers, which give the most delicious muscat-like flavour to this sorbet.

They are also good cooked with gooseberries or rhubarb and can be made into fritters, or syrup, or wine, or used dried as a tisane; they can also be put into various lotions. The berries have as many uses later in the year and the shoots and buds can be pickled.

Elder was often planted near cottages to protect the inhabitants from lightning and witches, and in Kent whole orchards of it were planted to provide berries for wine-making.

3	large lemons	3
2	oranges	2
575 ml	water	1 pt
300 g	sugar	10 oz
3–4	heads of elderflower	3–4
2	egg whites	2

Peel the lemons and oranges very thinly so that there is no pith but only the zest. Boil the peel, water and sugar together for five minutes to make a syrup, then take it off the heat and add the elderflowers. Let them infuse in the syrup until it cools completely. Combine the strained syrup and fruit juices. Freeze the mixture until it is mushy. Whip the egg whites to a stiff foam and fold it into the mush. Continue the freezing process.

AUTHOR'S NOTE: The mixture of orange and lemon juice may be exchanged for grapefruit juice, or the balance altered to accentuate the orange more than the lemon. Elderflowers may be replaced by an infusion of blackcurrant, mint or rose geranium leaves, or left out altogether if you want a plain fruit sorbet. To make a redcurrant or blackcurrant sorbet use the strained and sweetened juice of the lightly stewed fruit instead of the water in the recipe above, with the juice of a lemon to heighten the flavour.

Grassy Corner *(for 12)*

When I asked an octogenarian lady if she could remember anything outstanding about the May Weeks of her day (just after the Great War) she replied with great amusement: 'Only something called Grassy Corner – it was green and sweet and shiny, and possibly made at Trinity.' Remembering that this college is famous for its crème brûlée, I wrote to them and the following recipe came back. It was also used for the Boat Club dinner and is the same Grassy Corner as the one made there sixty years ago. (Grassy Corner is also the name of the Cambridge meadow where people meet to watch the boat races.) It is really a cross between a jelly, a trifle and a tipsy cake. When it is turned out it is indeed green, sweet and shiny, and also rather alcoholic.

Another version, made with strawberries and cream instead of sponge cake, follows this one.

You will need a lot of ice to set the jelly; a large plain mould of at least 1.85 litre/3½ pt capacity (the large pâté bowls sold by delicatessens suit well); and a sponge cake made according to the recipe on page 72, measuring slightly less across than the mould.

for the jelly

100 g	pistachio nuts	4 oz
100 g	sugar	4 oz
125 ml	water	¼ pt
half 15 ml sp	powdered gelatine	½ tbsp
4	limes (juiced) *or*	4
125 ml	lime juice	¼ pt
	a few drops of green colouring (optional, page 249)	
3–4	halved glacé cherries	3–4

Skin the pistachios by blanching them for one minute, then refreshing them in cold water and rubbing them well in a tea-towel. All the skins should come off easily. Chop the skinned nuts fairly finely.

Make the jelly by dissolving the sugar in the water, heating it to form a syrup and stirring in the gelatine. When it has all dissolved (without boiling) add the lime juice and, if you like, a few tactful drops of green colouring.

Let the jelly cool while you make a bed of ice for chilling the mould. As soon as the jelly becomes oily, coat the base and sides of the ice-cold mould, giving it several coats until all the jelly is used. Press the half-cherries, cut side up, in a pattern on the base. Scatter the pistachios all over the jelly and put the prepared mould in a cool place to set.

for the custard

275 ml	milk	½ pt
275 ml	whipping or double cream	½ pt
	piece of vanilla pod	
4	egg yolks	4
50 g	sugar	2 oz

Infuse the milk and cream with the vanilla pod and beat the egg yolks with the sugar. Pour the just-scalding milk and cream over the egg yolks, beating all the time. Strain the mixture and put it back into the pan to thicken over a low heat. As soon as it does so remove it before it can curdle and let it cool slightly. Set one half of the custard aside for the sauce.

	for the rest	
500 g	sponge cake (page 72)	1 lb
1 large glass	brandy *and*	1 large glass
1 large glass	curaçao *or*	1 large glass
2 large glasses	sweet white wine	2 large glasses
four 15 ml sp	apricot jam	4 tbsp
100 g	diced glacé fruit	4 oz
275 ml	whipping or double cream	½ pt
one 15 ml sp	powdered gelatine	1 tbsp

Slice the cake in half horizontally. In two soup plates, sprinkle both halves with half the brandy and half the curaçao or half the wine, then spread each cake with a thick layer of apricot jam. Put the gelatine to soften in a cupful of water.

Chop the glacé fruit into small pieces or cut it with scissors.

Whip the cream. Melt the gelatine by standing the cup in a pan of boiling water and stirring until all the powder is dissolved into a liquid jelly. Mix the whipped cream, the chopped glacé fruit and half the remaining brandy and curaçao or white wine with the cooled custard, then mix in the melted gelatine.

To assemble the pudding, pour one third of the cream-custard mixture into the jelly-lined mould and put it in the fridge to set.

When it has set, put one layer of the cake on top and cover this with the second third of the custard. Again, allow this to set, then put the second half of the cake on top and cover all with the last of the custard.

Stir the remaining brandy and curaçao or white wine into the custard that was reserved for the sauce.

Leave the pudding to set and turn it out just before serving it. Slice it like a cake and pass the sauce.

Instead of sponge cake the Oxford version of the pudding uses:

275 ml	raw, sieved strawberries	½ pt
75 g	caster sugar	3 oz
20 g	gelatine, dissolved in a cup of water	¾ oz
275 ml	lightly whipped double cream	½ pt

Mix the strawberry puree with the sugar. Add the melted, hot gelatine, then stir in the whipped cream.

Line the mould as before, with the jelly and the pistachios, then fill it with the plain custard made with cream and gelatine as before, and the strawberry cream in alternate layers. Purees of other soft fruit could be used equally well.

AUTUMN

An almost free Autumn lunch
High tea in Yorkshire
An English barbecue
A game dinner in the North

An almost free Autumn lunch

A sauté of wild mushrooms
Fried giant puffball
Stuffed clams or mussels
A sauté of cockles
Cockles with eggs

Rabbit and pork pudding
Pigeon pie

Fresh samphire
Autumn vegetables

Blackberry mousse
Damson syllabub
Autumn pudding
Crab-apple jelly with cream cheese

Walnut bread

Free food – food that grows wild and is therefore free for the picking – is the very opposite of convenience food, which is possibly why the gathering and preparation of it appeals so much to some people and so little to others.

You will never persuade a slouch or a soul with no gipsy in it that the pleasure of reaping a free harvest of nuts or berries or seafood is almost a reward in itself – the battles with undergrowth, brambles, and mud; the scratched faces, bent backs and stained hands are too much to pay, too taxing for them. But for those who feel a tinge of excitement, a primitive surge of glee at the discovery of a windfall of hazelnuts, a bush sparkling with ripe blackberries or a swathe of wild mushrooms where there were none the day before, the cropping of free food is almost an obsession. It also keeps the memory green for many traditional recipes. Autumn is the peak season for free food hunters; the places to look for it are anywhere in the country that has escaped the effects of modern farming, industrial pollution, re-afforestation and motorway engineering. Two places that I have found particularly fruitful are the New Forest and the Norfolk and Suffolk coasts.

There are three warnings: first, make sure that you don't pick the wrong things and poison your family or yourself – use a reliable identification book or consult an expert before eating anything unfamiliar; second, make sure that what you intend to eat has not been sprayed with pesticide or taken from polluted water – again, ask advice; third, don't trespass, break fences or hedges or leave farm gates open – the land may be private even if the food is free.

A sauté of wild mushrooms *(for 4)*

Edible wild mushrooms are most commonly found in late summer and autumn: the cep or cèpe (*Boletus edulis*) likes fairly open woodland; the chanterelle (*Cantharellus cibarius*) grows especially well on mossy banks under small deciduous trees; horse mushrooms (*Agaricus arvensis*), field mushrooms (*Agaricus campestris*) and giant puffballs (*Lycoperdon giganteum*) are all found on open grassland, in pastures and on garden lawns; parasol mushrooms (*Lepiota procera*) and shaggy inkcaps (*Coprinus comatus*) grow on grass verges, in little woods and sandy banks near the sea.

The New Forest is an exceptionally good place to look for wild fungi. Most large tracts of old woodland should harbour a few species; some shops even sell them. I have seen trayfuls of freshly picked wood blewits

(*Tricholoma nudum*) in a game shop in Derbyshire and boxes of oyster mushrooms (*Pleurotus ostreatus*) at a Greek shop in Camden Town.

Ceps and chanterelles are the best fungi for a sauté as they stay firm when cooked.

500 g	ceps, chanterelles or a mixture of both	1 lb
two or three 15 ml sp	olive oil	2 or 3 tbsp
	salt, pepper	
1 or 2	chopped cloves of garlic	1 or 2
	small handful of chopped parsley	
	small cupful of fresh white or brown breadcrumbs	
	toast or fried bread	

Pick over the fungi; wash them to get rid of grit and earth. Split the chanterelles into thin, lengthways slices. Remove the spongy gills from beneath the caps of the ceps, then slice the caps and the stems into neat pieces.

Heat the oil in a small frying-pan. When it is hot enough, throw in the mushrooms and cook them lightly. Add salt, pepper and garlic. As the juices start to run from the mushrooms add the parsley and breadcrumbs. Let it all heat through, stirring it as it does so, then serve it straight away with pieces of toast or fried bread.

Fried giant puffball

Two or three of these pure-white football-sized fungi grow near us by the same gate every year. We cut them up in thick slices, like bread, and fry them in bacon fat, taking the peel off after they are cooked. They can also be grilled (see the barbecue menu on page 127).

Stuffed clams or mussels *(for 4)*

Although clams have become naturalised here and are breeding at various places around the coast (page 56), you are unlikely to find them in any great quantities on an ordinary beach. Wild mussels, on the other hand, are quite common, especially on rocky or gravelly shores. Farmed mussels are grown on special rafts, and are usually allowed to reach a decent size before being harvested. The biggest landings of mussels are made in Lincolnshire, Norfolk, Devon, Cornwall and Wales.

For a first course for four people you will need 16–20 medium-sized clams (5 cm/2 inch)or 20–24 large mussels. If they are wild be sure that they come from an unpolluted source.

Open live clams with an oyster knife or a short, firm, cook's knife.

Use a cloth to protect the hand holding the clam. Insert the knife into the long side opposite the hinge, cutting through the two thick muscles that hold it firmly shut. Twist the shells to separate them and transfer the meat to one of the halves.

Alternatively, put the live clams in the freezer for two hours beforehand. They will then be very easy to open, as they will be dead but still fresh. They can now be stuffed.

Mussels opened raw are too soft and slithery to put a stuffing on. Open them by putting them into a large lidded saucepan with an inch or two of cold water. Put it over a high heat and take the mussels out as soon as they open, which they will do almost as soon as the water boils. Be careful not to cook them too much once they have opened or they will get tough. Discard any that stay closed. Put a plump, tender mussel in each half-shell.

You can either put the same stuffing in all the clams or mussels, or give a choice from the following. You will need about 100 g/4 oz of stuffing in all.

Garlic (or snail) butter: butter mashed with a clove of chopped garlic and parsley, with a dash of lemon juice and black pepper

Lemon butter: melted butter mixed to a paste with fresh breadcrumbs and lemon juice

Sherry or vermouth cream: breadcrumbs moistened with sherry or vermouth and cream

Cheese and cream: grated Cheddar cheese mixed with a little lightly sautéed onion, and parsley and cream

Put a little of the stuffing on top of each occupied shell. Arrange them in a gratin dish so that they can't tip sideways, and put them under a hot grill until the stuffing is bubbling and, if it contains cheese or breadcrumbs, is just beginning to brown.

Serve them very hot, with bread to mop up the juices.

AUTHOR'S NOTE: An elegant, but rather extravagant way to present this dish is to bed the shells down in a layer of coarse salt before cooking them. This looks pretty and keeps them upright.

A sauté of cockles *(for 4)*

Cockles (*Cardium edule*) are found at several places in great quantities along southern shores, as indeed they are wherever beaches are shallow and muddy. The Gower peninsula in Wales, Morecambe Bay, the Thames Estuary and the Norfolk coast are places where cockle-gathering is a real industry; elsewhere, scraping about on a suitable beach at low tide with a garden rake should provide enough cockles for a small family in a very short time. Take local advice about pollution, don't get stuck in the mud or caught by the tide, and take a big basket to carry the cockles home in. Jumble the cockles about in water to get rid of mud, and leave them in a bucket of clean, salty water when you get home; after a few hours they will have emptied themselves of a good deal of sand. Wash them well before cooking them.

Cooking the cockles enables you to take them out of their shells; this is also advisable if you have gathered them yourself in case they harbour harmful bacteria. But prolonged cooking tends to toughen them, so don't overdo it. Apart from the fact that they are free, the great advantage of live cockles is that you can eat them sautéed, straight from the shell.

	oil	
2 or 3	large chopped cloves of garlic	2 or 3
1 litre	cockles in their shells	1 quart
1	pinch of chilli powder (optional)	1
	chopped parsley (optional)	
	juice of a lemon	

Heat enough oil to cover the base of a large frying-pan, which should have a lid. When the oil is hot, sauté the garlic, then tip in the cockles. Keep the heat high and cover the pan to stop the cockles jumping out. They will open almost at once. When this happens, add the parsley and chilli, if you like, pour the lemon juice over and serve it, shells, liquor and all, in little dishes.

Cockles with eggs *(for 4)*

This recipe, which originally came from Wales, has a marked similarity to the Severn way of cooking elvers (page 25).

1 litre	cockles in their shells *or*	1 quart
150 g	shelled cockles	6 oz
one or two 15 ml sp	bacon fat	1 or 2 tbsp
4	beaten eggs	4
	pepper	
	toast or fried bread	

Put the cockles in a saucepan with enough water to cover them. Bring it to the boil and as soon as the cockles open take them out of the pan. Remove them from their shells, then dry them in a clean cloth.

Heat the bacon fat and warm the shelled cockles in it. Pour the beaten eggs over the cockles and stir as if making scrambled eggs, until they just set. Add black pepper and serve them on toast or fried bread.

Rabbit and pork pudding *(for 4–6)*

Wild rabbits appear to have grown immune to myxomatosis, and are as numerous as before, both in the New Forest and elsewhere. (In Norfolk they call them 'stump rabbits' because they seem to prefer living in stumpy undergrowth and in tree stumps, rather than underground, where the disease is more prevalent.) At all events, they are good to eat and are not protected by game laws.

Tame rabbits reared for the table are equally good for this recipe.

1 kg	rabbit pieces (from a rabbit weighing 1½ kg/3 lb)	2 lb
750 g	suet pastry (page 265)	1½ lb
50 g	seasoned flour	2 oz
100 g	cubed salt pork	4 oz
250 g	peeled small onions	8 oz
	salt, pepper	
275 ml	cold rabbit stock (see below)	½ pt

Bone the rabbit and make a stock from the liver, heart, head, neck and bones, flavouring it well with herbs, onion, celery stems and a carrot. Cool the stock before using it.

Line a 1½ litre/3 pint greased pudding-basin with the suet pastry, reserving one third for the top.

Flour the rabbit pieces and fill the basin in layers, starting with the rabbit, then the pork, and finally the onions. Season well and top up with the cold stock. Dampen the edges of the pastry and roll a circle from the remaining pastry for the lid, sealing it well.

Cover the top with greased paper and tie the whole thing in a cloth so that you can lift it in and out of the steamer.

Have ready a large pan of deep, boiling water to come three-quarters of the way up the sides of the basin. Put the pudding in it and cook it for at least 4 hours, never allowing the water to diminish or go off the boil (top it up with boiling water).

Serve it straight from the basin, with more gravy made from the remaining stock. Runner beans would go well with this dish.

AUTHOR'S NOTE: This recipe may be used to make the classic steak and kidney pudding: substitute 750 g/1½ lb of steak for rabbit and 150 g/6 oz of kidney for pork. Another popular filling, especially in Norfolk, is chicken and mushrooms.

Pigeon pie *(for 6)*

Wood-pigeons, like rabbits, can be shot at any time, as they are considered pests rather than game. Young ones are at their best in May, when they are just full-grown and are tender enough for roasting, but by the autumn it is better to stew them first and put them in a pie. Bacon and steak improve the pie's flavour; hard-boiled eggs are a traditional ingredient.

This recipe uses the breasts only; if you are dealing with feathered birds don't bother to pluck them, just skin them, feathers and all by cutting along the breastbone and peeling the skin back on either side.

6	plump pigeons	6
2	onions	2
2–3	celery sticks	2–3
1	carrot	1
	bay leaf	
100 g	strips of fat bacon, and rinds	4 oz
100 g	mushrooms, and trimmings	4 oz
375 g	chuck steak	12 oz
	seasoned flour	
	salt, pepper	
500 g	rough-puff pastry (page 266)	1 lb
6	hard-boiled eggs	6

Take the breasts (in two fillets) from each of the pigeons and make a stock with the rest of the carcases, or as many as you can be bothered to skin and clean completely. Add one of the onions, the celery and the carrot cut up, with the bay leaf, bacon rind and mushroom trimmings. Simmer the stock with a little seasoning for an hour.

Slice the breasts into pieces 1 cm/$\frac{1}{2}$ inch thick. Trim the steak into pieces of a similar size. Roll the meat in seasoned flour.

Put the bacon pieces in a heavy casserole and sauté them slowly until the fat runs out. Put them aside. Sauté the meat in the bacon fat, adding more fat if necessary. Add the second onion, chopped finely, and cook it a little; then return the bacon to the casserole. Pour enough stock in almost to cover the meat and add salt, if necessary. Cover the pan and simmer until the meat is tender – this will depend on its quality but it should be around $1\frac{1}{2}$–2 hours. Twenty minutes before the end add the mushrooms (left whole).

Allow the cooked meat to cool while you make the rough-puff pastry; let it rest before rolling it out to fit the top of a 1.5 litre/3 pint pie-dish. Put a pie funnel in the centre to let out the steam. Surround it with the meat, mushrooms and gravy. Arrange the halved hard-boiled eggs in the pie. Cover it with the pastry and decorate and glaze it as you like.

Bake it in a preheated oven at 220°C/425°F/gas 7 for twenty minutes to cook the pastry.

Serve the pie with the sort of food which pigeons like to eat themselves: peas, greens, cabbage or curly kale.

AUTHOR'S NOTE: By substituting steak and kidney for the pigeons you can use this recipe to make another classic English dish, steak and kidney pie (see also the recipe on page 150). In the past, rooks were baked like this as well.

Fresh samphire

Norfolk is the only place that recognises samphire as a food to the extent that it can actually be bought there, either at fishmongers or on market stalls. I have even heard of it on sale as far inland as Ely market, but it grows on low-lying mud-flats, particularly in Hampshire, Essex and

Lancashire, and is free for the picking, as long as you don't mind getting muddy. It looks like a greeny-grey cactus, fleshy without the prickles.

August is the best time for it, when it is fully grown and not too battered by the tides. It has quite a firm hold on the mud so cut it if possible.

Wash the samphire well before cooking it. Boil it in plenty of salted water for ten minutes, or until it is just tender, then drain it and eat it hot, with plenty of melted butter. (You have to pick it up in your fingers and strip off the soft green part with your teeth.) See also the recipe for pickling samphire (page 246).

AUTHOR'S NOTE: There are two kinds of samphire. The kind I am referring to here is *Salicornia europea*, also known as glasswort or marsh samphire. The other kind grows on rocky shores or shingle and is known as *Chrithmum maritimum* or rock samphire. It can be eaten in the same way.

Autumn vegetables

Although berries, fungi and nuts are at their peak in the autumn, the invigorating green leaves and the young shoots of the wild plants that made good salads earlier in the year have rather lost their appeal – they have become a bit too tattered and weather-beaten to be made into the dishes that were so enjoyable in the spring.

On the other hand, the vegetable garden is bursting with good things – baby and adult marrows, runner beans, giant pumpkins, sun-ripened tomatoes, outdoor cucumbers, lettuces and sweet-corn will be better and cheaper now than at any other time of the year.

Blackberry mousse *(for 4)*

Towards the end of August almost every roadside bramble hedge in the south of England has a holidaymaker in it, filling spare picnic bags and boxes with blackberries. No-one wants them after the first of October; the legend that from then on the Devil spits on them seems to be true, for they aren't nearly so good.

This mousse can be made with a puree of any soft fruit, but blackberries give it a beautiful purple colour.

500 g	blackberries	1 lb
100 g	granulated sugar	4 oz
	juice of a lemon	
15 g	gelatine	½ oz
two 15 ml sp	water	2 tbsp
275 ml	double cream	½ pt
2	egg whites	2
	mint leaves (optional)	

Reserve a few of the best-looking berries for decoration, then cook the rest, with the sugar, either in a covered dish in a low oven or in a double-boiler.

When the fruit is soft enough, sieve it, or put it through a food mill, to make a fine, pipless puree. Add lemon juice to taste.

Put the gelatine with the measured water in a cup and stand it in a pan of simmering water. Stir it all the time until it is quite thin and clear, then pour it at once into the puree, mixing well. Allow this to cool enough for the mixture to thicken.

Whip the cream very lightly, and fold most of it into the puree.

Whip the egg whites stiffly but not so that they become dry, and fold them in.

Fill four glass bowls or goblets. Once the mousse has set, decorate it with blobs of whipped cream and a few berries, and perhaps a little sprig of mint leaves as well.

Damson syllabub *(for 6)*

As readers of old cookery books will know, a syllabub was made by milking a cow directly over a bowl of sweetened ale, cider, port, sherry or white wine. The foam formed by the strong jets of milk was either spooned off into tall posset glasses or left as it was in the bowl, covered 'pretty high with clotted cream, grated nutmeg, pounded cinnamon and nonpareil comfits'.

As modern cows are milked by machine, a twentieth-century syllabub has to be made in some other way, but the old proportions of one part liquor to two or three parts cream, or creamy milk, should be kept (though if you use creamy cow's milk, the mixture will separate). The 'thin part' can either be left as it is, underneath the frothy cream, or strained off and turned into a flummery (see Sussex cream on page 84).

An authentic syllabub can also be made with fruit syrup instead of wine, cider or ale. The recipe here is made with fruit syrup and double cream and because it doesn't separate is called an 'everlasting syllabub'. It goes a beautiful dark pink. The juices of blackberries, plums, black- or redcurrants, raspberries or strawberries may be used instead of damsons. It doesn't matter if the fruit has been frozen.

500 g	damsons	1 lb
100 g	granulated sugar	4 oz
one 15 ml sp	lemon juice	1 tbsp
two 15 ml sp	brandy	2 tbsp
	grated nutmeg	
	powdered cinnamon	
575 ml	double cream	1 pt

Reserve four to six of the best-looking damsons for decoration. Put the rest in a double-boiler with the sugar and stew them until they are quite soft with the juices running copiously.

Strain the fruit through a sieve. There should be about 275 ml/½ pint of juice. Add the lemon juice, brandy and spices.

Put it in a large bowl, add the cream and whip gently, using a balloon whisk, until the mixture thickens just enough to make soft, droopy peaks.

Pour the mixture into 125 ml/¼ pint glasses and decorate with a blob of whipped cream topped by a stoned damson.

Autumn pudding *(for 6)*

This is an autumnal, hedgerow version of the well-known summer pudding (made with red- or blackcurrants and raspberries).

500 g	elderberries	8 oz
500 g	blackberries	8 oz
500 g	sugar	8 oz
725 g	crab-apples or windfalls	1½ lb
125 ml	water	¼ pt
	several slices of stale bread	
	cream	

Remove the stems from the elderberries and pick over the blackberries. Put them with half the sugar in a bowl in a low oven to heat through and give up a little of their juice. Roughly cut up the apples and cook them with the water until they are soft enough to puree through a sieve.

Sweeten the puree with the rest of the sugar, adding more if the apples are very tart. Strain off some of the juice from the berries and reserve it. Mix the berries into the puree, to make a fairly moist, but not sloppy, mixture.

Line a pudding-basin with trimmed slices of bread (white or brown), leaving no gaps. Fill it with the fruit. Cover the fruit with more sliced bread to make a lid and weight it down with a saucer.

Leave the pudding overnight; it should firm up enough to be turned out next day, a perfect basin shape and stained purple with the fruit juices.

Serve the pudding with cream and the reserved juice.

Crab-apple jelly with curd cheese

Crab-apple jelly (page 248) can be a delicate pudding if it is made in tiny jelly moulds, then turned out and served with a sweetened curd cheese (page 113).

Walnut bread

A recent glut of English walnuts encouraged a friend to make this walnut wholemeal bread. Unlike most English breads with nuts in, this is savoury rather than sweet. You could use hazelnuts or cob nuts instead of walnuts. This makes one large or two small loaves.

25 g	fresh yeast (or half quantity of dried)	1 oz
575 ml	warmed water	1 pt
one 15 ml sp	malt extract	1 tbsp
50 g	non-fat dried milk	2 oz
two 15 ml sp	butter	2 tbsp
two 5 ml sp	salt	2 tsp
525 g	wholemeal flour	1 lb 2 oz
250 g	coarsely chopped walnuts	8 oz
1	egg	1
one 15 ml sp	milk	1 tbsp

Cream the yeast with a little of the water, wait for it to froth up, then add the rest of the water. Mix in the malt, milk powder, butter and salt.

Put the flour in a large bowl and make a well in the centre, and gradually mix in the liquid.

Turn the dough onto a floured board or table top and knead it for about ten minutes, or until it is very smooth.

Leave it, covered, in a clean, well-greased bowl to rise for about 1¼ hours, or until it has doubled in size.

Return the dough to the table top and work it into a large flat oval.

Scatter half the nuts over the dough, then fold it over and knead them in. When they have all been incorporated, repeat the process with the rest of the nuts.

Divide the dough into two loaves, or leave it as one. Let it rest for five minutes before shaping it into a smooth flat ball (a cob shape). Leave it to prove on a greased baking-sheet, covered with a cloth, while the oven heats to 190°C/375°F/gas 5.

Make a glaze by beating the egg with the milk and brush this on top of the loaf. Make four long, shallow cuts across the top with a razor blade.

Bake small loaves for about 35 minutes; give large ones an extra ten minutes.

AUTHOR'S NOTE: This bread makes good toast once it has gone dry, which it does do, rather quickly.

High tea in Yorkshire

Rolled and baked herrings
Kippers
Cheese, ham and egg pudding
Yorkshire ham or bacon

Yorkshire tea-cakes – plain and fruit

Curd tarts
Mint pasties
Fat rascals

Vinegar cake
Yorkshire parkin

Ginger biscuits

Wensleydale cheese

Toffee apples

As in most farming communities, 'tea' means rather more to eat than a few elegant sandwiches and a little sponge cake. Here, the whole family, who have probably eaten a good two- or three-course lunch of soup, meat and pudding, sits down again at about six o'clock to a lighter, but even lengthier meal, the table loaded down with home-made breads, biscuits, cakes, potted meats, fish pastes, jams, jellies and pickles. The butter and cheese are either home-made or come from local farms, as do the ham, bacon and eggs; the same goes for the salads which follow and the milk and cream in the puddings at the end. Presiding over it all, with a vast tea-pot, is Mother, who usually bakes enough for the week in one great session, in good time for the weekend. (Mrs Lunn, a Yorkshire granny who gave me some of her recipes, bakes twice a year for two days on end and fills her freezer with enough to satisfy all her many grandchildren.)

Not content with all this, they usually have 'supper' in the form of a little something on toast, or a couple of sandwiches, just before bedtime.

Vast high teas are also eaten by Yorkshire townspeople.

Rolled and baked herrings *(for 6)*

These are sold by the Whitby fishmonger who gave me the recipe. How they got their golden tinge was a secret, he said, but it looked to me like a dab of kipper dye, brushed on before baking. The skin of the home-made version remains a bright silvery grey, but it tastes just as good as his. The manner in which he fillets his herring without using a knife remains a complete mystery.

6	herrings	6
	brine (1 litre/2 pt of water to 75 g/3 oz salt)	

Remove the heads and guts, and split the fish down the bellies. Flatten them and remove the bones and tails.

Preheat the oven to 180°C/350°F/gas 4. Soak the herrings in the brine for 15 minutes, then rinse them in cold water.

Roll them up, tail end first and skin side out, with the dorsal fin sticking up like a little shark's fin. Pack them closely in a baking dish and bake them, uncovered, for 20–30 minutes.

Eat them cold with green salad, brown bread and butter, apple chutney (page 248) or mustard pickle (page 247).

Kippers

Kippers, bloaters and red herrings are all made from the herring. Not long ago the North Sea was one of the best fishing grounds in the world for herring, and herring-curers were to be found in every East coast port.

Today it is a different story. Over-fishing, with the subsequent ban on herring fishing for all but a very limited quota in the North Sea, has led to the closure of many of the old-fashioned East coast fishmongers' shops with their own smoke-houses. At the same time people's tastes seem to have changed: they prefer boneless, skinless and frozen fish fingers to salted and smoked kippers complete with heads and tails as well as skin and bones. If they like kippers at all they like them dyed, skinned and filleted. If they like bloaters at all they will have a hard job finding them (but see page 163). As for red herrings, see page 163 too.

Mr Fortune of Whitby is one of the few old-fashioned kipper-curers left in that town. His shop is painted Yorkshire red (a sort of red umber) outside; inside the smoke-hole the walls and ceiling glisten black as the jet which is washed up on the beaches nearby. After splitting, gutting and brining his beautiful fat herring (bought mainly from Scotland or even Canada, these days), he smokes them over a smouldering fire of hardwood dust. He *never* dyes his kippers: they are thick, succulent and tawny. Yorkshire people fry them in butter on both sides, pressing them flat with a fish slice as they sizzle in a huge pan. Another way of cooking them is to grill them; or you can stand them head down in a large jug, pour boiling water over them and leave them for three or four minutes.

Cheese, ham and egg pudding *(for 4–6)*

Use your own curd cheese for this recipe (page 113), or cottage cheese.

500 g	cottage or curd cheese	1 lb
50 g	softened butter	2 oz
100 g	cooked and diced ham	4 oz
6	beaten eggs	6
	salt, pepper	
two 15 ml sp	finely chopped parsley	2 tbsp

Preheat the oven to 180°C/350°F/gas 4.

Beat the cheese vigorously with a fork, gradually incorporating the butter, to make a smooth and creamy texture.

Add the diced ham and carefully mix in the eggs. Check the seasoning and add the parsley.

Pour the mixture into a buttered, 1 litre/2 pt mould or pudding basin. Bake the pudding, uncovered, in a deep bain-marie for one hour or until it is completely set (it should not wobble when you shake the basin). Turn it out onto a serving dish and serve it hot or cold.

A fresh (or cooked) tomato sauce goes well with it (page 255 and page 257).

Yorkshire ham and bacon

There are two ways to cure hams and bacon: either you pickle them in brine, which is a wet cure, or you lay them on a bed of coarse salt, which is a dry cure. Thereafter the meat is washed and hung up to dry; it may or may not be smoked before drying. The skill comes in adding subtle amounts of sugar or molasses, or herbs and spices, to the salt or brine; in knowing how long to leave the meat at each stage; and in judging the right temperature and humidity in which all these processes must take place. Above all the raw material, the pig, must be a really good one, suitable for ham and bacon rather than pork, the right size for the customer and possessed of the right amount of fat. Its diet will also affect the flavour of the ham.

Home-cured hams are still made by a few farmers and butchers in the North but you have to book it months ahead if you want the genuine article.

York hams are dry salted. They are made only in the winter, though once made they can be kept for over a year. Small hams are ready in four months; large ones take longer. The salt, with a little saltpetre and sugar, is rubbed daily into the ham for three weeks. During the salting, some farmers' wives lay the ham on a bed of bracken on top of a stone slab with a hole in it for the resulting brine to run away. It is hung in the chimney to be smoked and then in the kitchen to dry.

Bacon also hangs in the kitchen boned, rolled and tied, to have slices (or collops) cut off when they're wanted. This is bacon as it ought to be, fat and salty and very crisp when fried, and quite different from the wet, fatless, sweet, soppy stuff we get today in plastic packets.

An economical way to cook a ham

This is the way recommended by an elderly customer of a Yorkshire butcher who cures his own hams. It is suitable for a whole ham or a piece.

Soak the ham all night in cold water to rid it of excess salt. Throw that water away.

Score the rind with a sharp blade and stick it with cloves.

Put it in a large oven-proof pot with a lid. Add two glasses of water and one of cider, an onion, a carrot and some herbs. Cook it in a moderate oven (180°C/350°F/gas 4) allowing 20–25 minutes to the half-kilo/pound for a piece weighing less than 5 kg/11 lb and 15 minutes to the half-kilo/

pound for a heavier cut. At the end of this cooking time raise the oven temperature to 220°C/425°F/gas 7. Remove the lid and cook it for a further 20–30 minutes, until the rind is dark brown.

Keep the rind on when it's cooked and eat the ham only when it's cold, slicing the rind off as you carve.

'To eat it hot is terribly extravagant.'

Yorkshire tea-cakes *(makes 16)*

Fruit tea-cakes are possibly more often sold and are therefore better known in the South than plain ones, but in Yorkshire both are equally common; one pork butcher in York sells hundreds of the plain kind every day, split open and spread with pork dripping.

The tea-cakes should be served hot from the oven or they can be split in two when cold, and toasted.

400 ml	milk	¾ pt
100 ml	water	¼ pt
75 g	butter	3 oz
2	beaten eggs	2
25 g	fresh yeast (or half quantity of dried)	1 oz
1 kg	plain flour	2 lb
two 5 ml sp	salt	2 tsp

Put the milk, water and butter in a small saucepan and heat them until lukewarm. Remove the pan from the heat and add the eggs and the yeast to the liquid. Leave it for about ten minutes or until the yeast begins to foam.

Put the flour and salt in a large bowl and make a well in the centre. Pour the liquids into the well and combine all the ingredients. Knead the dough on a floured surface and leave it in a greased bowl, covered with a cloth, to rise at room temperature.

Grease three baking-sheets, and preheat the oven to 180°C/350°F/gas 4.

Knock the dough back when it has trebled in bulk and divide it into 16 pieces. Shape the pieces into rounds about 2.5 cm/1 inch thick and 13 cm/5 inches across, then leave them on the baking-sheets in a warm place until they have doubled in bulk (about 20 minutes).

Bake them for 30–45 minutes or until they are golden, and serve them warm.

For fruit tea-cakes, you will need all the ingredients for the plain kind, plus 75 g/3 oz each of sultanas, currants and sugar. Mix the fruit and sugar into the flour before adding the liquid, and continue as above.

Curd cheese

One of the best ways of dealing with a surplus of milk is to turn it into cheese. Curd cheese is cheese at its simplest, and it lends itself to several different recipes. Yorkshire people are particularly fond of using it, both as a savoury and as a sweet ingredient.

To make curd cheese you need only do two things: first, encourage the milk to curdle; second, drain the curds from the whey.

There are three methods of doing this. You can *let the milk go sour and solid of its own accord*, which it will do easily enough in summertime. Once it has turned solid and as long as it is not putrid, you can drain it in the manner described below. This 'sour-milk cheese' will have a decidedly sharp flavour and be more suitable for eating as a savoury cheese than a sweet one.

The second method is to *add rennet to fresh milk*. Use plain, uncoloured and unflavoured rennet and follow the label's instructions for junket, without sweetening the milk. Drain the curds as described below. This makes a nice, sweetish, fresh-tasting cheese.

The third way is to *use cultured buttermilk* (some supermarkets sell it). To make 500 g/1 lb of curd cheese you need 2 litres/4 pints of fresh milk and one 15 ml sp/1 tbsp of buttermilk. This cheese is fairly sharp and is useful for all recipes.

Put the milk to warm slowly in a bain-marie, using a stainless steel, enamel, china or earthenware container. When it reaches 27°C/80°F add the buttermilk. Stir it well. Cover the milk and leave it for 24 hours in a warm room (around 20°C/68°F). The milk should have set like a junket.

Drain off the whey by spooning the curds into a muslin-lined sieve or colander over a bowl. Let the whey drain for about 4 or 5 hours, then tie the corners of the muslin together to make a bag and let it drip over a bowl for another 8 hours. The longer you hang it the drier the cheese will become, and the richer the milk you use, the creamier your cheese will be.

To eat sour curd cheese, mash salt into the curds. You can then add finely chopped herbs, spring onions, garlic, cayenne or chopped nuts and eat it spread on toast or bread, or have it with a salad. Also use it plain for the savoury cheese pudding (page 111).

To eat sweet curd cheese, mash it with sugar and serve it with fresh soft fruit or blackcurrant jam, or use it to make cheesecakes or curd tarts (see next recipe).

Curd cheese is also made on dairy farms from *beastings* (or beestings, or beaslings). This is the very rich, thick yellow milk given by a cow for the first three days after calving. The first milking is not used but the second and third days' milk can be made into curds simply by gently heating until it looks like scrambled eggs, then draining it. Yorkshire dairies used to sell beasting curds for curd tarts, but nowadays people make do with ordinary curd cheese.

If anyone should give you a present of beastings, do remember not to wash out the jug it came in before returning it as it would mean bad luck for the cow.

Beastings pudding is rather like a rich custard. To make it add 275 ml/ ½ pt of fresh milk to 575 ml/ 1 pt of beastings and pour it into a buttered pie-dish. Bake it in a bain-marie at 150°C/300°F/gas 2 until it is set. Eat it with thin cream and a little sugar.

Curd tarts

This recipe makes six small tarts or one large one (20 cm/9 inch).

100 g	currants	4 oz
four 15 ml sp	rum	4 tbsp
375 g	shortcrust pastry (page 264)	12 oz
100 g	butter	4 oz
50 g	sugar	2 oz
100 g	curd cheese (page 113)	4 oz
two 15 ml sp	chopped candied peel	2 tbsp
	pinch of cinnamon or nutmeg	
2	lightly beaten eggs	2

Soak the currants in the rum for half an hour. Preheat the oven to 200°C/400°F/ gas 6 and grease either six little saucers or a 20 cm/9 inch tart tin.

Line the saucers or tin with the pastry, rolled to about 0.5 cm/¼ inch thick. Prick the pastry all over.

Cream the butter and sugar until they are light and fluffy, then add the cheese, peel, spice and the rum-soaked currants. When everything is well mixed, stir in the eggs – the mixture may curdle but it doesn't matter.

Spoon the filling into the pastry and bake it (with the saucers standing on a baking-sheet) for 30–40 minutes, when the filling should be set.

AUTHOR'S NOTE: Yorkshirewomen like to cook these tarts in china saucers in the traditional way, but you get more filling per mouthful if you use deeper tart tins.

Mint pasties

These, like Chorley cakes and Eccles cakes, are made of pastry with a sweet filling. They are really good only if made with fresh mint; their season is therefore limited to the time between spring and the first frosts. They have a lovely refreshing flavour.

50 g	currants	2 oz
250 g	rough-puff or shortcrust pastry (pages 266 and 264)	8 oz
	big bunch of mint	
two 15 ml sp	caster sugar	2 tbsp
25 g	chopped peel (optional)	1 oz
25 g	butter	1 oz

Preheat the oven to 220°C/425°F/gas 7, and grease a baking-sheet.

Soak the currants in water while you prepare the pastry. Roll the pastry out to a rectangle which will fit the baking-sheet when it is folded in half. Lay one half on the sheet.

Chop the mint finely. Drain the currants, but leave them damp. Put them in a bowl and mix them with the mint and sugar, and chopped peel if you like.

Leaving a 1 cm/½ inch margin on three sides, spread the mixture over half the pastry, and dot it with the butter.

Dampen the edges of the pastry and fold the other half over the top. Close the edges by pressing them firmly together. Make a scalloped edge if you like, by denting it into loops with the back of a knife. Brush the pastry with a little milk or beaten egg and sprinkle it with caster sugar. Prick little holes in the top for the steam to escape.

Bake it for 20 minutes, allow it to cool, then cut it into fingers or squares.

Fat rascals *(makes 12)*

How these very popular, scone-like little cakes came by their name, no one seems to know, but the similarity between the word 'rascal' and 'rusk', plus the inclusion of lard (fat) in the recipe, is my explanation. A friend who lives near Whitby tells me that on the local moors they are known as 'turf cakes' as they used to be cooked on bakestones over the turf fires found in every farmhouse and inn. The lard would come from their own pigs, and the fruit would be dried bilberries which also come from the moors, and were used during the last war instead of currants. This is my friend's recipe.

100 g	lard	4 oz
250 g	self-raising flour	8 oz
75 g	caster sugar	3 oz
50 g	currants	2 oz
25 g	sultanas	1 oz
	large pinch of salt	
	water or beaten egg	

Preheat the oven to 190°C/375°F/gas 5, and grease a baking-sheet. Rub the lard into the flour and add the dry ingredients. Mix to a soft dough with the water or egg.

Roll it out to about 1 cm/½ inch thick and cut it into 8 cm/3 inch rounds. Put them on the greased baking-sheet and bake them for 12–15 minutes or until they are brown. Or, even better, if you have a bakestone or griddle, cook them on top of the stove, turning them over as their undersides brown.

Vinegar cake

This is a good cake to make if you are short of eggs. The vinegar, whether malt, wine or cider, makes no difference at all to the flavour, but it is used because its reaction with the bicarbonate of soda produces a remarkably good 'rise'.

250 g	butter	8 oz
500 g	plain flour	1 lb
one 5 ml sp	baking powder	1 tsp
250 g	brown sugar	8 oz
250 g	currants	8 oz
125 g	raisins	4 oz
1	beaten egg	1
three 15 ml sp	distilled vinegar	3 tbsp
175 ml	milk	6 fl oz
one 5 ml sp	bicarbonate of soda	1 tsp

Preheat the oven to 190°C/375°F/gas 5.

Rub the butter into the flour until the mixture is crumbly. Add the baking powder, sugar and fruit, and then the egg.

Put the vinegar into a large jug and add the milk, reserving a spoonful or two. Warm the reserved milk and add the bicarbonate of soda, stirring until it is dissolved. Add this mixture to the vinegar and milk and quickly add it to the flour, being careful as the liquid will froth up.

When all the ingredients are well combined, pour them into a lined and greased cake tin (22 cm/9 inch). Bake the cake for 30 minutes, then lower the heat to 150°C/300°F/gas 2 and bake it for an additional 30 minutes or until the cake is firm to touch.

Yorkshire parkin

This combination of oatmeal, treacle and ginger has dozens of different permutations; some people add eggs, some add candied peel, and some caraway. What it should be is soft and sticky, characteristics that improve with a day or two of keeping in a tin. It is *the* traditional cake to eat round the bonfire on November 5th. Guy Fawkes (whose attempt to blow up the House of Commons nearly 400 years ago is so spectacularly commemorated on this day) went to school at St Peter's in York; this institution deliberately ignores the occasion (they don't burn effigies of their old pupils). Needless to say, like so many other relatively modern festivities, this occasion has connections with far more primitive ones – in this case, the Vikings' Thorfeast.

250 g	plain flour	8 oz
500 g	medium oatmeal	1 lb
100 g	brown sugar	4 oz
one 5 ml sp	ground ginger	1 tsp
150 g	butter and lard, mixed	6 oz
250 g	black treacle	8 oz
250 g	golden syrup	8 oz
2	eggs	2
one and a half 5 ml sp	bicarbonate of soda	$1\frac{1}{2}$ tsp
	dash of vinegar	

Preheat the oven to 180°C/350°F/gas 4. Grease and line a baking tin (20 × 30 cm/8 × 12 inches) or two tins (18 × 18 cm/7 × 7 inches).

Mix the flour, oatmeal, sugar and ginger in a bowl and make a well in the middle.

Melt the fats in a pan and then add the treacle and syrup. Let the mixture warm through a little and stir it into the dry ingredients. Add the eggs and mix well. Put the bicarbonate of soda in a cup and add enough vinegar to make it fizz; pour it at once into the bowl.

Pour the mixture into the tin(s) to about 2.5 cm/1 inch depth and bake it for $1-1\frac{1}{2}$ hours.

Ginger biscuits *(makes 24)*

250 g	butter or margarine	8 oz
250 g	sugar	8 oz
two 15 ml sp	golden syrup	2 tbsp
300 g	plain flour	10 oz
one 5 ml sp	bicarbonate of soda	1 tsp
one 15 ml sp	ground ginger	1 tbsp

Cream the butter and gradually add the sugar. Stir in the golden syrup. Sift the dry ingredients together and fold them into the butter and sugar mixture. Refrigerate the dough for a few hours or overnight as it will be too soft to work with straight away.

Preheat the oven to 150°C/300°F/gas 2 and grease a baking-sheet.

Roll the dough out on a floured surface to a thickness of about 0.25 cm/ $\frac{1}{8}$ inch. Stamp the dough with a 6 cm/ $2\frac{1}{2}$ inch circular cutter or a glass. Transfer the biscuits to the greased baking-sheet. Bake them for ten minutes or until they are slightly puffed and golden. Remove the biscuits to a wire rack to cool, before storing them in an airtight tin.

AUTHOR'S NOTE: The dough may be stamped out with decorative cutters, then decorated before baking with currants where appropriate.

Wensleydale cheese

Be sure to have some Wensleydale on the high tea table (page 243).

Toffee apples *(makes about 18)*

Most children like something to suck or chew at a party, especially if the circumstances are slightly awe-inspiring. Toffee apples are very soothing for firework parties.

Choose small, sweet apples. Trim out the stems and the blossom end. Wash and dry them well. Push round, wooden skewers firmly into each one (these can be bought from an obliging butcher), then twirl them quickly in a toffee mixture made as follows:

125 g	butter	4 oz
250 g	golden syrup	8 oz
500 g	brown sugar	1 lb
one 15 ml sp	vinegar or lemon juice	1 tbsp

Melt the butter in a saucepan. Add the rest of the ingredients and stir until the sugar has melted, then boil the toffee fast until it turns from golden to brown and will set hard on a saucer (soft crack 140°C/275°F on a sugar thermometer). Turn the heat right down to keep the toffee fluid.

Lay each apple on greased foil or paper to set.

AUTHOR'S NOTE: The vinegar or lemon helps to prevent the toffee crystallising but doesn't affect the flavour.

An English barbecue

Home-smoked trout with horseradish sauce
Barbecued fish in seaweed
Salt-grilled fish

Barbecuing a large piece of meat
Butterflied leg of lamb
Grilled spiced chicken with hot chilli mint sauce

Marinated and grilled skewers of monk-fish, meat and vegetables

Roast onions
Grilled puffball
Barbecued sweet-corn

Bulgar salad

Roast apples
Roast walnuts
Cheese in vine leaves

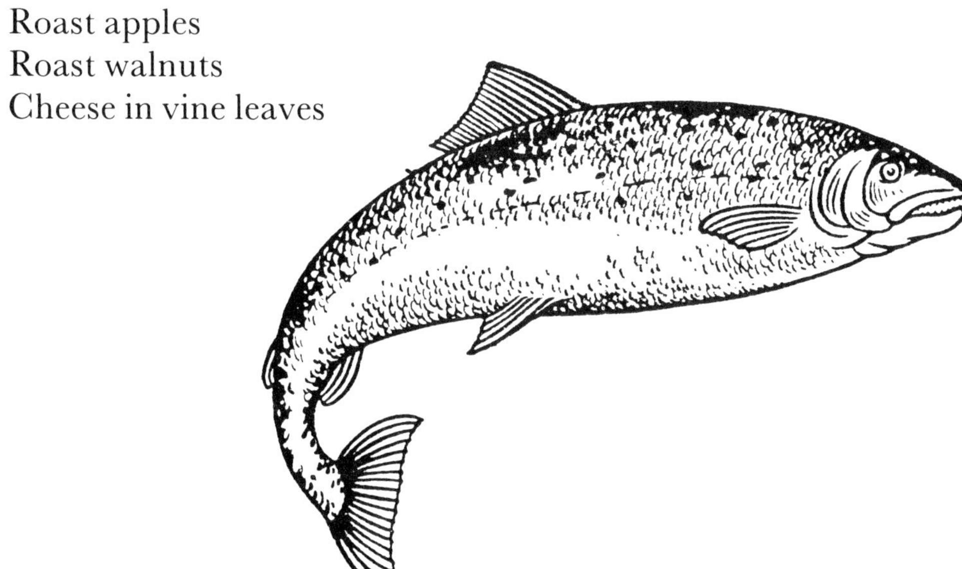

The English have always enjoyed cooking out of doors; stewing things up in billy-cans, toasting freshly caught fish on sticks and baking potatoes in the ashes of a camp-fire used to be the style, but over the past twenty years the charcoal grill has become an accepted part of our backyard or garden furniture and a typical English barbecue now combines elements of American, Indian and Greek taverna cookery.

Some judgement is called for in building a charcoal fire and cooking the food in the proper order, so that everything is done and ready at the right time. Charcoal can take a good three-quarters of an hour to get hot enough to cook meat, but skewers of marinated vegetables, or whole peppers, halved aubergines and onions can be grilled first, before the heat builds up to its maximum temperature. They can be put into a dressing of oil and lemon juice to make a salad while you cook the meat. Fish also needs less heat than meat, so this can be the first course. Potatoes need a long time and should be started early. After the meat is cooked, the heat of the ashes lasts for ages; this should be used for your roasted pudding of apples, nuts and cheese in vine leaves.

Find room on the grill to heat up some pitta bread (page 62), or have plenty of crusty white or wholemeal bread (page 230) on hand; Staffordshire oatcakes (page 13) are useful too.

Green salad and cold rice (page 204) or bulgar salads make good accompaniments, and if the menu includes hamburgers or highly spiced meat, provide pickles and chutneys as well (see pages 245–248, for instance).

Home-smoked fish

If you have the kind of barbecue that is made out of nothing more complicated than a few bricks set in a box shape with a metal foot scraper of the kind found by the back door for a grill, it is not much work to turn it into a smoker. You just need a few bamboo canes, a large barrel (topless and bottomless), a few more bricks, a sheet of metal large enough to cover the fire, and a piece of sacking to cover the barrel.

Drill holes in opposite sides of the barrel and push the canes across (these are for hanging the food from).

Put the barrel on a brick plinth at one end of the fire box and take out a brick or two at that end, so that smoke can go up the barrel. Make a fire with a kindling of wood, then cover it with sawdust or chips from any hard wood (oak is the best, but fruit trees, elm and sycamore will do). Ask for sawdust at a sawmill, but avoid pinewood dust as it is too resinous. On the other hand, the green twigs and leaves of herbs like fennel or rosemary add a delicious flavour and smell. Once the fire is smouldering you can cover it with the metal sheet (an old metal draining board is ideal) and direct the smoke up the barrel.

To smoke fish, gut and scale them, but leave the heads on. Make a fairly strong brine and soak small fish in it for an hour or two; give large fish longer. Rinse them clear of the brine, then hang them up and allow them to dry as much as possible before hanging them with hooks through their gills, in the smoking barrel. The heat of the smoke will probably be quite cool, in which case the fish will take on the flavour of smoke but remain raw. They should then be grilled, but if the smoke is hot enough to cook them as well as smoke them you can eat them just as they are, hot or cold. Cover the barrel throughout with a damp sack, to keep the smoke in. Half an hour will give a strong smoky flavour to a small fish but timing depends on the heat and density of the smoke and the size of the fish. Serve the fish with horseradish sauce (page 257).

There are also commercial smokers, little metal boxes, which are quite useful, but not so versatile.

Barbecued fish in seaweed

Fish cooks remarkably well over an open fire if it is enclosed in a really damp wrapping. I found a recipe for cooking freshly caught trout this way in a little book dated 1866. '. . . Take the trout just as it is, fill the mouth with salt, roll it in two or three folds of paper (a bit of *The Times* will do), screwing the ends up tight. Put the fish, paper and all, into water, until the paper is saturated, then lay it in the hot embers, and when the paper is well charred, the fish will be cooked enough.'

What really happens is that the fish steams in its wrapping. Over one hundred years later the chefs of *nouvelle cuisine* have rediscovered the method. Michel Guérard recommends steaming a sea-bass in a wrapping of seaweed well soaked in sea-water. A fish weighing about 800 g/ 1¾ lb will take about 20 minutes over a good fire. If you can't get seaweed use any edible herb that grows near water: fennel leaves, dill, sorrel, watercress or wild mint would be good, as long as they are well dampened first. Clean the fish but do not scale it. Salt the fish inside and out first, if you are using herbs.

Sea-bass is a delicious fish, with a texture rather like chicken; it used to be very cheap and plentiful, but has lately become fashionable, and is now hard to find and expensive when you do. Alternative fish could be sea bream, grey mullet, sole, sea trout, fresh water trout, perch or pike.

Serve the fish whole, unwrapped from the seaweed, or skin and fillet it, and serve it with melted butter, watercress puree (page 191), sorrel sauce (page 257) or fresh tomato sauce (page 255).

Salt-grilled fish

The inspiration for this way of cooking fish is Oriental; they have a way of grilling it with a liberal covering of salt. The result is a delicately well-cooked fish, not at all over-salty in flavour (and not burnt to a frazzle, which is what usually happens if you cook a whole fish directly over charcoal without any protection). It is suitable for most sorts of firm-fleshed fish, both oily and non-oily. Whole fish big enough for one person look very good cooked this way. Try it with mackerel, sea bream, sardines, trout or red or grey mullet. Pieces of monk-fish, sea-bass, eel, or cuts from larger specimens of any of the fish above may also be treated similarly.

You need two fine skewers for each fish if you are grilling them whole, and plenty of coarse salt. You could use the kind sold in large blocks (from Cheshire) or the flaky kind (from Maldon, in Essex).

Wash, clean and scale the fish but leave their heads, tails and fins on. Calculate about 20 g/$\frac{3}{4}$ oz salt per kg/2 lb of fish and sprinkle it all over. Leave it for about 30 minutes, when it will have dissolved into a brine. Wipe the fish dry.

Insert the first skewer (oiled) through the head, just below the eye. Pass it through the centre of the body and let it emerge on the same side as it went in, in front of the tail. Pass the second skewer through the fish a little below the first one. This makes the fish rigid and easier to cook and turn over.

Just before cooking the fish, salt it again, liberally, taking care to rub some into the tail and fins. This protects them from burning to a cinder before the rest of the fish is cooked, as salt has a higher resistance to fire than the fish itself. Cook it on both sides until it is done, about six to ten minutes in all for a small fish.

Remove the skewers and serve the fish with lemon wedges.

To barbecue a large piece of meat

Very large pieces of meat need a great deal of heat, and a long time to cook, preferably on a spit. A leg of lamb can be filleted, then spread flat (see how to butterfly a leg of lamb, below) and a short wing-rib of beef can be cooked whole, as long as it is not too thick. A rib weighing more than 1.4 kg/3 lb and over 5 cm/2 inches thick is not recommended as it is liable to be very raw inside, unless you want to finish it in the oven.

Butterflied leg of lamb

One leg of lamb is enough to feed a fair number of people, especially if there are other tit-bits to be had. The best way to deal with it is to bone it so that it can be opened out as a single butterfly-shaped piece of meat; it will take only 45 minutes to one hour to cook.

Unless your butcher knows how to do this, you will have to do it yourself. Don't let him whack through the shank bone – this needs to be kept intact to form a sort of handle.

First, trim most of the surplus fat from the outside of the leg to reduce the amount of flaring and smoking that it can cause. Then, starting at the top, take out the 'aitch' or pelvic bone with a sharp boning knife. Keeping the inside of the leg upwards, trim out the next bone (the thigh bone).

When you get to the next joint, cut carefully so as to leave the little knee-cap bone in its place. If you remove it the 'butterfly' is very likely to fall apart in cooking. Leave the next bone (the shank) in place as well.

Open out the meat and cut deep gashes in the thickest parts, but from the inside only. Finally beat it flat with a mallet. It is now ready to marinate.

for the marinade

2	garlic cloves, cut into strips	2
four 15 ml sp	olive oil	4 tbsp
	juice and grated peel from a lemon	
	rosemary, thyme, crushed bay leaves, sage	

Insert a few strips of garlic into each side of the meat. Rub both sides with the olive oil, lemon juice and grated peel. Sprinkle over the herbs and press them well into the meat. Cover it and leave it to marinate in a cool place until you are ready to cook it (an hour or more, if possible: overnight is not too long).

When the charcoal is just right, put the meat on an oiled grill, and turn it every five minutes or so. Continue to brush it with oil as it cooks, about 45 minutes to an hour, depending on the heat of the coals and the way you like your meat. A rare piece of meat is done when it resists a poke from the blunt end of a skewer. (A meat thermometer should read about 50°C/125°F.) Remove the meat to a carving board and let it rest for about ten minutes before carving, to allow the juices to retreat back into the meat. Carve it in such a way that everyone gets a share of the delicious burnt outside part.

Serve it with sauce béarnaise (page 256) or herb butter.

AUTHOR'S NOTE: This method of marinating and cooking can also be applied to a single short fore-rib of beef.

Grilled spiced chicken *(for 4–6)*

This recipe is based on the formula used by good Indian restaurants (in England at least) for their tandoori chicken. The only thing missing is the red colour which you can add with the appropriate powder if you like, or with paprika. Tandoori ovens are like Ali Baba jars with hot coals at the bottom. A charcoal grill is not a bad substitute. Instead of skewering a whole marinated chicken on a poker, as the Indians do, it is easier to cut the chicken into pieces first. If you put boned pieces of marinated chicken on skewers, you will have the equivalent of chicken tikka.

Use a fairly large chicken and cut it into eight pieces.

	salt	
	lime juice	
125 ml	plain yoghourt	¼ pt
one or two 5 ml sp	crushed cumin seeds	1–2 tsp
one or two 5 ml sp	grated fresh ginger	1–2 tsp
1	de-seeded, minced, fresh green chilli pepper	1
	red colouring (optional)	

Skin the chicken pieces and gash the large pieces here and there. Sprinkle them with salt and a little lime juice and leave them for one hour.

Combine all the other ingredients and coat the chicken in this mixture. Leave it for 24 hours before grilling on the barbecue.

Serve hot chilli mint sauce (page 258) with it, and if you can't make chapatis or nan, eat it with pittas (page 62) or Staffordshire oatcakes (page 13).

Marinated and grilled skewers of monk-fish

Monk-fish (also known as angler fish) is usually the ugliest fish on the slab, that is if you get the chance of seeing it whole – it is most often sold bereft of its huge head, and skinned, leaving a strange cone-shaped tail of pinkish white flesh with no bones save for a gelatinous spinal column. It is therefore extremely easy to fillet.

Put the two fillets from a monk-fish tail weighing about 750 g/ $1\frac{1}{2}$ lb in a marinade of oil, lemon juice, salt and pepper for about half an hour before you want to cook. Cut them into cubes and thread them onto skewers with whole mushrooms and pieces of green pepper (also marinated) between the pieces of fish. Grill them over charcoal for six to ten minutes, turning them from time to time.

Marinated and grilled skewers of meat

The same marinade, with perhaps the addition of a few herbs such as bay leaf, thyme, rosemary or marjoram, can be used for cubed lamb (from the shoulder), pork, beef steak, liver or kidney.

Salt is best added at the last minute as it tends to draw the juices if it is left on for any length of time, and meat benefits from longer marination than fish. If you have some strong, woody rosemary branches, use them instead of skewers for the meat.

Marinated and grilled skewers of vegetables

Mushrooms, red or green sweet peppers, onions, tomatoes and aubergines are particularly suitable; they can be seasoned in advance by sprinkling them with a few spoons of olive oil and lemon juice. Fresh or dried herbs can be added for extra flavour. Onions should be halved downwards and the layers separated. As a rough guide, allow one medium skewer of vegetables per person.

Alternate cubes of aubergines, squares of sweet pepper, onions, whole or halved tomatoes (previously marinated for about one hour) on the skewers, and grill them for about ten minutes on each side, or until the vegetables are soft and have browned a little. The vegetables may be basted with the remaining marinade as they cook. Season them with salt and pepper.

Small whole tomatoes and mushrooms are two good vegetables to grill together. Toss them in a marinade, skewer them and grill as above.

Cut green tomatoes into small cubes, marinate in olive oil and freshly grated ginger. Leave them for about one hour before grilling.

Marinate small cubes of aubergines and small whole onions. Wrap each cube of aubergine in a small piece of bacon before assembling them onto the skewer, alternating with the onions. Grill as above.

Roast onions

Wrap onions, either peeled or not, in foil, and bake them in the charcoal for about 30 minutes, or until they are tender. Remove them from the heat, and serve them still wrapped in foil. Eat them with butter, salt and pepper.

Grilled slices of puffball

Slice a firm, fresh puffball into 2.5 cm/1 inch thick slices. Stick a few slivers of garlic into each slice, rub them with olive oil and leave them to marinate for about 15 minutes before grilling them. Season with salt and pepper and grill for about five minutes on each side or until they are golden in colour.

Barbecued sweet-corn

A variety of sweet-corn suitable to this climate can now be grown in our gardens, and it flourishes on many acres in the south of England. This is tender sweet-corn as opposed to the somewhat tougher maize which is also grown here as animal fodder.

Provide one freshly picked cob for each person.

The leafy husk should be pulled back and the silky tassels removed before barbecuing the corn. Next dip the cob in cold water, then push back the husk and bake the whole thing on a rack over the fire, turning often. It will take about 15 minutes to cook – don't overcook it or it will become tough. Eat it as usual, with butter, salt and pepper.

Alternatively, remove the husk and tassels completely, smear the cob with butter, wrap it in foil and roast it in the same way.

Bulgar salad *(for 6)*

Bulgar (bulgour, burghul, bulgur) is a Middle Eastern preparation of boiled, pre-soaked whole wheat grains which are then dried, de-husked and cracked into coarse pieces. It is, fortunately, now sold all over the country, in wholefood shops as well as in Greek groceries, and could become as much a part of our diet as rice. It makes an excellent alternative to rice and has become a very popular salad, since it has a good fresh clean taste and requires no further cooking, just soaking in water and embellishing with a dressing and a few raw vegetables. This salad is also known as tabbouleh.

250 g	bulgar	8 oz
1	finely grated large onion	1
	salt, pepper	
1	large bunch of parsley and mint	1
	juice of a lemon	
four 15 ml sp	olive oil	4 tbsp
	salad items, lemon quarters, and so on	

Soak the bulgar in water for about half an hour in a basin that will allow it to double at least in size.

Drain it dry and then squeeze out what is left of the moisture with your hands. Still using your hands mix in the grated onion, working it in well by squeezing it as you do so. Add salt and pepper to taste, then mix in the herbs, lemon and oil. Add more lemon or oil if you think it needs it.

Heap the bulgar up in a serving dish on a bed of lettuce leaves. Garnish it with strips of cucumber, or green or red pepper, radishes, olives, quarters of lemon and tomato, and so on. It can be made to look very festive.

Roast apples

Wrap whole eating apples in foil and put them around the edges of the fire, turning them once or twice during the cooking time. After cooking them for about 30 minutes, test for doneness by poking through the foil with a fork. Serve them in the foil and let each person add sugar and butter as they like.

Alternatively, core the apples, and fill each one with a little butter flavoured with sugar and cinnamon. Wrap them in foil and cook as above.

Roast walnuts

Crack a number of walnuts, but do not remove the shells. Wrap the nuts in foil, about a dozen per package, and put them right on the fire. Heat them for about ten minutes. Serve them with apples and cheese.

Cheese in vine leaves *(for 4)*

This curious item is best suited to very firm or slightly dried-out pieces of hard cheese. Fresh vine leaves give the best results, but those that have been preserved in brine may be used after soaking and drying.

12	2.5 cm/1 inch cubes of cheese	12
12	fresh or brined vine leaves	12

Wash (or, if brined, soak) the leaves, dry them and remove their stems. Put a piece of cheese in the centre of a leaf and fold the sides of the leaf over the cheese, then roll up the leaf to form a package. Continue with the remaining pieces of cheese and leaves. Put the packages, seam side down, on an oiled rack and brush them with oil.

Grill them for five to seven minutes on each side or until the cheese appears to have melted and the leaves are crisp.

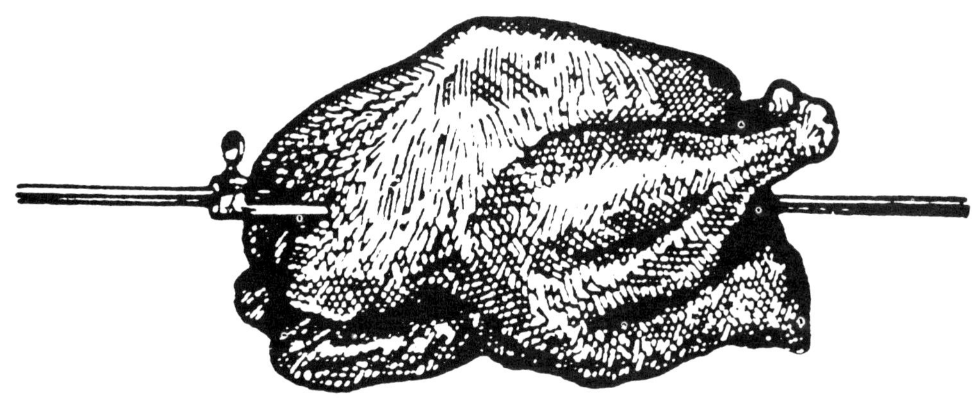

A game dinner in the North

Carlins

Clear game consommé
Fresh trout
Potted trout or potted char

Grouse pie
Pot-roast pheasant
Ragout of wild duck with pears
Venison escalopes with walnut sauce
Hare in cider

Forcemeat balls

Glazed carrots
Puree of leeks
Roast potatoes

Bilberry pie
Fried apple slices

Rum butter
Singing hinnies
Stotty cakes
Oatcakes (havercakes, clapbread and riddlebread)

Cotherstone cheese

The moorlands, rivers and lakes of Northumberland, Cumberland and Westmorland, as well as North Yorkshire, are rich in game; almost every furred, finned and feathered creature that you can legally stalk, catch or shoot can be found here, and while the sportsmen's lunches may be nothing better than a can or bottle of beer with a sandwich in the lee of a Land Rover on a windy hilltop, the dinners later in the evening in shooting lodges and country houses are magnificent. With luck the hunters, shooters, stalkers or fishermen are home in time for tea first, so I've included a few of the many Northern specialities for that meal too at the end of this section.

Workaday Northern meals are not always quite as grand as this, but they are as sustaining (see for instance the Football Supper on page 148 and the High Tea in Yorkshire on page 109). There are other recipes for game on pages 167 and 192.

Carlins (or carlings)

These are also known as maple peas, pigeon peas and horsehead beans and are similar to Lancashire's parched peas. They are small, round, greyish dried peas, obtainable at some wholefood shops, and on Tyneside people eat them to celebrate the second Sunday in Easter (Carlin Sunday). The legend is that on this day, some centuries ago, the city of Newcastle was besieged by the Scots. The people were starving and were saved by the appearance on the River Tyne of a stranded French ship carrying a load of these grey peas. Another more recent story is that people took to eating them in the Depression, as they were very cheap and sold mainly as pigeon feed. Whichever story is right, they make nice appetisers with drinks before dinner – local pubs serve them (free) in twists of paper, with salt and vinegar. They can also be put into stews or soups. They may be the original ingredients of old-fashioned 'bean feasts' although they don't grow here.

The peas should be soaked overnight, then cooked for about an hour, when they will be tender. Drain them and either eat them as in the pubs, with salt and vinegar, or else as a sweet, sprinkled with rum and a little brown sugar.

Clear game consommé

Make a consommé (page 87) with the carcases of roast game (grouse and pheasant are particularly good). Clarify it and flavour it with a little sherry or white wine. Add small pieces of cooked game and a little boiled rice as garnishes.

Fresh trout

The plainer and fresher the trout, the better. North-Country people usually fry them in butter, after cleaning them. They put them on a hot dish and deglaze the pan with a little lemon juice and pour this over the fish, which is sent to table with a sprinkling of fresh parsley.

Some cooks roll the fish in fine oatmeal before frying it, others use flour, or a mixture of flour and oatmeal. Trout may also be brushed with melted butter, then grilled.

Try this way too: roll the cleaned and washed trout first in flour, then dip it in a bath of melted butter, then coat it with fine oatmeal. This is to be fried in hot butter or lard until it is golden.

Potted trout or potted char *(for 4–6)*

Trout and char are, with salmon, indigenous to the North. Char are related to salmon and trout, and though rare in other freshwater lakes and rivers in England, local fishermen still find them in Windermere. This method of potting them can be used for salmon too. It makes a nice first course, served cold with hot buttered toast.

4	trout or char (about 150 g/6 oz each)	4
	salt, pepper	
	powdered cloves and mace to taste	
250 g	clarified butter (page 264)	8 oz
	cayenne pepper	

Wash the trout or char and remove the heads and tails. Split the fish down the back and remove the backbones with the ribs. Sprinkle the fish inside and out with salt, pepper, cloves and mace and leave them overnight.

Next day preheat the oven to 150°C/300°F/gas 2. Arrange the fish head to tail, and bellies up in a baking dish that is just large enough to hold them, and pour half the clarified butter over them. Cover the dish and bake the fish for an hour, or until they are soft.

Turn them out of the dish and drain the liquid from them. When they are cold open them and scrape the seasoning away from them. Sprinkle a little cayenne pepper inside them, close them up again and pack them tightly in a dish (in the olden days special white china 'char pots' were made for this) on their sides, again head to tail. Pour a little of their cooking liquid in first, then put the rest of the clarified butter over them. The butter should cover them completely. Let it set, then serve the fish.

AUTHOR'S NOTE: Another recipe (the way they were done for the late Lord Lonsdale) states that 'char seasoning' used to be sold at Boots the Chemist in Bowness-on-Windermere. This recipe leaves the fish whole until after they have been very slowly cooked for eight to ten hours in the manner described above. When they are cold the heads and bones are carefully removed. The fish are then laid in the char pot and covered, as above, with clarified butter.

Notes on cooking game birds

Provided the birds are young they can be roasted and are best cooked this way. If it is late in the season, or you suspect the birds of being past their prime, it is better to pot-roast or casserole them. In all cases roast game birds in a pan of good dripping to baste them with in a hot oven – set it at 200°C/400°F/gas 6 for three-quarters of the time given overleaf, then reduce the heat a little to finish them off.

Land birds need little in the way of preparation. If they are sold with a barding of fat or bacon, remove it towards the end of cooking and baste them, then sprinkle them with a little seasoned flour so that the breast browns. A few sprigs of thyme, a clove of garlic and a slice of lemon or orange, with seasoning, can be put inside to improve their flavour.

Water birds sometimes have a rather muddy or fishy flavour. Some cooks think that roasting them with a raw peeled potato and an onion inside the cavity helps to counteract this; others give them a basting with plain water for half their cooking time (the water is then thrown away). Note that water birds are not hung, but eaten as fresh as possible.

Specific notes on cooking various types of game birds are to be found on the next two pages.

Grouse pie *(for 6–8)*

This pie is better cold than hot. It is made in exactly the same way as a pigeon pie (page 103), but the ingredients here are a brace of well-hung grouse divided into four breast portions and four legs, and a large slice of gammon cut into 2.5 cm/1 inch squares. The grouse carcase and skin are used to enrich a good beef stock and the meat is simmered in it. The pie is covered in rough-puff or shortcrust pastry (pages 266 and 264) which is glazed with egg and prettily decorated.

Game birds cooking chart

Set the oven to 200°C/400°F/gas 6; reduce it to 180°C/350°F/gas 4 for the last quarter of the cooking time, and remove any bacon at the same time to let the breasts brown.

bird	*season*	*servings per bird*	*preparation*
Blackcock	August 20 to December 10	3–4	season and baste
Capercailzie	October 1 to January 31	6	cover breast with bacon, stuff with beefsteak
Grouse	August 12 to December 10	1–2	cover breast with bacon, baste
Partridge	September 1 to February 1	1–2	as grouse
Pheasant	October 1 to February 1	2	cover breast with bacon, stuff with apple, herbs
Pigeon	all year round	1	as grouse
Ptarmigan	August 12 to December 10	1–2	as grouse
Quail* (brace)	all year round	1	wrap in vine leaves and then bacon
Snipe	August 12 to January 31	1	don't draw, cover with bacon, baste
Wild duck**	September 1 to February 20	3–4	cover breast with bacon, stuff with onion and potato, salt well, cook at first with water to baste
Woodcock	October 1 to January 31	1	don't draw, leave head on and impale legs with beak

*Quail are protected and are only reared on farms for eating.
**Includes: Teal, Mallard and Widgeon.

cooking time in minutes	*how to serve and with what garnishes*	*bird*
45–60	on buttered toast, with gravy, bread sauce (page 260), buttered breadcrumbs	Blackcock
60	with gravy, bread sauce (page 259), buttered breadcrumbs and watercress salad	Capercailzie
30–35	with toast that has caught drips while roasting, and accompaniments as above	Grouse
30	as grouse, with redcurrant or rowan jelly (pages 249–50)	Partridge
40	as capercailzie, sometimes with fried apple rings too, or redcurrant or rowan jelly (pages 249–50)	Pheasant
20–30	on fried bread, with watercress or a sharp sauce (page 260)	Pigeon
30–35	on toast, as grouse	Ptarmigan
12–15	with toast, as grouse, and vine leaves or not, as liked	Quail* (brace)
15	with toast that has caught drips while roasting, and the entrails spread on it	Snipe
25–30	with a port wine or orange sauce, watercress and orange salad (page 226)	Wild duck**
15	as snipe	Woodcock

Note that this chart refers to shooting dates; birds which have been hanging will be available for up to two weeks after the last date.

Pot-roast pheasant *(for 4)*

While pheasants are in season country people get quite blasé about them as they are so much more plentiful than any other game. Fortunately, there are almost as many recipes for them as there are for chicken. This one comes from North Yorkshire. The pheasants should be well hung, then skinned, feathers and all, which is easier than plucking them.

	salt	
1	brace of pheasants	1
6–8	rashers of streaky bacon	6–8
500 g	trimmed button mushrooms	1 lb
500 g	peeled pickling onions	1 lb
	butter for frying	
two or three 15 ml sp	calvados or brandy	2–3 tbsp
275 ml	double cream	½ pt
2–3	sliced, sweet apples fried in butter	2–3

Preheat the oven to 200°C/400°F/gas 6.

Salt the insides of the pheasants, then put them side by side in a large, lidded, buttered casserole with the bacon rashers over their breasts.

Sauté the mushrooms and onions in a little butter and put them in the casserole. Add half the calvados or brandy. Cover the pot tightly, first with foil and then with the lid and pot-roast the birds for 45 minutes (cook older birds a little longer). Joint them neatly and keep the pieces warm, in a serving dish, with the bacon rashers and the vegetables nicely arranged beside them.

Strain the gravy and reduce it a little by fast boiling. Flambé the rest of the brandy or calvados and add this to the sauce. Add the cream to the sauce and heat it gently. Taste for seasoning and pour some of it over the pheasants. Keep the rest to serve in a sauce boat at table.

Arrange the fried apple rings around the dish, and serve.

Sprouts or runner beans go well with this dish, and roast potatoes (page 141).

Ragout of wild duck with pears *(for 4)*

1	wild duck weighing 2–2.5 kg/4–5 lb (with giblets)	1
	butter for frying	
1	finely chopped carrot	1
1	finely chopped onion	1
275 ml	white wine	½ pt
	duck stock (see below)	
1	bouquet garni	1
4	small, peeled pears	4
	salt, pepper	

Make two slits down the duck's back on either side of the backbone. Lift the bone out and reserve it for the duck stock, along with the wing ends.

Clean the gizzard if you still have it, and add it with the neck to the stock ingredients (see below).

Cut the duck into four pieces, giving more breast meat to the wing portions than to the leg portions so that all the pieces will be approximately equal. Remove any excess fat. Prick the skin all over with a skewer and sauté the pieces in butter in a large, heavy pan. They will require about ten minutes on each side to turn golden. Transfer them to a lidded casserole.

Drain most of the fat from the pan and add the carrot and onion. Sauté the vegetables until they are soft and lightly coloured. Add the wine and stock (see below) to the pan and bring it slowly to the boil. Transfer the liquid to the casserole and add the bouquet garni. Cover the casserole and simmer the duck for about one hour or until the flesh seems tender when poked with a skewer. Set the pieces aside, strain the sauce and lift off any excess fat. Return the duck to the sauce and keep it warm.

Halve or quarter the pears and gently sauté them in a little butter for ten minutes or so, just to heat them through. Place the duck pieces on a warmed serving dish and arrange the pears round them. Taste the sauce for seasoning and pass it separately.

AUTHOR'S NOTE: To make the duck stock, sauté a finely chopped onion and a few finely chopped carrots in a deep pan. Add the neck, backbone, wings and gizzard. Sauté all the giblets until they are well browned. Add enough water to cover them, add salt and simmer for an hour. Strain and degrease the resulting stock before using it for the cooking liquid for the duck. This recipe can also be used for an ordinary duck but it will probably take less time to cook.

Venison

Like the New Forest, Exmoor and various other tracts of wild moorland and forest, the Keilder Forest in Northumberland is the home of the wild red deer. Herds of smaller deer are also kept in parks, partly for decoration, but also, through carefully controlled culling, as food. There is even a method of raising deer like farm animals and feeding them intensively for their meat. Venison, whether red, fallow, roe, sika or muntjack, is in season all the year round, though different species are in season at different times. At one time 90 per cent of it was exported to Western Europe, mostly to Germany, Austria and Switzerland but lately we have been eating more at home. Any butcher with a game licence can sell venison.

As shot today, venison is usually young and tender enough to eat without hanging; old and tougher animals will become more tender with hanging. It is also necessary to hang venison if you like the flavour of high, rather than fresh, game. The traditional way is to skin the joint first, then hang it somewhere cool and very draughty for anything up to two months. The result is a piece of meat that has developed a skin like boot leather and has lost a deal of weight, but the flavour and texture have become superb.

When cooking venison, remember that although it might be tender, it does not have enough fat to keep it moist. It benefits from marinating, and should be barded with fat, then pot-roasted with a little wine or water if you are eating it in a large piece. It is also good in casseroles. Cold pot-roasted venison is nice in salads, but best of all are venison steaks or escalopes – these can be treated like the best veal or beef and grilled or fried quite rapidly.

Venison escalopes with walnut sauce *(for 6)*

The steaks for this dish will have to be cut either from a large haunch (weighing about 10 kg/22 lb) or from a boned loin (ask for the eye piece). The slices should be cut diagonally across the grain. The sauce can be made with any sharp astringent jelly that is usually eaten with game – rowan, redcurrant, medlar or sloe and apple jelly will do very well (see pages 249 and 250). The original inspiration for this walnut sauce was, in fact, an Iranian dish called *fezanjan* which uses a preparation based on pomegranates that is unobtainable here.

1	finely chopped small onion	1
25 g	butter	1 oz
100 g	shelled, chopped walnuts	4 oz
100 ml	sharp jelly (see above)	4 fl oz
one 15 ml sp	lemon juice	1 tbsp
100 ml	beef or game stock	4 fl oz
	salt, pepper	
	nutmeg	
6	venison escalopes, each weighing about 150 g/6 oz and about 1 cm/½ inch thick	6
	oil, salt and pepper for a marinade	
	oil and butter for frying	

Sauté the onion in the butter until it is golden. Add the walnuts (which should be chopped about as finely as coarse breadcrumbs), the jelly, lemon juice, stock, salt, pepper and nutmeg. Simmer this sauce for ten minutes, then put it to one side.

Marinate the escalopes in a little oil, salt and pepper for about 20 minutes before you want to cook them.

Melt the oil and butter in a frying-pan and sauté each escalope for about three to four minutes on each side. As they are cooked remove them to a serving dish and keep them warm.

When they are all cooked, put the sauce in the pan and mix it with any juices that may have come out of the meat. Heat it through and serve it in a sauceboat with the escalopes.

Serve game chips or mashed potatoes, and buttered spinach (page 238) with this dish. A crisp green salad is a nice addition; so are glazed carrots (page 140).

Hare in cider *(for 6–8)*

This recipe makes use of the bits of the two hares that are left when the saddles have been used for another dish (see page 167). The blood should be kept too, if possible, to thicken the sauce (mix it with a little cider vinegar to prevent it curdling). The hares will need to be marinated first.

for the marinade

550 ml	rough cider	1 pt
125 ml	olive oil	$\frac{1}{4}$ pt
2	bay leaves	2
1–2	sprigs of rosemary and thyme	1–2
	a few crushed juniper berries	
	salt, pepper	
2	crushed cloves of garlic	2

Mix all the ingredients together and marinate the back legs, trimmed ribs and shoulders of the hare overnight. Make some stock from the head and trimmings of the hare, but reserve the liver and the blood (see introduction).

for cooking the hare

165 ml	strained and reduced marinade	7 fl oz
two or three 15 ml sp	seasoned flour	2–3 tbsp
	dripping or oil for frying	
125 ml	cider	$\frac{1}{4}$ pt
	stock (see method)	
12	small, whole, peeled onions	12
500 g	small mushrooms	1 lb
500 g	small peeled carrots	1 lb
	butter	
	a small chopped head of celery (or 6 stems of celery, chopped)	
1	peeled and cut-up cooking apple	1
	little rolls of fried streaky bacon to garnish	

Preheat the oven to 140°C/275°F/gas 1. Drain and dry the hare pieces. Reduce the strained marinade by fast boiling. Meanwhile coat the meat with the seasoned flour and brown each piece in dripping or oil before putting it in a heavy casserole. Deglaze the pan with the glass of cider and pour that over the meat. Add the marinade and enough stock to cover the meat. Put the lid on the casserole. Cook it in the oven for $1\frac{1}{2}$–2 hours, when the meat should just be tender.

Sauté the onions, mushrooms and carrots very briefly in butter, then add them with the celery and apple to the casserole and cook it for another 45 minutes. Twenty minutes before the end, cook small dumplings on top of the stew (page 170) or make forcemeat balls (page 140). To finish the sauce mash the liver finely and mix it with the blood. Strain some of the cooking liquid onto it, stir well and return this mixture to the pot to finish cooking. Serve the casserole garnished with the rolls of fried bacon, mashed potatoes and redcurrant jelly (page 249).

AUTHOR'S NOTE: This dish can also be made with venison.

Forcemeat balls

These accompany roast meat or game and should be made with fresh herbs so that they are bright green when they are cut open. Mix together finely chopped bacon, finely chopped chives, marjoram and parsley, fresh breadcrumbs and salt and pepper. Bind the mixture with one or two beaten eggs and form it into small balls about the size of a large marble. Fry them until they are brown and serve them separately at the same time as the gravy.

Glazed carrots

Choose good, mature, but not woody carrots and slice them diagonally, rather than down or across.

Put them in a pan with just enough slightly salted water to cover them. Add a generous knob of butter and a sprinkling of sugar. Cook them uncovered until the water has almost all evaporated and the butter and sugar have combined to give each slice of carrot a shiny glaze. Serve them sprinkled with finely chopped parsley.

AUTHOR'S NOTE: This method can also be applied to small, whole or quartered turnips.

Puree of leeks *(for 6)*

North-Country gardeners, particularly in Durham, compete with one another to grow the largest leeks. This is one way of making use of them.

750 g–1 kg	leeks	1½–2 lb
50 g	butter	2 oz
	salt, pepper	
2 or 3	sprigs of fresh mint (or an equivalent amount of dried)	2 or 3
one 15 ml sp	double cream	1 tbsp

Trim the roots and the darkest, coarsest parts of the green leaves from the leeks. Make a cross in them from the green end to about halfway down and leave them in a bowl of cold water for the grit to soak out.

Starting at the green end slice the leeks, with a good sharp cook's knife, into the finest pieces you can manage. Rinse them well in a colander.

Melt the butter in a saucepan and cook the drained leeks in it, uncovered, stirring occasionally. Add salt and pepper to taste.

They should become quite tender and most of the moisture should have evaporated after 20 to 30 minutes' cooking. At this point add the finely chopped mint and the cream. Heat through and serve.

AUTHOR'S NOTE: If you want to leave out the cream and butter, use a little stock instead.

Roast potatoes *(for 6)*

1.25–1.5 kg	potatoes	2½–3 lb
	good dripping	

Peel the potatoes and cut them into halves or quarters to make them all roughly the same size.

Heat enough dripping in a large frying-pan to cover the bottom to a depth of about 0.5 cm/¼ inch and fry the potato pieces in it until they are nicely coloured.

Take them out of the fat and put them into an oven-proof dish without any more fat. Bake them in the oven for about 45 minutes at the same temperature as your roast meat.

AUTHOR'S NOTE: This method of roasting potatoes has two advantages over the more usual way of either roasting them under the meat after par-boiling them, or roasting them entirely under the meat: it is quicker and neater. The preliminary frying seals the outside and the centres cook faster with their locked-in pockets of steam.

Bilberry pie *(for 4–6)*

Bilberries, also known as blueberries and whortleberries, grow on squat, spreading bushes on Northern moors and hillsides (and on Dartmoor), in exactly the same heathery habitat as that enjoyed by grouse. This bilberry pie is traditionally made on August 12th to celebrate the start of the grouse-shooting season. Serve it with thick cream and sugar.

750 ml	washed bilberries	1½ pt
100 g	caster sugar	4 oz
250 g	shortcrust pastry (page 265)	8 oz
	egg white to glaze	

Preheat the oven to 200°C/400°F/gas 6.

Mix the drained bilberries with the sugar and put them into a deep pie dish with a pie funnel in the centre. Cover the dish with the pastry, leaving a hole for the funnel and glazing the top with lightly beaten egg white.

Bake it for twenty minutes to cook the pastry, then reduce the heat to 180°C/350°F/gas 4 to cook the fruit for another 15-20 minutes. (Put a large dish beneath the pie in case the juice overflows.)

AUTHOR'S NOTE: Some recipes suggest adding the pulp of one or two cooked apples.

Fried apple slices *(for 4)*

This is the time of year when apples are so plentiful that they can hardly be given away. If you have a sackful of soft, tart cooking apples, make the bruised and misshapen ones into purees and pies and keep a few of the best for these batterless 'fritters'. They look smart enough to be served at a dinner party.

2	large, unblemished cooking apples	2
two 15 ml sp	rum or brandy	2 tbsp
two 15 ml sp	lemon juice	2 tbsp
one 15 ml sp	caster sugar	1 tbsp
50–75 g	unsalted butter	2–3 oz
4	crustless slices of bread, cut into fingers	4
50 g	plain flour	2 oz
	caster sugar	
	cinnamon powder	

Peel and core the apples, then cut them into thin rounds.

Mix the rum or brandy with the lemon juice and sugar and soak the apple slices in it for two or three hours.

Melt half the butter in a frying-pan and fry the bread until golden. Arrange these croûtons around a warmed serving dish and keep them warm.

Drain the apple rings and reserve the marinade. Flour each ring before frying them in the rest of the butter. Turn them over so that they are quite a dark brown and slightly crisp on both sides. Arrange them in an overlapping pattern in the warmed dish.

When they are all cooked put the marinade in the pan, cook it an instant until it thickens, then pour it over the apples. Sprinkle them with a mixture of sugar and cinnamon and serve them very hot, with cream.

Rum butter

The Lake District makes more use of rum, brown sugar and dried fruit and spices than any other part of England. The reason for this is the trade which started in the 18th century between Cumbria and the West and East Indies. Cotton cloth, and wool for carpet-making, grown by the shaggy moorland and fell sheep that are still reared here today, were the English exports.

Southerners think of rum butter as an accompaniment to mince pies, Christmas pudding and nothing else, but in Cumberland it is called 'brown jam'. It is associated with christenings in particular, with tea-time in general, and is sold at every shop and cafe in the area. It is extremely good spread on bread and butter, warm scones (page 13) or oatcakes (page 145). After a christening or the birth of a baby, visitors to the house are offered a glass of wine or ale spiced and mixed with rum to drink the baby's health. Biscuits spread with rum butter are passed around as well. (There is a saying that the first woman to taste it is the next to have a baby.) Rum butter is also eaten with a very filling steamed pudding called rum dog.

250 g	unsalted butter	8 oz
500 g	soft brown sugar (called Scotch moist or Barbados)	1 lb
one 5 ml sp	grated nutmeg	1 tsp
60 ml	rum	$2\frac{1}{2}$ fl oz

For this *Westmorland* version of *rum butter*, soften the butter and beat the sugar into it. Add the nutmeg and slowly incorporate the rum, stirring well. Put it into little bowls or glass dishes and let it set.

AUTHOR'S NOTE: If you want to make *Cumberland rum butter*, the ingredients are the same as above, but the rum and sugar are beaten together first. Then the butter is melted and stirred in until the mixture is well amalgamated. It is put into bowls with the nutmeg grated on top. It keeps for up to three months in a covered dish in a cool place.

North-Country baking

This tradition is far from dead, especially in the country, where oatcakes, scones and pikelets are still made at home, along with cakes, baked pies and biscuits. Some kitchens still have a special arrangement for mixing doughs. A North-Country friend describes it: 'They prepare and mix the ingredients for pastry and dough in a kind of open-ended drawer. This is placed on the table to work in. The ones I have seen never seem to get washed – they are well seasoned with flour. They roll out pastry too, for pies and tarts, in the confines of the drawer.'

Bakestones, griddles or girdles are still considered an essential part of kitchen equipment. They were originally actually made of stone, a fine, soft, micaceous stone, and were flat, oval and portable. Today they are made of cast iron. The large rectangular iron bakestones set into old kitchen ranges have mostly disappeared, and have been replaced by small round, portable ones which are easy to use, even on electric cookers.

Singing hinnies *(for 6–8)*

The derivations of this pretty name for a Tyneside griddle scone are rather fanciful, but 'hinny' means (in Geordie dialect) 'honey' in the affectionate sense, and 'singing' is the sound made by the cakes as they sizzle on the girdle or bakestone. 'Is it ready to eat yet mother?'; 'No, it's just singing, hinnies', is a tale given as explanation of the name. Recipes vary, but the result should be a griddle-sized cake, 20 cm/8 inches across and about 2 cm/$\frac{3}{4}$ inch thick. Proper Northumbrian kitchens have pairs of wooden 'hands' shaped like ping-pong bats, to turn the cakes over.

250 g	plain flour	8 oz
one 5 ml sp	baking powder	1 tsp
	pinch of salt	
50 g	butter	2 oz
50 g	lard	2 oz
75 g	currants	3 oz
	milk to mix	

Sift the flour with the baking powder and salt, rub in the fats and add the currants. Add enough milk to make a soft dough. Roll it into a cake about 1 cm/$\frac{1}{2}$ inch thick (it will rise a little), prick the top and mark it into eight sections. Bake it on a hot, greased griddle for about eight minutes on each side until it is golden on both sides. Eat it warm, the wedges split in half and generously buttered.

Stotty cakes *(makes 4)*

Stotty cakes are to the Northumbrian what the pasty is to a Cornishman. They are sold in vast numbers in the North-East, ready to be sliced open and filled with whatever you like, for lunch. They look like soft, sloppy berets, with a dent in the middle instead of a tassel. The same sort of bread is made in Yorkshire where it is called a 'bottom cake' because it is baked on the oven floor.

To make stotty cakes use the same recipe for dough as the one given on page 35 for cabbage bread rolls adding 25 g/1 oz lard and using half milk and half water. Let the dough rise, then knock it down and form it into four balls. Roll each one into a flat round about as big as a dinner plate and leave them to prove on greased baking-sheets in a warm place while the oven heats up to 200°C/400°F/gas 6. Just before you put them in the oven, dust them with flour and push your thumb down hard in the centre. Bake them for 15 minutes, then reduce the heat to 190°C/375°F/gas 5 for another 15 minutes.

Oatcakes *(makes 16)*

These are known as havercakes, haverbread and clapbread, and are similar to the oatcakes made on the other side of the North Sea in Scandinavia. *Hafri* is the old Norse word for oats, which are still grown in these parts. These oatcakes (see below) are the crisp kind, sold sometimes as small saucer-sized rounds, and sometimes as flat quadrants known as 'farls'. The name clapbread derives from the way they are made, the dough being 'clapped' into its flat, thin shape on a board.

Another kind of oatcake called riddlebread is made from a thinner yeasted oat-based batter. It is flung onto the heated bakestone in such a way that it forms a long, flat oval, rather than a round. These are soft enough after baking to be hung up to dry over special wooden rails (the same rails are used to dry clothes above the range in North-Country kitchens). These oatcakes are not to be confused with yet another kind of yeasted oatcake, Staffordshire oatcakes (page 13) which are kept soft and pliable, and not allowed to dry.

50 g	lard	2 oz
500 g	fine oatmeal	1 lb
two 5 ml sp	salt	2 tsp
225 ml	warm water	8 fl oz

Rub the lard into all but a handful of the oatmeal and salt and add the warm water, gathering in the dry ingredients as you do so. Knead the dough well – it should be a little loose at first, but it will become firmer after a little more kneading. Break off one quarter of the dough, and keep the remaining dough covered

Roll the piece of dough out as thin as possible on a board sprinkled with oatmeal. If you cannot roll out a perfect circle, cut off the ragged edges, using a large plate as your guide. Continue to make circles with the remaining dough. Divide each one into four quarters or 'farls'. Bake the oatcakes on a hot, well-greased griddle, giving them about five to seven minutes a side. Transfer the cakes to a rack and leave them to dry for several hours, before storing them in a tin.

AUTHOR'S NOTE: If you want to keep them flat, cook them on one side only on the griddle and dry them off in a low oven.

Cotherstone cheese

This would be a good local cheese, soft and fresh-tasting, to eat with your oatcakes (page 243).

WINTER

A Lancashire football supper
Dinner for a cold day in Norfolk
Christmas Day
A St Valentine's Day dinner

A Lancashire football supper

Fish pie
Huddersfield fish-cakes
Grilled smoked haddock or cod

Steak and kidney pie
Lancashire hot-pot
Tripe with butter beans
Fried tripe
Tripe wiggle

Stuffed 'taters
Leek pie
Nettle champ

Bread-and-butter pudding
Apple or gooseberry pie
New College puddings

Blackburn cracknels and Lancashire cheese
Pikelets

Lancashire is the home of many famous dishes: Simnel cake, Morecambe Bay shrimps, Eccles and Chorley cakes, tripe and onions, steak and cow-heel pie, black puddings – they eat well in this county. It also seems to have more football clubs than anywhere else. This menu is planned to give the hungry fans something to eat when they come home from the match; elated or downcast, they will be hungry. These dishes, rural in origin, but now traditional also in mostly industrial areas, are the kind that can wait a little in the oven until they're wanted.

Fish pie *(for 6)*

'I always make enough fish pie for two dinners,' said a wise old lady, married to a fisherman and used to cooking for a large family. 'You have it first as a pie and then you make what's left into fish-cakes' (page 16).

750 g	ling, cod or whiting	1½ lb
	salt, pepper	
2	sliced onions	2
65 g	butter	2½ oz
40 g	flour	1½ oz
425 ml	milk	¾ pt
125 ml	fish stock (see method)	¼ pt
3	sliced, hard-boiled eggs	3
750 g	potatoes boiled and mashed with salt, milk and butter	1½ lb

Salt the fish overnight; wash it off the next day. Heat the oven to 180°C/350°F/gas 4. Cook the fish in lightly salted water for 20 minutes. Drain it, remove any skin or bones and flake the fish coarsely. Reserve 125 ml/¼ pt of the liquor for the sauce.

Sauté the sliced onions in a third of the butter until they are soft and golden.

Make a béchamel sauce (page 254) with the flour, remaining butter, milk and fish stock and season it well. Grease a pie-dish and put the fish in first. Follow with the onions, then the sliced hard-boiled eggs. Pour the sauce over all, then cover it with the mashed potato. Bake the pie until it is well-heated through and brown on top (about half an hour).

Huddersfield fish-cakes *(for 4)*

These are also known as 'Staffordshire Swallows', though anything less like a swallow is hard to imagine – they are very solid and satisfying. The fish is sandwiched between two slices of potato and the whole thing is coated in batter, then deep-fried.

You need only a bit of practice to tell when the temperature of the fat is right, and how long to cook the fish-cakes. You want the batter to be dry and crisp, the potatoes to be soft and cooked through, and the fish to be moist and juicy.

1	egg	1
three 15 ml sp	flour	3 tbsp
100 ml	water, or milk and water mixed	4 fl oz
	salt	
1	large potato weighing about 500 g/1 lb	1
500 g	fillet of cod or haddock	1 lb
	oil for frying	

Make a batter from the egg, flour, water and a little salt, and leave it to stand for at least an hour if possible.

Cut the peeled potato into eight slices not more than 0.75 cm/¼ inch thick. Skin the fillet and cut it into four equal-sized pieces. Sandwich each piece of fish between two slices of potato.

Heat the oil in a deep-fat-fryer to between 160°C and 170°C/325°F and 340°F.

Dip the 'sandwiches' in the batter and fry them, one or two at a time, for 15 minutes, turning them over at half-time. Drain them well and serve them with tomato sauce (page 257), or ketchup.

Grilled smoked haddock or cod *(for 6)*

Choose a plump, freshly smoked fillet for this dish. It is very quick and simple to prepare. Serve plenty of tea with it as it makes you very thirsty.

750 g	smoked fillet of haddock or cod	1½ lb
50–75 g	butter	2–3 oz
50–75 g	grated Lancashire cheese (or Cheddar)	2–3 oz
6	large rashers of bacon	6

Heat the grill so that it is red-hot.

Butter a shallow fire-proof dish just big enough to take the fish. Cut the fish into six equal portions and put it in the dish, skin side down. Dot it with the butter. Grill the fish for five minutes, when it should be well browned. Cover the surface with the grated cheese and return the dish to the grill. As soon as the cheese has melted (in about one or two minutes) arrange the rashers (rinds removed) on top of the cheese and baste them with the juices from the fish. Put the dish under the grill again and leave it for a few more minutes to cook the bacon. It is ready as soon as the bacon is crisp.

AUTHOR'S NOTE: Sliced tomatoes dotted with butter can be substituted for the bacon.

Steak and kidney pie *(for 8)*

This pie, made regularly to order at weekends in a pub high in the Pennines, uses cheap cuts of stewing beef and ox kidney for the filling. It is ideal for warming up just as the hungry customers arrive, as it is made in a flat pie plate with pastry above and below the meat, rather than in the traditional deep pie-dish, which has a crust only on top.

	seasoned flour	
1 kg	trimmed and cubed stewing steak	2 lb
375 g	trimmed and sliced ox kidney	12 oz
	dripping	
	salt, pepper	
	stock or water	
	bunch of herbs	
1 kg	rough-puff pastry (page 266)	2 lb
	beaten egg	

Put the seasoned flour into a paper bag with the pieces of steak and kidney and shake it about to coat the meat with the flour. Brown the meat in the dripping, in a frying-pan, then transfer the pieces to a casserole or saucepan, adding stock or water to cover, and the bunch of herbs, with salt and pepper to taste. Simmer it gently until the meat is tender – depending on the quality of the meat this will take 1½–2½ hours. Let it cool and make the pastry.

Heat the oven to 220°C/425°F/gas 7. Grease two 23 cm/9 inch pie plates and line them with half the pastry. Spoon in the filling and cover it with the rest of the pastry, sealing the edges well. Cut slits in the tops for the steam to escape and glaze the pies with beaten egg.

Bake them for 20 minutes and serve them cut in quarters, with mushy peas. The pie reheats very well, if cooked completely beforehand.

Lancashire hot-pot *(for 6)*

The liking for this simple stew of lamb, potato and onion is not confined to Lancashire – it is regarded as almost a national dish. It should be cooked in a tall, straight-sided earthenware pot. It is usually made with neck of lamb, which is fairly bony. If the butcher has any small, cheap cutlets, they are very good for a hot-pot too.

2.25 kg	potatoes	2½ lb
1.125 kg	onions	1¼ lb
2–3	lambs' kidneys	2–3
575 ml	stock	1 pt
2.25 kg	cutlets or middle neck of lamb	2½ lb
	salt, pepper	
	a little dripping	

Peel the potatoes and slice about two-thirds of them very finely. The remaining third should be about the size of an egg (halve or quarter large ones if necessary). Peel and slice the onions finely. Skin the kidneys and slice them. Warm the stock.

Arrange a few of the cutlets at the bottom of the pot. Cover them with a layer of onions, a few slices of kidney and a layer of the sliced potatoes. Season this layer and fill the pot with similar layers. Pour in the stock and put the whole or quartered potatoes on top. Dab them with a little dripping. Cover the pot and bake it in the oven at 160°C/325°F/gas 3 for three hours, removing the lid for the last half-hour to brown the potatoes.

Cooked this way, the sliced potatoes and onions combine to form a gravy-thickening mush, while the top potatoes remain whole. Serve the stew very hot with greens and pickled cabbage (page 246).

Tripe

Like black pudding, tripe is as popular in the North of England as it is in the North of France, which gives support to the theory that it was introduced to England by the Normans (the influence of Norman culture seems to have been stronger in the fortified towns of the North than it was in the South). All the same, tripe as eaten these days in the North of England bears little resemblance to the same thing in Normandy.

In northern England tripe is almost invariably stewed with milk and onions and then eaten with a thickened sauce made from the milk – this is a soothing but rather bland dish. It is also almost always sold ready-cooked so that it can be eaten cold with vinegar or with a jelly made from cow-heel.

In Derbyshire, it is cooked with cow-heel, onions and pork sausages, the liquor from the stew being thickened with flour.

In Northumberland and East Anglia a large piece of partly cooked tripe is sewn round a boiled onion, sage and breadcrumb stuffing, then roasted with rashers of bacon on top (this is called Dressmaker tripe).

A 17th-century recipe from Dorset recommends simmering strips of partly cooked tripe in a mixture of white wine and veal stock, then thickening this with egg yolks and lemon juice – a very continental-sounding recipe.

In spite of its cheapness, the demand for tripe is now so low that many southern butchers don't stock it at all, or if they do, it is only sold as pet food. Its unpopularity is possibly due partly to the dullness of most English recipes though it is admittedly an acquired taste. This recipe originally came from Milan but it uses ingredients which are all quite common in England. Note that most tripe is sold half-cooked in the South, and that it is more often sold wholly cooked in the North; the cooking times will therefore have to take this into account, so ask your butcher. It is also unfortunately invariably sold bleached, which does not improve flavour or texture.

Tripe with butter beans *(for 4–6)*

This can be made thick for a stew or thin for a soup, depending on the quantity of liquid.

	oil or butter	
1–2	sliced carrots	1–2
1–2	sliced sticks of celery	1–2
1	medium-sized peeled potato, cut into 2.5 cm/1 inch cubes	1
1	roughly chopped medium-sized onion	1
	shredded leaves of a very small cabbage	
500 g	tripe, thick or thin, half-cooked and cut into 2.5 cm/1 inch squares	1 lb
75 g	butter beans (soaked overnight)	3 oz
	beef stock to cover	
	salt, pepper	
	grated Lancashire or Parmesan cheese	

Heat 2–3 spoonfuls of good oil, or oil and butter, in a large, heavy pan and lightly sauté all the fresh vegetables. Add the tripe and let it cook a little. Add the drained butter beans and enough stock to cover everything well. Season, cover, and cook over a very low heat for 1½–2 hours, or until the butter beans are tender. The tripe should be tender too, but with a little 'bite'. Taste it for seasoning and serve it with grated cheese passed round at table.

It is extremely good (if not better) reheated the next day.

Fried tripe

This also makes a good starter. Cut cooked tripe into pieces measuring about 5 cm/2 inches by 7.5 cm/3 inches. Soak them for a little while in a marinade of equal quantities of oil and vinegar. Drain them, dry them, then coat them in flour and either egg and breadcrumbs or batter before frying them in good oil or lard.

Tripe wiggle *(for 6–8)*

This version of tripe can be made with clams, oysters or peeled prawns. It makes a nice start to a meal, served in small quantities.

750 g	cooked tripe	$1\frac{1}{2}$ lb
12	raw oysters or clams *or*	12
150 g	cooked peeled prawns	6 oz
425 ml	béchamel sauce (page 254) made with milk and the clam or oyster liquor, and tripe liquor if you have cooked it yourself	$\frac{3}{4}$ pt
	salt, pepper	
	lemon juice	
	ground mace	

for serving

parsley
lemon wedges
fried bread

Cut the tripe into small pieces. Add it, along with the oysters, clams or prawns to the sauce, and season it with salt, pepper, lemon juice and mace. Heat the mixture through, but don't overcook it or the oysters and clams will go tough. Serve it with a sprinkling of chopped parsley and lemon wedges and slices of fried bread.

Potatoes

A great many dishes combining potatoes with meat or fish are to be found in Lancashire, possibly because it was here in the early 18th century that potatoes were first grown in England, encouraged no doubt by the large numbers of Irish people who came to work and settle here (Ireland was the first area of Britain to grow potatoes). It was also in Lancashire that fish and chips were first thought of; Lancashire too (like the rest of the North) is the home of Britain's oddest and most filling sandwich – the chip butty.

A Hallowe'en speciality, rather good for Guy Fawkes parties as well, is a baked potato stuffed with sausage-meat. To make these 'stuffed 'taters' for eight people bake four large floury potatoes. Cut them in half lengthways, scoop out the middles, leaving about 1 cm/$\frac{1}{2}$ inch of potato round the edges, and mix it with 375–500 g/12 oz–1 lb good sausage-meat (page 19), which has been well sautéed with herbs and a finely chopped onion. Put the meat and potato mixture back into the potatoes, and brown the halves in a hot oven for about twenty minutes.

Leek pie *(for 4)*

This recipe appears to be common to both Lancashire and Cornwall (where it is called likky pie). It is a substantial pie which is good enough on its own to make a warming lunch or supper dish. The proportion of bacon to leek can be altered to suit your taste.

4	large leeks	4
	salt	
275 ml	creamy milk	½ pt
2	beaten eggs	2
6	rashers of unsmoked bacon	6
	butter	
	pepper	
300 g	suet crust (page 265)	10 oz

Preheat the oven to 200°C/400°F/gas 6.

Cut the leeks into 2.5 cm/1 inch lengths and wash them well to get rid of any grit, then blanch them by putting them in a colander and pouring boiling water over them; drain them well. Put them in a saucepan, season them with a little salt, and cook them with the milk until they are just tender. Strain the milk onto the beaten eggs as if you were making a custard. Allow both the leeks and the custard mixture to cool. Trim the rinds from the bacon, cut the rashers into 2.5 cm/1 inch pieces. Sauté them lightly in a little butter.

Butter a 1 litre/2 pt pie-dish and put a pie funnel in the centre. Arrange the leeks and bacon in the dish in alternate layers, pour over the custard and season it with a little pepper. Cover the dish with the suet crust and bake it for 20–30 minutes. Serve it hot (the custard should be quite firm).

AUTHOR'S NOTE: I have taken liberties with the traditional recipes, which recommend cooking the leeks and bacon in the pie-dish on top of the stove first (not easy), then, after the crust has baked, lifting it off to add the eggs to the contents, and baking it for another ten minutes.

Nettle champ

This is another Lancashire dish based on the potato, related to the 'champ' that is eaten in Ireland which is made of potatoes mixed with chopped spring onions. Lancashire country people make nettle champ with a bunch of young nettle tops, trimmed of their hairy stalks and roughly chopped, then boiled in a little milk. This is added to the already boiled and hot mashed potatoes with salt, pepper and a little butter. Cooked green cabbage and chopped parsley are also good ingredients for making champ.

Bread-and-butter pudding *(for 4)*

This is an old nursery favourite, which remains so even when the babies have grown up. It is also a good way of using up stale bread. The brandy or rum gives it a touch of adult luxury.

50 g	raisins	2 oz
25 g	candied peel	1 oz
two 15 ml sp	brandy or rum	2 tbsp
	juice of half an orange	
575 ml	milk	1 pt
50 g	sugar	2 oz
	grated nutmeg	
3	eggs	3
	butter	
4	well-buttered crustless slices of bread	4

Soak the fruit in the brandy or rum and orange juice for an hour. Make a custard with the milk, sugar, nutmeg and eggs (page 262). Heat the oven to 160°C/325°F/gas 3. Cut each slice of bread into four fingers, and put them in a buttered pie-dish in layers with the fruit and the juice. Pour over the custard and let it soak in for ten minutes, lightly pressed down with a weight. Grate more nutmeg over the top and bake the pudding, without a weight, in a bain-marie for about an hour.

Gooseberries

Lancashire, Cheshire and North-Midland cotton-workers and weavers had a tradition, still alive today, of growing fruit and vegetables to huge sizes, particularly leeks, onions and gooseberries. In fact, gooseberry competitions were so popular that no fewer than 155 gooseberry exhibitions were held in 1863. Competitors belonged to gooseberry clubs and hundreds of new varieties were bred with names like Brundit's Tickle Toby, Farrow's Roaring Lion, or Dan's Mistake, their colours ranging from red and green to white or yellow. Their prize-winning weights were two ounces or more. The high rainfall of this area is very advantageous to the growing of prize specimens; it may also cause disaster, and many a time the prime contenders have had the misfortune to burst in their boxes just before the show. The prizes today are mostly money, but in Victorian times one champion competitor won 103 prizes in a single year, including silver cups, cream jugs and teaspoons, a pig, a ham and a rocking-chair.

Gooseberries are also grown to be eaten and are very popular in pies (see for instance the version on page 34).

Apple pie *(for 8)*

Lancashire people eat Lancashire cheese (page 242) with their apple pies, just as Yorkshire people have Wensleydale cheese with theirs. On both sides of the Pennines they make apple pies in an enamelled dish that is not as deep as a china pie-dish, nor yet as shallow as a tin pie-plate. It gives the ideal proportion of crisp pastry to juicy apple.

250 g	rough-puff or shortcrust pastry (page 266 or 264)	8 oz
1 kg	peeled and cored cooking apples	2 lb
two 15 ml sp	demerara sugar	2 tbsp
one 5 ml sp	ground cinnamon, cloves or ginger	1 tsp
	caster sugar	

Preheat the oven to 220°C/425°F/gas 7, while you make the pastry. Let it rest while you prepare the apples. Slice them thickly and put them in a 23 cm/9 inch round pie-dish with the sugar and spices, and a pie-funnel in the middle. Make a pastry rim round the dampened edge of the pie-dish and dampen it in turn so that the pastry lid adheres to it.

Bake it for 20 minutes to cook the pastry, then lower the heat to 190°C/375°F/gas 5, to finish cooking the apples (another 20 minutes).

Sprinkle the top with caster sugar and serve the pie either hot or cold, with Lancashire cheese and whipped cream.

AUTHOR'S NOTE: Grated lemon rind and a little lemon juice can also be added to the apples. About 750 g/1½ lb of gooseberries, topped and tailed and mixed with plenty of sugar, would also make a good fruit pie, using the same shaped dish as above, but don't fill it too full, as gooseberries make more juice than apples and the pie may boil over.

New College puddings *(for 8)*

This recipe dates from a cookery book of 1698. It was known even then as New College puddings after the Oxford college. Now, as then, it satisfies hungry lads.

250 g	minced beef suet	8 oz
250 g	currants	8 oz
125 g	fresh breadcrumbs	4 oz
	grated rind of a lemon	
	nutmeg	
one 5 ml sp	salt	1 tsp
125 ml	double cream	¼ pt
3	beaten eggs	3
	caster sugar	

Combine the suet, currants, breadcrumbs and seasonings in a large bowl. Stir in the cream and the eggs and mix just until all the ingredients are combined to make a stiff paste. Add more breadcrumbs if the mixture is too loose, or cream if it is too stiff. Shape the mixture into eight large ovals the size of goose eggs, and refrigerate them for at least one hour or overnight before cooking. Sauté the puddings in a heavy frying-pan for about five minutes on each side or until golden all over. It is not necessary to add any fat to the pan as the mixture already contains a sufficient amount.

Dust the puddings with caster sugar and serve them with custard (page 261).

Blackburn cracknels *(makes about 24)*

These are to be eaten with Lancashire cheese. Cracknel is a very old word for biscuit; they were first made by boiling wheat paste, then rolling it, cutting it out and frying the rounds. These are only baked.

125 g	lard	4 oz
500 g	sifted plain flour	1 lb
15 g	baking powder	½ oz
	pinch of salt	
250 ml	warm milk	½ pt

Preheat the oven to 160°C/325°F/gas 3. Rub the lard into the flour and add the baking powder and salt. Add the milk and make the mixture into a dough. Knead it well, then roll it out 0.25 cm/⅛ inch thick. Cut it into rounds about 7.5 cm/3 inches across. Put the cracknels on greased baking-sheets, prick the tops and bake them for 30 minutes.

Pikelets *(makes 30–40)*

These are the North-Country, Lancashire and Yorkshire version of southern crumpets and Scottish drop scones: a cross between the two.

half 5 ml sp	caster sugar	½ tsp
15 g	fresh yeast (or half quantity of dried)	½ oz
250 ml	warm milk	½ pt (scant)
250 g	plain flour	8 oz
	pinch of salt	
1	beaten egg	1

Mix the sugar and yeast together, then add the milk. Put the flour and salt in a bowl, making a well in the centre. Gradually incorporate the milk mixture, then add the egg. Beat the batter well to remove any lumps of flour, and leave it in a warm place for one hour to rise.

Heat a greased griddle or heavy frying-pan and drop the batter in large spoonfuls onto it. When the top shows little holes in the surface turn the pikelets over to cook the other side. Both sides should be a pale gold. Keep them warm in a folded cloth and serve them hot with butter and jam or honey. Any left over can be toasted the next day.

Dinner for a cold day in Norfolk

Broiled eels with sage
A matelote of eels
Red herrings and bloaters
Turbot fillets with shrimp sauce
Baked latchett
Herrings pickled in mustard

Roast saddles of hare
Norfolk pig's fry
Boiled beef and carrots

Norfolk dumplings

Gratin of potatoes
Pease pudding
Sweet glazed parsnips

Eve's pudding
Ipswich almond pudding

Suffolk rusks

This menu is designed to provide you with two courses only, because the dishes in it contain so much fat and carbohydrates, to help keep out the bitter winds that sear into the flat, marshy countryside direct from the North Sea.

The food is also rather simple, based mostly on what farming people ate and still eat and less on what the gentry eat; accordingly, choose either fish or meat for the main course. The area is still predominantly agricultural, with vast, unfenced fields of grain, sugar-beet, potatoes, mustard and cabbages. Poultry-keeping is an old East Anglian tradition, as are milling, fruit-growing and brewing. Game abounds and the coasts are still rich inshore with magnificent fish and shellfish. Local dishes make use of all these things, but tastes are plain. I have rather daringly included one or two recipes (from elsewhere) using wine, in spite of the assurance from more than one Norfolk person that 'if wine has to be poured on it there's either something wrong with the food or else something wrong with the cooking.'

Norfolk fish

The north Norfolk coast is famous for shellfish, the offshore seas are (or were) renowned for sole, turbot, herring and sprats and the inland rivers and the Broads are rich with pike, perch, tench, and above all, eels.

Cromer crabs are best during the summer months, but winkles, whelks, mussels, oysters and cockles are gathered all the year round. Served plainly boiled, taken from their shells and seasoned with a dash of vinegar, they make tasty snacks, either with drinks, or with bread and butter for tea. One recipe recommends cockles coated in flour, then fried in bacon fat.

The creeks round the north coast also harbour tiny dabs, called 'butts' by the locals. They shine with phosphorus at night and their diamond shape looms up just below the sand as the tide goes out. One old man remembers the tale of an aunt and three of his uncles going out butt-pricking as children (spearing them with a toasting fork) when they should have been in bed. But all they got for their naughtiness was a sight, by the light of the harvest moon, of the Norfolk shuck, which is a famous, floating ghost in the shape of a huge black dog. If they had caught any butts they'd have had them fried, with parsley sauce.

Norfolk ghost stories also concern eel-catchers and are so terrifying as to put you off eels altogether. This may be why very few people eat them in Norfolk, sending them to London instead. They are caught in the Waveney river in a variety of basket-like traps, and also for fun, with a bunch of worms tied to a line: this is called 'eel-babbing'.

Norfolk eel-catchers are not very imaginative about ways in which to cook eels – unlike their counterparts on the other side of the North Sea who make them into delicious matelotes, or smoke them (one of the greatest luxuries I know). A Geldeston man said he liked them cut up and boiled with seasoning, parsley, onions and potatoes. He drains the broth into a basin for soup and eats that with bread after he's eaten the eels. The Londoner's jellied eel or hot eel with parsley sauce is likewise good, but plain. Small wonder that we do a roaring trade exporting both eels and elvers to the Continent.

Eels are best bought live, or eaten when freshly caught. However, they are extremely lively and slippery, and killing them is no joke. Nor is skinning them, as they wriggle like live serpents even after death. There are as many tips on how to skin an eel as there are eels themselves, but being too squeamish to try any of them myself, I recommend that you ask the eel-catcher or fishmonger to do it. Some recipes require the eels to be boned too. To do this leave the eel whole after skinning, then slit it up the belly and flatten it out. The spine should come out all in one piece.

Broiled eels with sage *(for 3 or 4)*

The Victorians appreciated eels more than we do. This is one of Eliza Acton's recipes.

1	large skinned eel	1
	salt, white pepper	
	fresh sage leaves	
	oil or clarified butter for frying	
	juice of a lemon	

Cut the eel into about six or eight finger lengths. Rub them with the salt and pepper and leave them for half an hour.

Wipe them dry and wrap them in sage leaves. These will need to be tied on with thread.

Brush the pieces with oil or melted clarified butter, squeeze lemon juice over them and then grill them gently until they are brown all over. Serve them with a sauce made from:

one 15 ml sp	chilli sauce	1 tbsp
one 15 ml sp	tarragon vinegar or wine	1 tbsp
one 15 ml sp	water	1 tbsp
50–75 g	butter	2–3 oz
	salt	

Heat the liquid ingredients, but don't let them evaporate, then, away from the heat, whisk in the butter. Add salt if necessary. Pour the sauce over the eels.

A matelote of eels *(for 4–6)*

A matelote, as the name suggests, has marine connections: it is a fish stew, with wine and onions. It suits large, fatty eels very well.

2	large eels	2
	seasoned flour	
	butter and oil for frying	
2	chopped onions	2
1	finely chopped clove of garlic	1
1	diced carrot	1
½ bottle	red wine	½ bottle
	bunch of herbs	
	peppercorns, salt	
12	button onions	12
12	button mushrooms	12
2–3	thick rashers of bacon, cut into small pieces	2–3
1	egg yolk	1
two 15 ml sp	double cream	2 tbsp
	fried bread	

Have the eels skinned and cut into 5 cm/2 inch pieces. Dip them in the seasoned flour and sauté them in a little butter and oil. Transfer them to a shallow heavy saucepan. Sauté the chopped onions with the garlic, adding more fat if necessary. Add the carrot and cook everything for a few minutes. Transfer the vegetables to the saucepan and deglaze the frying-pan with the wine, leaving it to reduce a little.

Pour the wine over the eels and add the herbs, peppercorns and salt to taste. While the eels cook, gently sauté the button onions, mushrooms and the bacon pieces in more oil and butter, in the frying-pan. When the eels are tender (after about 20 minutes), remove them to a warm serving dish.

Mix the egg yolk and cream and strain the cooking liquid into the same bowl. Heat the resulting sauce in a small pan until it thickens a little. Pour it over the eels and surround them with the mushrooms, onions and bacon pieces.

Decorate the dish with triangles of fried bread.

Bloaters and red herrings

Both of these are, like the kipper, a form of cured herring and both are traditional to and still processed at Lowestoft, an East Anglian port just south of the border between Norfolk and Suffolk. In fact I have not found red herrings anywhere else, though bloaters are still made in London by one fishmonger at least.

Both fish are cured whole, with the guts left in; the bloater is silvery grey, juicy and rather gamey. It is delicious grilled, then split open and spread with freshly made mustard, or mashed into a paste (page 17). When people had open ranges to cook on they used to toast them in front of the red-hot coals, with a dish to catch the drips, thus avoiding the trouble of washing a grill afterwards (it becomes very strongly fishy – the biggest drawback to cooking a bloater). Bloaters are not smoked for long; red herrings are left high up in the coolest part of the smoke-hole for six weeks. At the end of this time they are quite shrivelled, tawny-red and as stiff and as dry as a board. They will keep more or less for ever in a dry place and were once exported in large quantities to West Africa. In Norfolk they reconstitute them by splitting them open and pouring boiling beer over them. After soaking for half an hour they can be eaten with scrambled eggs and mashed potatoes. They are also toasted, unsoaked, like bloaters.

In the old days they would be sold at threshing time to the farm workers by men who travelled the country with a horse and cart. The labourers cooked them on a shovel over the fire-box of the threshing machine and ate them with boiled potatoes or parsnips.

Red herrings are immensely popular with publicans: some Norfolk pubs still serve them as accompaniments to drinks, as their saltiness makes for a great thirst. Admirers of the red herring compare it to ham (it is still called ham-dried herring by some) but it smells very strongly of kipper and would presumably make a good lure to draw hounds off the scent of a fox.

Lowestoft, besides being famous for its red herrings and bloaters, is also the port that lands the biggest catches of turbot in England. I include a recipe for this fish too, but you probably won't be able to buy it locally – like the eels it's all sent to London or even to Europe, where people are more prepared to pay the high prices it can command.

Turbot fillets with shrimp sauce *(for 4)*

Chicken turbots weighing about 2 kg/4 lb each are delicious poached whole, then served with this sauce. If you haven't got a turbot-shaped fish kettle, bone and skin the fish and cook the fillets like this:

4	skinned fillets of turbot weighing about 250–300 g/8–10 oz each	4
	salt, pepper	
	butter	
100 g	sliced button mushrooms	4 oz
2–3	chopped spring onions or shallots	2–3
1	lemon	1
125 ml	reduced fish fumet (page 263) made from the head and bones of the fish	¼ pt

Preheat the oven to 180°C/350°F/gas 4.

Butter a gratin dish big enough to accommodate all the fillets if they are folded in three. Season the fillets and put them aside. Lightly sauté the mushrooms in a little butter with the spring onions or shallots and put them in a gratin dish.

Peel the lemon so that the flesh is exposed and detach four of the sections with a sharp knife, leaving their covering skin behind. Chop the fruit fairly finely and spread it over the fillets. Fold them in three (skinned side out) so that they make neat bundles. Lay them on the bed of mushrooms and spring onions. Pour in the fish fumet and dab the fillets with a little more butter.

Cover the dish in foil, or butter paper, and bake the fish for about 30 minutes. Drain the liquor from the fish when it is cooked and keep the fish warm.

for the sauce

25 g	butter	1 oz
25 g	flour	1 oz
	fish liquor (see above)	
125 ml	milk	¼ pt
125 ml	cream	¼ pt
100 g	potted or peeled and chopped shrimps	4 oz
	salt, pepper	
	cayenne	

Melt the butter and stir in the flour. Cook it a little, then gradually add the fish juices, the milk and the cream, stirring all the time to make a smooth sauce. Add the shrimps and taste for seasoning. Pour the sauce over the fish and, just before serving, brown it a little under the grill.

If this is to be a main course serve it with buttered spinach (page 238) or Swiss chard leaves.

Baked latchett *(for 4)*

The fishermen of small East Anglian ports like Aldeburgh and Southwold sell their catch directly from the boats on the beach: wonderful sole and plaice in summer and cod and sprats in winter. There is no better way to cook sprats than to leave them whole (see page 15). But the fish that really brings light to the eyes of a Norfolk fisherman is the yellow-grey safferine gurnard or, as they call it round Yarmouth and Beccles, the latchett. It is in season in the summer, but this recipe suits other types of gurnard too. Latchetts have their very poisonous fins removed by the fishmonger. They are then filleted and baked with onions and beef dripping, which is also sold by local fishmongers, and is served with a brown gravy made from the pan juices.

1	large filleted gurnard (about 1.5 kg/3 lb) or 2 small ones	1
	salt, pepper	
1	large sliced onion	1
	beef dripping for frying	
one or two 15 ml sp	flour	1 or 2 tbsp
	water	

Season the fillets with salt and pepper and put them aside for half an hour. Preheat the oven to 180°C/350°F/gas 4.

Fry the onion very gently in the dripping until it is golden and softened. Strew it as a bed for the fish in a shallow, greased oven-proof dish. Put the fish, skin side up, on top and dab it with a little more dripping.

Bake it for about 20–30 minutes, or until the fish feels tender. Remove it to a warm serving dish and put the onion and the juices from the fish into a small saucepan. Mix in enough flour to make a soft brown roux and cook it for a minute or two. Add enough water to make a pouring sauce, simmer it for a few minutes, adjust the seasoning and pour it over the fish. Serve the latchett with mashed potatoes.

AUTHOR'S NOTE: A Cornish version uses suet instead of beef dripping. I found this recipe excellent for sea-bass too.

Herring pickled in mustard *(for 4)*

This is intended as a first course only and should be made a good two days ahead. It is well worth making a larger amount than that given here as it keeps for at least a week in a fridge. The ingredients make use of two of the best products of Norfolk – mustard and (until the herring fishing ban at least) herring. The recipe, however, seems to have Scandinavian origins. The herring are very good washed down with aquavit or schnapps or, if you prefer it, a locally brewed ale.

2	large filleted herrings (or 4 small ones)	2
four 15 ml sp	freshly made English mustard	4 tbsp
1	sliced lemon	1
1	sliced medium-sized onion	1
two 5 ml sp	capers	2 tsp
	white wine vinegar	
one 15 ml sp	mustard seed	1 tbsp

Cut each of the fillets in two lengthways and spread them generously with the mustard. Fold each one in half and put them in a stoneware pot, making layers with the sliced lemon, onion and capers. Pour over enough vinegar to cover the contents and sprinkle the mustard seed on top. Press the fillets down well to expel the air and seal the lid firmly. Leave the pot in a cool place for two days, during which time the mustard and vinegar will transform the herrings.

Mustard

The proximity of Norwich City's football club to the mustard mills of Jeremiah Colman means of course that this team's colour is a bright canary yellow (and they are called the Canaries). Also yellow are the acres of fields in June both around Norwich and in the *Nine Tailors* country that lies to the east of the M1 and to the south of the Humber. This is when the mustard plant flowers (it looks confusingly like flowering rape, which is grown as animal fodder).

The seeds are harvested in August, and are of two kinds: brown for the reverberating pungency and white for the sting and bite. (The latter is in fact the same seed that we grow on damp flannels for the mustard of mustard and cress.) At Colman's the seeds are milled to a powder, then mixed with a little flour for sale in those familiar yellow tins. 'Made mustard' is also sold, with a variety of vinegars and flavourings; it is worth experimenting with your own concoctions at home (grind whole seeds as well). Mustard, in spite of its heat, is a faithful conveyor of other flavours, whether of herbs, vinegar, onion, anchovy, olive, or citrus juices. The heat moreover is totally dispelled in cooking, so if you want a sauce to be bitingly hot, add the mustard after the sauce is cooked. The leaf, not only in seedling form but fully grown, is also good in salads.

Horseradish

Horseradish is another speciality of Norfolk. It is cropped for its long, tenacious root and is to be found wild on many a railway siding and canal bank (planted originally to help hold these banks together); gardeners often regret having it as it is almost ineradicable. The same volatile oil that makes mustard hot is present in the root. To make it into a sauce it has to be grated – a tearful job and possibly the reason for whole horseradish being almost unobtainable nowadays. It used to be sold in greengrocers' shops and market stalls in the winter. The sauce you make yourself is far more powerful and satisfactory than the commercial kind. If you don't grow it try to get some for the sauces on pages 257 and 258.

Roast saddles of hare *(for 4)*

Norfolk is famous for its game: the Broads are the home of every kind of waterfowl, and swan and wild goose may even appear on some menus (though the circumstances under which they were shot are not necessarily permitted elsewhere). Pheasant and partridge inhabit every copse, and the wilderness of the Breckland is practically a game reserve in itself. There is even one animal that I have never encountered in a recipe book before: this is the South American coypu. It looks like a beaver but is related to the porcupine. It was once bred in captivity for its fur (known as nutria) but has now become a naturalised escapee, living wild in Norfolk's river banks and devastating them. For this reason it is being exterminated; if you do get the chance to cook one that has been humanely killed without being gassed or poisoned, treat it like rabbit; cook it in a casserole, or make it into a pâté with pig's liver, ham or pork. It is not a meat or fish eater, but a vegetarian. The meat was actually imported at one time, and sold as 'Argentine hare'.

However, it is Norfolk hare, along with pheasant, that makes up most of the bags sent to London. This recipe needs two saddles, which, when paired up and roasted together make a moister and more generous dish than one saddle on its own. Use the rest of the hares to make jugged hare, or hare in cider (page 139).

	the saddles of 2 large hares	
1	large glass of red wine	1
1	bay leaf	1
	salt, pepper	
1	crushed clove of garlic	1
50 g	finely chopped mushrooms	2 oz
1	finely chopped small onion	1
	butter and oil for frying	
	parsley	
two 15 ml sp	double cream	2 tbsp

Prepare the saddles by peeling off the silvery membrane with which they are covered. Discard the flaps that hang either side, with the kidneys. (You need a very sharp, pointed and flexible knife for all this.) Next remove the meat from the bones so that you have two long fillets from each saddle. Try to keep the meat which lies below the spine attached to the meat on top.

Put the four fillets into a bowl and cover them with a marinade made from the wine, bay leaf, salt and pepper and the crushed clove of garlic. Leave them for two or three hours.

Heat the oven to 200°C/400°F/gas 6.

Make a duxelles by sautéing the very finely chopped mushrooms and onions with the oil and butter. Add the finely chopped parsley, and season well.

Butter a large square of foil. Take the fillets out of the marinade and dry them with kitchen paper. Lay two side by side on the foil and spread the duxelles mixture on top of them. Lay the second pair of fillets on top of this. Put two or three generous dabs of butter on the meat and then wrap the foil round it, sealing the join tightly. Put the foil parcel into a fire-proof dish and bake it for 40 minutes.

While the hare is cooking, strain the marinade into a small pan and reduce it to a couple of large spoonfuls.

When you undo the parcel you will find that the meat has made quite a lot of gravy. Keep the meat hot and put the gravy into the small pan with the reduced marinade. Heat the gravy through and add the cream but don't let it boil.

Carve the meat lengthways into fine, slender pieces; pour the gravy over them and serve them with mashed or sautéed potatoes and buttered spinach (page 238) or slices of hot, cooked beetroot to which you have added a little lemon juice mixed with sugar and soured cream. Redcurrant jelly is a traditional accompaniment to hare (see page 249).

Norfolk pig's fry *(for 4)*

'Fry' in this recipe means the mixture of pig's offal which used to be sold ready prepared for this dish all over East Anglia. I did find one butcher in Bungay selling it, complete with the caul fat to cover the dish, but he thought he was about the only one to keep the tradition today. It makes a filling, rural meal.

The ingredients should include pig's liver, heart, kidney, sweetbread, brain, tongue and the skirt (mesentery or frill). They should be cut up quite small and trimmed into neat pieces; you can arrange the proportions according to what you like most of, or what is available.

	seasoned flour	
750 g	pig's fry (as above)	$1\frac{1}{2}$ lb
100 g	belly of pork	4 oz
	lard or dripping for frying	
2	large sliced onions	2
2	peeled and sliced large potatoes	2
	a few sage leaves	
	salt, pepper	
	stock or water (see below)	
	caul fat (if available)	
	or back fat to cover	
	cornflour (optional)	

Preheat the oven to 150°C/300°F/gas 2.

Flour the pieces of meat and offal and fry them in a little of the fat. Transfer them to a shallow casserole.

Lightly fry the onions and add them to the meat. Arrange the slices of potato around the sides of the dish and season it with salt, pepper and sage. Add enough water or stock to come halfway up the meat. Cover it with the caul fat or very thin slices of back fat and then with a lid, and bake it 'from dinner time' (i.e. midday) 'to tea-time' (i.e. five or six p.m.). Thicken the gravy, if you like, by straining it off and mixing it with cornflour.

Serve it with more potatoes (mashed) and dumplings (see next page). In Lincolnshire boiled onions and greens are traditional accompaniments. In Yorkshire the fry is cooked without the potato or caul fat but the lid is hermetically sealed with a flour and water paste. It is then served on a bed of fried bread, encircled by mashed potato and garnished with parsley.

Boiled beef and carrots *(for 8)*

I give this recipe, not just because it is one of England's most traditional, but because it is a good excuse for eating dumplings as well. It is best made for large numbers of people as a small joint shrinks and loses too much moisture before it can cook properly. The cold meat is very good too; it is exactly the same as 'bully beef', that is to say, boeuf bouilli: perhaps the recipe is not so English after all.

2–2.5 kg	salt brisket or silverside, soaked overnight if necessary, and tied with string	4–5 lb
1 kg	peeled and halved large carrots	2 lb
8	peeled, medium-sized onions	8
	cloves	
1–2	cubed turnips	1–2
	bunch of herbs, peppercorns	

Soak the meat for a few hours (or overnight) in plain water if you suspect it of being very salty. Put it in a large saucepan with fresh cold water to cover it. Bring it very slowly to the boil and skim off any scum as it rises.

When the water is clear add one or two of the carrots, one of the onions stuck with cloves, half the turnips, and the herbs and peppercorns. Cover the pan and let it cook, barely simmering, for $2\frac{1}{2}$ hours.

Remove the original vegetables and replace them with the remaining, uncooked ones. Continue to cook until both they and the meat are quite tender – about another three-quarters to one hour. Cook potatoes and dumplings (see below) in the same pot for the last 20 minutes if you have space; if not, use another pan, or a steamer fixed over the stewing pot.

Serve the meat with the gravy, the vegetables and plenty of freshly made mustard, and sharp sauce (page 260).

Norfolk dumplings

To hear them talk, you'd think Norfolk people had invented the dumpling; they call them floaters or swimmers and are often called 'dumplins' themselves. They eat them with soups and stews as well as roasts, and also as a pudding, with a fruit vinegar or cream and treacle ('thunder and lightning'), or brown sugar and melted butter. A middle-aged publican, whose father was a baker from North Norfolk, recalled that in the twenties and thirties, before people in country districts had reliable ovens or electricity as they do now, the bakehouse oven was used by the whole village for the Saturday lunch, which was either a roast or a stew. The baker's mother positioned everyone's dinner to suit the dish and the customers would buy a penn'orth of dough for the dumplings.

At home the dough would be shaped, either as one big ball, or else in smaller ones about the size of tennis balls. The dough would be left to rise and then, twenty minutes before dinner time, it was cooked either on its own in a steamer or on top of the boiled potatoes (and potatoes were always served, as well as dumplings). The large dumplings would serve two or more people, but the smaller ones, which when cooked ended up as large as a croquet ball, were intended only for one. Smaller ones still were made for soups.

As to eating them, dumplings are never cut with a knife – that traps the steam inside, and they go soggy; they must always be torn apart with two forks.

Dumplings are still eaten in Norfolk today, but the baker's dough has been superseded by doughs made with suet and self-raising flour or baking powder. They are no less filling.

Norfolk dumplings (*for 4*)

with bread dough

250 g	flour	8 oz
half 5 ml sp	dried yeast (or a lump of fresh yeast the size of a sugar cube)	½ tsp
half 5 ml sp	salt	½ tsp
125 ml	warm water	4 fl oz

Mix all the ingredients together, knead them well and leave the dough to double in size. Form it into four balls (they should be the size of tennis balls) and leave them for a little while to prove.

Boil or steam them in a covered pan for 15 to 20 minutes. Don't lift the lid until the end or they will deflate and go soggy. Serve them at once.

AUTHOR'S NOTE: If you are making bread anyway, you could use 375 g/12 oz of the dough for the dumplings.

with suet

250 g	flour	8 oz
60 g	suet	2 oz
half 5 ml sp	salt	½ tsp
half 5 ml sp	baking powder	½ tsp
125 ml	water	4 fl oz

Mix all the ingredients together and knead the resulting soft dough very lightly. Form it into four balls and steam or boil them as above for 15 to 20 minutes.

with self-raising flour

250 g	self-raising flour	8 oz
half 5 ml sp	salt	½ tsp
125 ml	milk or water	4 fl oz

Mix the ingredients together and proceed as above.

AUTHOR'S NOTE: The addition of fresh or dried herbs or horseradish to any of the dumpling mixtures is a pleasant variation.

Potatoes, pease pudding and parsnips

Although the rich, dark-earthed flat Fenlands to the south and east of the Wash are the source of some of the best vegetables in England, most of them are destined to end up in plastic packages for the nation's freezers: the fresh green peas, the specially bred miniature sprouts and cauliflowers, the slender beans and dark green spinach are gobbled up by the freezing plants. Only the unfreezables, or the less easily frozen, are to be bought in local shops – wonderful potatoes, succulent asparagus, beautiful carrots, celery, celeriac and parsnips, huge and handsome leeks and onions, and football-sized cabbages. In spite of the rich variety of vegetables grown here, chips, mushy peas and parsnips are still favourite in Norfolk.

To give the family a change from potatoes boiled, mashed, baked, roasted or fried, serve them sliced and baked in milk, as a gratin. The recipe is French, but it goes extremely well with roasts or casseroles.

Gratin of potatoes *(for 4–6)*

	butter	
750 g	finely sliced white potatoes	1½ lb
1–2	finely chopped cloves of garlic	1–2
	salt, pepper	
425 ml	milk	¾ pt
200 ml	double cream	7 fl oz
half 5 ml sp	flour	½ tsp

Preheat the oven to 190°C/375°F/gas 5.

Butter a round earthenware casserole. Make a layer of the potatoes in the bottom, cover it with a little chopped garlic, salt and pepper and continue to fill the pot with layers like this. Heat the milk and just as it comes to the boil, pour it over the potatoes. It should just come up to the top of them.

Mix the flour with the cream and pour it over the potatoes – this makes for a nice brown top. Bake them for 50 minutes, when they should be golden on top and soft within.

Pease pudding *(for 6–8)*

People were eating peas, fresh in summer and dried in winter, long before Sir Walter Raleigh introduced them to the potato. Norfolk's neighbouring county of Lincolnshire grows most of those that end up as mushy peas in tins, or as a delicious pease pudding. Use whole 'marrowfat' peas (of the kind used by boys in a peashooter) rather than the split variety, which are not so starchy. Cook them in a muslin bag in the same pan as a piece of boiling salt pork, bacon, ham or salt beef.

500 g	dried peas	1 lb
1	peeled, medium-sized potato	1
	salt, pepper	
1	egg (optional)	1
	butter (optional)	

Soak the peas in water for an hour or two. Cook them with the potato for about an hour, when they should be tender.

Puree them, using a little of the cooking water to help them along. Add seasoning if necessary. You can serve the puree as it is, or go on to make a traditional pease pudding, in which case, add an egg and a good lump of butter, mix them in well and turn the puree into a greased pudding-basin. Cover it and steam it for an hour. It can then be turned out and served in slices.

Any left-over slices can be fried for breakfast, with rashers of bacon.

Sweet glazed parsnips *(for 4)*

500 g	parsnips	1 lb
50 g	butter	2 oz
two 15 ml sp	sugar	2 tbsp
	juice of an orange	
	juice of half a lemon	
	salt, pepper	
	chopped parsley	

Peel and cut the parsnips into equal-sized pieces, either in fingers, chunks or slices.

Steam or boil them until they are just tender. Drain them and return them to the pan with the rest of the ingredients (except the parsley). Cover, and cook them over a low heat for approximately ten minutes, when they should be surrounded with a syrupy sauce.

Arrange them on a serving dish and sprinkle them with chopped parsley.

Eve's pudding *(for 6–8)*

Apples are grown for both cooking and eating on many Norfolk fruit farms, but the old-fashioned D'Arcy Spice, Sturmer Pippin, Norfolk Beauty, Biffin and Blenheim have almost disappeared, giving way to the more commercially popular Cox's Orange Pippin and Bramley Seedling. How is it that today these two varieties of English apple together represent over 60 per cent of the total tonnage grown in this country, when there are no fewer than 65 varieties of dessert apples and 69 cookers listed in a fruit-grower's hand-book of 1926? The accountants no doubt have the answer, but as a consumer I regret the lack of choice.

Norfolk Biffins, also known as a Beaufins or Beefings, are cooking apples. Bakers used to preserve them by drying them slowly, unpeeled, under weights in a cooling oven. The resultant flattened reddish brown discs would be covered with melted sugar and sold as sweets. No one seems to do this any more.

For this filling recipe (taken from a jingle allegedly written by Sydney Smith, the wit and one-time Canon of St Paul's) you can use dessert apples or cookers. It contains no fat, nor does it need any, and as he says: 'Three hours let it boil without hurry or flutter, And then serve it up without sugar or butter', but modern families will probably want cream or custard.

6	small, peeled and grated apples or 4 large ones	6
150 g	fine, fresh breadcrumbs	6 oz
150 g	currants	6 oz
150 g	sugar	6 oz
2	large beaten eggs	2
	pinch of salt	
	pinch of nutmeg	

Mix all the ingredients together, and put them in a buttered 1 litre/2 pt pudding-basin. Cover it and boil it for three hours.

Serve the pudding hot, turned out of the basin. Left-overs can be fried.

Ipswich almond pudding *(for 6)*

Although this pudding is credited to Ipswich in the neighbouring county of Suffolk, puddings and cakes made with almonds are to be found in recipes (especially very old ones) from all over the country. Having made this one I saw that what we were eating was almost exactly the same as the filling for a Bakewell tart. Further research revealed that the original recipe, written by Hannah Glasse in 1747, did indeed have the pudding baked in a puff paste.

As for almonds, they were probably introduced by the Romans; although almond trees are admired here for their blossom, they rarely produce ripe nuts. These come mostly from southern Europe, Australia, South Africa or California and their importation is nothing new – in 1286, apparently, the Royal Household consumed 28,500 pounds of them.

Modern appetites will probably prefer this pudding without the pastry, but if you want to try it the old-fashioned way, begin by lining an 18 cm/7 inch buttered pie-dish with 150 g/6 oz puff pastry (see page 266). Spread this with jam, pour in the filling and bake it at 230°C/450°F/gas 8 for fifteen minutes, then reduce the heat and bake it at 180°C/350°F/gas 4 for half an hour.

To make the pudding without the pastry you will need:

40 g	fine white bread or cake crumbs	1½ oz
275 ml	double cream	½ pt
50 g	ground almonds	2 oz
two 5 ml sp	orange flower water	2 tsp
4	egg yolks	4
50 g	sugar	2 oz
2	egg whites	2
50 g	melted butter	2 oz
	a few slivered almonds	

Preheat the oven to 180°C/350°F/gas 4.

Butter an oven-proof porcelain mould, gratin dish or soufflé dish measuring 18 cm/7 inches across.

Steep the crumbs in the cream. Mix the almonds with the orange flower water and add the egg yolks and sugar. Stir in the soaked crumbs. Beat the egg whites stiffly and fold them into the mixture. Stir in the melted butter.

Fill the mould and carefully lay the slivered almonds on the top. Bake the pudding with the dish standing on a metal sheet, for 40–45 minutes, until the suriace is a nice brown and the centre feels resistant when you prod it gently. Serve it warm or cold, with cream or an orange or lemon sauce (page 261).

Suffolk rusks *(makes about a dozen)*

These are also made in Norfolk where they are called Norfolk rusks of course, but they seem to be more popular in Suffolk. They are made with a scone dough, baked once, then split in half and baked again (true *biscuits* in fact). Unkind critics have declared that they are nothing but stale scones, toasted to use them up, but no self-respecting Suffolk baker would ever do such a thing. This recipe comes from the turkey-pluckers of Worlingworth. Eat the rusks spread with butter.

50 g	margarine	2 oz
50 g	lard	2 oz
250 g	self-raising flour	8 oz
half 5 ml sp	salt	½ tsp
1	large egg	1
	milk to mix	

Preheat the oven to 180°C/350°F/gas 4.

Rub the fat into the flour with the salt and bind the mixture with an egg, adding milk if necessary to make a soft dough. Roll it out to a thickness of 2 cm/¾ inch and cut it into little rounds with a small glass. Put them on a greased baking-sheet and bake them for 20 to 25 minutes until they are well-risen and golden.

Cool them slightly, then slice them across and return them, cut sides up, to the oven which should be lowered to 150°C/300°F/gas 2. Leave them for about 30 minutes, until they are lightly browned.

AUTHOR'S NOTE: To make cheese-flavoured rusks (a modern innovation) add 50–75 g/2–3 oz of grated cheese to the mixture at the same time as you add the egg.

Christmas Day

Smoked salmon
Oysters
Stilton soup

Roast turkey with various stuffings
Roast beef with Yorkshire pudding
Roast goose with potato stuffing

Braised celery
Brussels sprouts with chestnuts
Braised red cabbage

Watercress and beetroot salad

Ginger sorbet
Elizabethan orange tart
Chestnut pudding
Christmas pudding

Ripon spice cake

Stilton cheese

We used to have terrible problems over Christmas dinners – the family included the very old and the very young (as most families do); an evening dinner was too late for them but if the meal was to be ready for lunch-time it meant starting to cook at breakfast, which is tough on the cook. The solution came to me long after the babies had grown up, but at least the grandparents were still with us; we now have Christmas dinner at around six o'clock, which gives the cook a leisurely day beforehand and everyone has a long evening afterwards in which to digest all this rich food before going to bed. Christmas dinner as we know it today was largely influenced by Prince Albert; it is still rather Germanic and Victorian in style, from the chestnuts with the Brussels sprouts to the candles on the Christmas tree.

Smoked salmon

The best fish for smoking are Scotch salmon, the larger the better, but Irish and English are excellent too. Each of these countries smokes its salmon in a similar way, and each claims to smoke it the best, but I have never been able to tell the difference between one well-smoked salmon and another. A London-smoked Scotch salmon is as good as any for me.

If you can afford a whole side (and they do come quite small) buy it like that – it is so much more succulent freshly sliced and keeps well in a cool place, as well as being cheaper. Use a very sharp knife to cut it, starting from the tail end, carving towards the tail. Don't forget to extract the little rib bones first.

Eat it sliced as thinly as possible with brown bread and butter, with wedges of lemon.

Oysters

Perhaps it is rather more a French habit to eat oysters at Christmas (they eat them on Christmas Eve) but why not here too?

English natives – the flat, round oysters with sharp crinkly edges – are delicate molluscs, vulnerable to frost, disease, predators, excesses of salt, excesses of fresh water . . . is it any wonder that they are now one of the most expensive luxuries, as supply can never, it seems, keep up with the demand for them?

To help satisfy our appetites for them, English oyster growers also rear the more sturdy oval *Pacifica gigas* oyster (also erroneously called 'Portuguese'). These are natives of warmer waters and therefore cannot breed here, but they are robust and can be eaten all the year round, whether there is an 'r' in the month or not. This prohibition applies to our own natives because they spawn in summer.

The most famous and traditional breeding and fattening grounds for oysters are at Colchester in Essex, at Whitstable in Kent, and at Port Navas on the Helford river in Cornwall. All vie with one another to produce the best, but even experts say that it is well nigh impossible to distinguish one from another.

Enjoy them, freshly opened and alive, with a glass of white wine or stout. They are much too precious to be put into soups, steak pies, lamb stews or the insides of turkeys as they once were when plentiful and cheap. If you do want to add a savoury fishy touch to these dishes, use clams instead.

To open oysters, you need an oyster knife or, failing that, a short, inflexible, stubby knife with a sharp point. First scrub the shells (which should be tightly closed). Hold the oyster in a cloth that covers your hand as well as most of the oyster. Arrange it so that the hinge shows with the flat shell uppermost. Push the point of the knife in between the shells to one side of the hinge. Twist the knife so that the shells are prised apart. Hold the oyster over a bowl to catch the juice and twist off the top shell, slicing the meat free from the inside. Slice the meat from the lower, more rounded shell and leave the oyster in it, with as much juice as possible and no chips of shell.

Make a bed of crushed ice for the opened oysters to lie on and serve them with lemon wedges, brown bread and butter and a spot of cayenne for those who like it.

Stilton soup *(for 4)*

This is perhaps more suitable for after Christmas, when the Stilton cheese is reaching its end.

two 15 ml sp	butter	2 tbsp
1	finely chopped medium-sized onion	1
2	finely chopped celery sticks	2
one 15 ml sp	flour	1 tbsp
1 litre	chicken stock (page 264) or turkey stock	2 pt
575 ml	single cream	1 pt
150 g	crumbled Stilton	6 oz
	salt	
	white pepper	
	croûtons	

Melt the butter in a large pan and sauté the onion and celery until they are soft but not brown. Stir in the flour and when it begins to foam, whisk in the stock. Simmer the mixture, covered, for about 30 minutes. Add the cream and the Stilton and allow the cheese to melt as the mixture comes to the boil.

Give the soup a turn in the liquidiser or food processor and put it back in the pan to reheat it. Correct the seasoning.

Serve the soup hot with croûtons.

Roast turkey

Advice on how to roast the turkey is never more freely available than at Christmas. If the idea of cooking a turkey makes you anxious, relax and simply regard the thing as an extremely large chicken. The stuffing takes time to prepare, so try to do that the day before. If the bird is frozen it is definitely best to thaw it slowly, in the fridge, but remember that a large bird will take three days; give it half as long at room temperature.

It is also best cooked slowly, especially if it is over 5.5 kg/12 lb. Once it is cooked, allow plenty of time for the bird to rest before you carve it.

It is quite easy to remove the wishbone from the inside of the bird before it is cooked if you sever the joints at the shoulder with a very sharp knife and work along both sides of the bone with your fingers, using the knife once again at the tip. Do this from the inside without cutting the skin before you cook the bird. This makes it much easier to carve the breast. Keep the breast meat moist by cooking the bird upside down for all but the last quarter of its cooking time. Cover the bird with foil if you are cooking it fast, or with a piece of muslin soaked in melted butter if you are cooking it more slowly. The foil will have to be removed towards the end, but the bird will brown beautifully and stay moist if you leave the muslin on throughout the cooking.

As for the stuffing, this can be varied as you like. It can be fruity, meaty, herby or nutty; the important thing is that it should be fatty, tasty and moist enough to enhance the turkey meat, yet not be sloppy or overpowering. Don't forget to serve bread sauce (page 259) and roast potatoes (page 141), and make a gravy with the pan juices.

Roasting times are roughly as follows; it is not easy to predict how long a large bird will take to cook.

Fast cooking time	*Weight of bird (including stuffing)*	*Slow cooking time*
(190°C/375°F/gas 5)		(170°C/325°F/gas 3)
2¼–2¾ hours	3.6–4.5 kg/8–10 lb	3½–3¾ hours
2¾–3 hours	5–6 kg/11–13 lb	3¾–4 hours
not recommended	6.3–7.3 kg/14–16 lb	4½–5 hours

Stuffings for turkey

The three stuffings that follow are enough for a small 5 kg/11 lb turkey. If you have any over use it to fill the cavities of small, cored eating apples and bake them for the last hour with the turkey.

Orange and apple stuffing

275 g	grated apple	10 oz
	grated rind of an orange	
100 g	fresh breadcrumbs	4 oz
four 15 ml sp	brown sugar	4 tbsp
75 g	chopped walnuts	3 oz
one and a half 15 ml sp	orange juice	1½ tbsp

Mix all the ingredients together and stuff the turkey, not too firmly.

Traditional sausage-meat stuffing

425 g	sausage-meat	14 oz
425 g	chopped, skinned and par-boiled chestnuts	14 oz
100 g	fresh breadcrumbs	4 oz
1	large, beaten egg	1
	salt, pepper	

Mix everything together and stuff the turkey.

Herb and raisin stuffing

200 g	seedless raisins	7 oz
1	large glass of port	1
375 g	sausage-meat or minced fatty pork	12 oz
	butter for frying	
1	chopped turkey liver	1
12	soaked, stoned and chopped prunes	12
	dried or fresh thyme	
	salt, pepper	

Soak the raisins in the port for a few hours. Sauté the sausage-meat or pork in the butter and mix in the rest of the ingredients. It is then ready to use.

Roast beef

This is still considered to be one of the best things you could possibly eat in England, beef from Aberdeen Angus or Hereford steers having an almost legendary reputation. But the fact is that most English beef cattle are now crossed with those gigantic, beige-coloured French Charollais cattle. This is an animal that has an astounding growth-to-feed ratio: a three-year-old, fully mature Charollais bull, for example, weighs 3,000 lb while a fully mature Hereford of the same age weighs half that. However, the Charollais has a low percentage of fat and a high percentage of meat, which means the flavour is less good. Herefords have lots of fat, and Aberdeen Angus beef is liked so much because the meat is finely marbled with fat. Beef is now so expensive that it could well be regarded as a Christmas treat. Hot or cold, a standing rib of beef (sirloin, wing or forerib) looks magnificent.

Roast rib of beef *(for 8)*

2.5–3 kg	rib of beef on the bone	5–6 lb
	salt, pepper	
	dry mustard	
	dripping	

Have the meat chined by the butcher so that it will be easier to carve. Rub the fat with a mixture of salt, pepper and dry mustard. Preheat the oven to 220°C/425°F/gas 7 and roast the meat, fat side uppermost, for 20 minutes to the half-kilo/pound with 20 minutes over, basting it with extra dripping from time to time. If you like the meat rare, and have a meat thermometer, cook it until the reading is 60°C/140°F (best for cold meats). If you like it medium-rare, cook it until the reading is 70°C/160°F. Well-done meat will read 80°C/170°F (but this will be too dry to serve cold). If you have no thermometer, press the meat with your finger: if the meat is very soft, it is rare; if it is firm it is well done.

Be sure to allow at least 20 minutes after the meat has finished cooking for the joint to 'rest' and the juices to set. Leave it in a warm place.

To cook a boned and rolled joint (from the ribs)

Prepare the meat by seasoning it as for the roast rib of beef and cook it at the same temperature, in the same way, but allow 25 minutes to the half-kilo/pound with 25 minutes over. The absence of bone means that the heat will not be conducted to the centre of the joint so well, which is why it needs longer to cook. You can obviously allow for less wastage with boned joints.

Beef can also be roasted more slowly, at a lower temperature, with possibly less shrinkage. Heat the oven to 190°C/375°F/gas 5 and allow 27 minutes to the half-kilo/pound, with 27 minutes over, for joints on the bone; give boned joints 33 minutes to the half-kilo/pound, with 33 minutes over.

Accompaniments for hot roast beef

Make gravy by deglazing the roasting-pan (after pouring off the fat) with a glass of wine, port or sherry, and then adding good beef or vegetable stock. Strain it and serve it hot with any of the following: freshly made English mustard; either of the horseradish sauces on page 257; forcemeat balls (page 140), and most important of all, Yorkshire pudding.

Yorkshire pudding *(for 8)*

Mix the batter well in advance of the meat going into the oven.

150 g	plain flour	6 oz
2	beaten eggs	2
	pinch of salt	
200 ml	milk *and*	7 fl oz
200 ml	water (or $\frac{2}{3}$ milk and $\frac{1}{3}$ water)	7 fl oz

Put the flour into a large basin. Make a well in the centre and beat in the eggs, not necessarily incorporating all the flour at this stage. Add the salt and slowly add the milk, mixing it in carefully so that you have no lumps. Beat it well and leave the batter to stand while the meat cooks.

As soon as the meat is done, and resting in a warm place, drain off enough dripping to cover two large baking-tins, turn the oven to 220°C/425°F/gas 7 (if it is not already at that temperature) and heat the dripping in the tins. As soon as it is smoking, pour in the batter. Bake it for about 20 minutes, when it should be well risen and crisp. Serve it cut into squares. If you have enough little tins it can be baked in them and served individually.

Roast goose with potato stuffing *(for 6–8)*

Potato makes an excellent stuffing for goose because it absorbs a lot of the surplus fat which makes it delicious.

750 g	potatoes	$1\frac{1}{2}$ lb
100 g	lean salt pork or bacon	4 oz
	oil for frying	
1	medium-sized chopped onion	1
four 15 ml sp	chopped parsley	4 tbsp
	dried marjoram	
	dried sage	
	salt, pepper	
	butter	
5 kg	goose	11 lb

Preheat the oven to 220°C/425°F/gas 7.

Cut the potatoes into small cubes and boil them for ten minutes in salted water. Drain them and set them aside.

Finely chop the salt pork or bacon and sauté it in a little oil until it is crisp. Set the bacon aside and sauté the onion in the same fat until it is soft and golden.

Return the bacon to the pan, add the potatoes and the herbs and season the mixture to taste. Leave it to cool before stuffing the bird. Remove the wishbone from the goose (page 179) and pull out any excess fat from the cavity. Loosely fill the bird with the stuffing and truss it.

Sprinkle the skin with salt and rub a generous amount of butter all over. Roast the bird for 45 minutes, and then reduce the temperature to 160°C/325°F/gas 3 and continue to cook it for 2–$2\frac{1}{2}$ hours, basting the bird every 20 minutes or so. The goose is cooked when the juices run out clear from the thickest part of the thigh when it is pricked with a skewer.

Remove the bird from the pan and allow it to rest for 20 minutes before cutting the trussing strings and carving it. Use the pan juices to make gravy. You could also serve apple sauce (page 258).

Braised celery

Cut off the leaves and wash the celery. If the heads are small, cut the sticks in half. If they are large, cut each stick into 7.5 cm/3 inch pieces. Place the celery in a sauté pan, dot it with a little butter, sprinkle it with salt and add just enough boiling water or stock barely to cover the celery.

Cover the pan and cook it for 15–20 minutes or until it is tender.

Transfer the celery to a warmed serving bowl. Add a little cream to the cooking liquid, taste for seasoning and pour it over the celery.

If you like, sprinkle a few slices of slivered almonds over the top.

Brussels sprouts with chestnuts

Cook some Brussels sprouts in salted water. Drain them, and refresh them in cold water to keep their colour bright and to stop them cooking more. Just before serving them, sauté them in butter or goose fat with an equal quantity of lightly boiled, peeled chestnuts (page 186).

Braised red cabbage

Shred a cabbage finely, discarding the outer leaves and core. Melt some butter in a large pan and coat the cabbage, lightly sautéing it. Add a sliced apple, a sliced onion, a little grated orange rind, a few caraway seeds, a crushed clove of garlic, a pinch of cinnamon and a grating of nutmeg, some salt, two spoonfuls of brown sugar, and a glass of red wine or wine vinegar. Cover the pan tightly and let the cabbage cook very slowly for at least $1\frac{1}{2}$ hours. Add a little warm water if it shows signs of drying up. It reheats well.

Watercress and beetroot salad

This salad looks like holly wreaths.

With a 1 cm/$\frac{1}{2}$ inch melon-ball-cutter, scoop out balls from about 500 g/1 lb of a cooked and peeled beetroot. Trim and discard the coarse stems from three bunches of watercress and divide it among salad plates, arranging it in wreaths. Divide the beetroot balls among the plates, arranging them on the wreaths like berries, and dress the salads with a vinaigrette (page 255).

Ginger sorbet *(for 5–6)*

This will cleanse the palate and refresh you, so that you can face the next course. Make a sorbet base with orange and lemon juice, according to the recipe on page 93 for elderflower sorbet, leaving out the elderflowers and making up a portion of the syrup with the syrup from a jar of crystallised ginger. Add some slivers of crystallised ginger and a whipped egg white before you freeze it.

Elizabethan orange tart

3	large, thin-skinned oranges	3
125 ml	water	$\frac{1}{4}$ pt
two 15 ml sp	honey	2 tbsp
375 g	rich shortcrust pastry (page 265)	12 oz
575 ml	double cream	1 pt
	caster sugar	
	sprigs of mint (optional)	

Scrub the oranges and slice them into thin rings, removing the pips and the end slices. Soak them overnight in the water and honey. Next day, poach the oranges in their liquid for 25–30 minutes. Transfer the slices to a rack to drain, and reduce the remaining liquid to a thick syrup by boiling it fast.

Heat the oven to 190°C/375°F/gas 5.

Roll out the pastry, line a 20–23 cm/8–9 inch flan tin, and bake it blind (page 265) for 15–20 minutes or until it is golden-brown. Leave it to cool completely.

Lightly whip the cream with sugar to taste and spread it over the pastry case. Arrange the orange slices over the cream, starting at the outside, overlapping the slices in one direction for the outer circle and in the opposite direction for the inner circle. Brush the warmed syrup glaze onto the oranges and decorate the top with a few sprigs of mint if you like. Serve the tart as soon as possible.

Author's note: Pastry cream (page 268) may be substituted for the whipped cream.

Chestnut pudding *(for 6–8)*

750 g	chestnuts (or 375 g/12 oz of tinned unsweetened chestnut puree)	$1\frac{1}{2}$ lb
100 g	caster sugar	4 oz
100 g	grated bitter cooking chocolate	4 oz
	rum (optional)	
100 g	butter	4 oz
125 ml	double cream	$\frac{1}{4}$ pt
	vanilla essence	
2	egg whites	2
two 5 ml sp	icing sugar	2 tsp
	grated chocolate for sprinkling	

Peel the chestnuts by making a small cut on the rounded side of each one; then either bake them in a very hot oven for 10–15 minutes, or put them in a pan of boiling water and cook them for 2–3 minutes; refresh them in cold water. The shells and skins are then relatively easy to remove. Put the peeled chestnuts back into a pan with cold water to cover them. Simmer them, covered, for 20 minutes, until they are soft enough to put through a sieve or food mill – they will become a light pink mass. Let it cool a little while you melt the grated chocolate in a little water over a double-boiler. Add the butter to the chocolate and when it has melted too, blend this mixture with the chestnuts.

Dissolve the sugar in a little water and boil it until you have a caramelised syrup. Whisk it into the chestnut mixture.

Oil a shallow dish (about 20 cm/8 inches round). Spoon the chestnut mixture into it. It should be about 4 cm/$1\frac{1}{2}$ inches deep when it is smoothed out. Leave it in a cool place to solidify.

Whip the cream with a few drops of vanilla essence. Then whip the egg whites until they hold peaks and fold them into the cream with a fork. Stir in the icing sugar. Pile the cream on top of the chestnut mixture and sprinkle the top with grated chocolate.

AUTHOR'S NOTE: As it is Christmas, you could add a little rum to the chestnut mixture when you melt the chocolate. The chestnut mixture is also the basis for a yule log cake – to make one, shape the mixture into a short, fat log by rolling it up in a piece of waxed paper. Refrigerate it for five hours, then unwrap it and put it on an oval dish. Make streaks along it with the prongs of a fork, not forgetting a knot or two. Stick a sprig of holly or mistletoe in at one end, and cover the top with sifted icing sugar for the snow. If you have a Christmas robin, perch him on top of the log as well.

Christmas pudding *(makes 2.4 kg/$5\frac{1}{4}$ lb)*

No Christmas dinner is complete without a Christmas pudding; its appearance in the darkened dining-room with its sprig of holly about to be consumed by dancing blue flames always raises a cheer and although it is the most filling pudding imaginable, everyone always manages to make room for just a little. As I mention elsewhere (page 228) its antecedents are to be found way back in a dish of frumenty. It has gradually become more and more solid, reaching its present state in the time of George I. Puddings used to be boiled in a cloth, and turned out as big, black and round as cannon balls. Modern ones are almost always steamed in a basin. They should have silver charms hidden in them for luck, and everyone in the house should have a turn at stirring, again for luck. The tradition of making them, the mincemeat and the cake in mid-November has some sense in it too; it gets them out of the way in good time, as well as allowing them to mature.

This fruity, fatless recipe dates from 1923 and is from Senn's *Century Cookery Book* which was dedicated to Queen Mary. M. Senn was once chef at the Reform Club, in the days when gentlemen's clubs served particularly good food.

500 g	white or wholemeal breadcrumbs	1 lb
100 g	shelled, finely chopped Brazil nuts	4 oz
25 g	blanched, skinned and finely chopped almonds	1 oz
250 g	grated cooking or dessert apples	8 oz
	grated rind and juice of a lemon	
250 g	sultanas	8 oz
250 g	currants	8 oz
100 g	chopped, mixed peel	4 oz
2	peeled and chopped bananas	2
250 g	stoned and chopped dates	8 oz
250 g	demerara sugar	8 oz
one 5 ml sp	salt	1 tsp
two 5 ml sp	mixed spice (optional)	2 tsp
two 15 ml sp	rum or brandy (optional)	2 tbsp
3	beaten eggs	3
225 ml	milk	8 fl oz

Mix all the ingredients together, adding the eggs and the milk last. Stir the mixture well and put it into either two well-buttered 1 litre/2 pt basins or one 2 litre/4 pt basin, covering them in the usual way. Steam them for at least three hours immediately, or give them one hour in a pressure cooker. Steam them for two more hours on Christmas Day. The long boiling is what makes them dark. Serve the pudding with rum butter (page 142) or Camperdown sauce (page 260).

Ripon spice cake *(makes 2 large cakes)*

This cross between a bread and a cake has festive connections in Yorkshire, the festival being Christmas, when callers are given a slice with a glass of ale or sweet home-made wine and a chunk of Wensleydale or Stilton cheese. The spice is sometimes only nutmeg; the leavening was always yeast in the past, but nowadays it is more often baking powder. Early recipes give only currants; this one is much fruitier. This cake is also known as 'Yule cake' or even 'Yule doo' ('doo' meaning 'dough').

The recipe for the celebration cake on page 209 can also be used for a Christmas cake.

250 g	butter	8 oz
300 g	caster sugar	10 oz
3	eggs	3
125 ml	milk	¼ pt
50 g	candied peel	2 oz
50 g	glacé cherries	2 oz
250 g	currants	8 oz
250 g	raisins	8 oz
50 g	ground almonds	2 oz
two 5 ml sp	mixed spice	2 tsp
500 g	plain flour	1 lb
	pinch of bicarbonate of soda	
one 15 ml sp	baking powder	1 tbsp
	pinch of salt	

Preheat the oven to 150°C/300°F/gas 2. Grease and line two loaf tins measuring 25 × 10 cm/10 × 4 inches.

Cream the butter and sugar together until the mixture is light and fluffy. Beat in the eggs, one at a time, until they are well amalgamated. Toss the fruit in a little flour to prevent it sinking. Stir in the milk, all the fruit, and the almonds and spice. Sift the remaining dry ingredients together and fold them into the mixture.

Turn the mixture into the prepared tins, and bake the cakes for 1½ hours or until a cake-tester comes out clean.

A St Valentine's dinner

Smoked salmon quenelles with watercress puree
and Valentine croûtes

Sautéed tenderloin of pork
Partridge with cabbage

Gratin of potato, onion and cheese
Braised chicory

Salad of chicory, lamb's lettuce and orange

Orange caramel custard
Pears in red wine
Chocolate cake

The food in this menu is chosen for the ease with which you may prepare most of it well in advance, so that you can concentrate on your loved one during the meal. There are no particularly traditional dishes for this day, though sometimes cakes are given as presents. The quantities can be multiplied for orgies or larger dinner parties. Drink champagne throughout the meal.

Smoked salmon quenelles *(for 2)*

Good quality, oily smoked salmon is recommended for this dish, but it need not be cut in fine slices. Cheap scraps off a good salmon are ideal. The quenelles can be prepared and shaped the day before. Serve them warm with the watercress puree and heart-shaped toasts.

100 g	smoked salmon	4 oz
125 ml	double cream	$\frac{1}{4}$ pt
one 15 ml sp	lemon juice	1 tbsp
	paprika or cayenne pepper	
	salt, pepper	
	toasts or Valentine croûtes (see opposite)	

Reduce the salmon to a puree, either in a food processor or with a pestle and mortar. Pass the puree through a fine sieve set over a bowl and discard any stringy flesh remaining in the sieve. Cover the bowl with plastic film and refrigerate it for about an hour.

With a wooden spoon, beat the cream in vigorously, about a spoonful at a time. Be sure that each spoonful is thoroughly incorporated before adding the next. The mixture should remain very firm. Beat in the lemon juice at the end and taste for seasoning.

To make the salmon mixture into quenelle shapes, dip two small spoons into cold water and scoop up some of the mixture with one of the spoons. Transfer the mixture from spoon to spoon until you get the proper shape. Put each 'egg' on a tray and continue working until all the mixture is shaped. You can prepare the recipe in advance up to this point.

To cook the 'eggs', drop them into a large pan of simmering water and let them cook for about five minutes. Turn them over once during that period to ensure uniform cooking. Remove the quenelles from the water with a slotted spoon and transfer them directly to warmed plates or, if you like, onto a bed of hot watercress puree. Sprinkle the quenelles with paprika or cayenne. Serve them with warm toasts or 'croûtes'.

AUTHOR'S NOTE: If you are in a great hurry, or if the quenelles prove too difficult to make, or fall apart in the boiling water, pack the mixture into little pots, chill, and serve it as a spread for the toasts.

Watercress puree *(for 2)*

Once blanched, the taste of watercress soon fades, so make this as near to the time it is to be eaten as you can.

2	bunches of watercress	2
	butter	
	salt, pepper	

Trim the watercress of all thick stems and dead or wilted leaves, then plunge it into a pan of boiling salted water.

Cook it for three minutes, drain it well and refresh it in a colander by running cold water over it until it is quite cool.

Reduce it to a puree by chopping or liquidising it.

To serve it, melt a knob of butter in a small pan, stir the watercress puree into it, season to taste and just allow it to heat up without cooking at all.

Valentine croûtes

3	thin slices of firm white or wholemeal bread	3

Stamp or cut out two heart shapes from each slice of bread. Toast the croûtes for a few minutes until they are golden brown.

Serve them immediately with the quenelles and the watercress puree.

Sautéed tenderloin of pork *(for 2)*

The tenderloin of pork is also known as the fillet. It comes from the underside of the loin and is only sold when the rest of the pig has been cut up for bacon.

375 g	pork fillet or tenderloin	12 oz
	salt, pepper	
	half a lemon	
	oil and butter for frying	
1 small glass	white wine or sherry	1 small glass
	stock (page 263, optional)	
	chopped parsley	

About an hour before you want to eat it, slice the meat into 0.5 cm/$\frac{1}{4}$ inch rounds. Season them with salt, pepper and the juice from the half-lemon. Leave it to absorb the flavours. This part can be prepared in advance.

Heat sufficient oil and butter to cover the base of a thick frying-pan. When the fat is hot and sizzling, throw in the meat. Turn it and shake the pan about, and put the meat on a serving dish as soon as it has all changed colour. The whole operation should be as quick as cooking an omelette.

Deglaze the pan with the wine or sherry, adding a little stock if you like plenty of gravy. Pour this over the meat, sprinkle with parsley and serve it.

Partridge with cabbage *(for 2)*

This is the last moment for much of the game that has been in season since the autumn; the shooting of pheasant and partridge ends on February 1st, so these birds will either be very well hung by now, if fresh, or making way for something else in the freezer. They may well be rather elderly too; if so, this recipe suits them.

2	partridges	2
1	onion	1
1	carrot	1
4	sticks of celery	4
	bunch of herbs	
75–100 g	salt pork or fat bacon	3–4 oz
	oil or butter for frying	
1	small Savoy cabbage	1
	juniper berries	
	salt	
	bay leaf	

Well in advance of the cooking time cut the birds into serving pieces so that you can use the backs and giblets (if you have them) for the stock. Fortify its flavour with trimmings or pieces of the onion, carrot and celery and add a bunch of herbs and the bacon rind.

Heat the oven to 160°C/325°F/gas 3.

Make a mixture of the finely chopped onion, carrot, celery and bacon or salt pork (a mirepoix) and sauté it in oil or butter in a frying-pan. As soon as it is lightly coloured tip it into a medium-sized iron or earthenware casserole.

Melt some more oil and butter in the pan and sauté the pieces of partridge to brown them on all sides. Put them on a plate when they are ready.

Cut the cabbage leaves away from the central core, using a sharp, pointed knife. Blanch them, whole, in boiling salted water, then drain them well and shred them finely.

Put a layer of cabbage over the mirepoix and lay the partridge pieces on top. Scatter a few juniper berries and salt over them and add a bay leaf. Cover with the rest of the cabbage. Pour the warmed stock over all so that it comes almost to the top of the cabbage.

Cover the casserole and bake it for at least three hours. This dish is good if it is cooked the day before and then re-heated.

AUTHOR'S NOTE: Pheasant, pigeon or guinea-fowl can be cooked the same way.

Gratin of potato, onion and cheese *(for 2)*

375 g	potatoes	12 oz
1	medium-sized onion	1
	salt, pepper	
100 g	grated Cheddar cheese	4 oz
50 g	butter	2 oz

Preheat the oven to 180°C/350°F/gas 4.

Peel and thinly slice the potatoes and onion. Butter a small gratin dish and arrange half the potatoes in a layer. Sprinkle them with salt and pepper and then place half the onion on top of the potatoes. Cover the onion slices with half the cheese, dot with butter, and repeat the sequence.

Bake the dish in the oven for 45–60 minutes until the top is bubbly and golden. Serve it immediately.

Braised chicory *(for 2)*

2 or 4	heads of chicory	2 or 4
50 g	butter	2 oz
	a pinch of sugar	

Put the chicory heads close together in a suitably sized buttered fire-proof dish or saucepan.

Dot them with butter, and sprinkle them with sugar. Cover them with buttered paper and then with a lid.

Cook them in a moderate oven or over a very low heat (with the aid of a heat-diffusing mat) for about 40 minutes.

Salad of chicory, lamb's lettuce and orange

Cut a head of chicory into 2 cm/1 inch lengths, separate the lamb's lettuce leaves (mâche) and chop the orange segments, being careful to exclude all skin and pith and to collect any juice in a bowl. (The best way to deal with the orange is to peel off the skin and pith together, and then to run a sharp, pointed knife down the sides of each segment, leaving the transparent skin that covers them attached to the central core.)

Make a salad dressing with the collected juice, a couple of spoonfuls of sunflower or grapeseed oil, salt, pepper and a dash of cream. Pour the dressing over the salad just before serving it.

Orange caramel custard *(for 2)*

This is the time of year when imports of citrus fruit are very welcome, providing us with winter supplies of vitamin C and, while Seville oranges last, the means of making marmalade (page 251). If you have bought Sevilles, and like their very tart flavour, let the juice of one make up part of the quantity needed for the custard.

This must be prepared the previous day.

for the caramel

100 g	caster sugar	4 oz
four 15 ml sp	water	4 tbsp
one 15 ml sp	lemon juice	1 tbsp

for the custard

3	eggs	3
75 g	caster sugar	3 oz
	grated rind of half an orange	
125 ml	freshly squeezed, strained orange juice	¼ pt

Make the caramel by putting the sugar, water and lemon juice into a small, heavy pan. Heat the mixture slowly and cook it until it turns a nice amber colour.

Coat the inside of a ½ litre/1 pint oven-proof dish with the caramel. Hold it with gloved hands as the caramel is very hot, and rotate it so that the sides as well as the base are lined. (If you have a heart-shaped mould for this occasion, so much the better.) Leave it to cool and set while you make the custard.

Heat the oven to 180°C/350°F/gas 4.

Beat the eggs and sugar together until they are thick and creamy in colour (this takes about ten minutes by hand). Add the grated orange rind and the orange juice and stir until they are well mixed.

Pour the custard mixture into the caramel-lined dish. Put the dish into a deep baking tin and surround it with enough boiling water to come three-quarters of the way up the sides.

Bake it for about 45 minutes, or until the custard is set.

Take the dish out of the water and let the custard rest overnight – this makes for a nice firm texture.

Next day turn the pudding out onto a shallow dish, spooning the liquefied caramel all round it. Decorate it, if you like, with candied fruits such as glacé cherries and angelica.

AUTHOR'S NOTE: The main difference between this and the classic crème caramel is that the milk is replaced by orange juice. Other fruit juices could be used instead of orange juice, but don't make them too sweet.

Pears in red wine *(for 2)*

The pears for this recipe should be just-ripe, dark green slender ones mottled with gold and known as 'Conference'. The conference from which they take their name was an International Pear Conference held in Chiswick, in 1885. Out of 10,000 entries they were the only ones to win a certificate and the judges therefore named them 'Conference'.

4	small Conference pears	4
575 ml	red wine	1 pt
	scrap of orange peel (dried if possible)	
5 cm	stick of cinnamon	2 inch
	a few cloves	
50 g	sugar	2 oz

Peel the pears, but leave the stems on, and put them at once into an oven-proof china dish with the wine, orange peel, spices and sugar. Arrange them so that the wine completely covers them, and leave them to soak for an hour or two before you cook them. This will give the pears a nice red colour.

Heat the oven to 180°C/350°F/gas 4, and bake the pears in the wine until they are tender. This will take one to two hours, depending on their ripeness.

When they are done, put them aside. Strain off the wine and remove the flavourings, then reduce it by fast boiling until it becomes syrupy.

Let it cool, then pour it back over the pears. Eat them cold.

Author's note: If you are doing this for a larger number of people arrange the cooked pears, stems upward, in an elegant pyramid.

Chocolate cake

100 g	plain chocolate	4 oz
50 g	unsalted butter	2 oz
100 g	caster sugar	4 oz
3	separated eggs	3
	pinch of sugar	
50 g	sifted flour	2 oz
50 g	finely ground almonds	2 oz
	whipped cream	

Preheat the oven to 160°C/325°F/gas 3. Melt the chocolate in a bain-marie, and leave it to cool.

Cream the butter and gradually add the sugar. Beat in the yolks, one at a time, incorporating each one well into the mixture before adding the next. Stir in the melted chocolate.

Beat the egg whites with a pinch of sugar until they are firm. Add half the quantity of flour, almonds and egg whites to the batter and gently fold them in. Repeat with the remaining ingredients.

Spoon the mixture into a well-buttered 16–18 cm/6–7 inch mould (preferably a heart-shaped tin) and bake the cake for about 45 minutes or until it is firm to touch and an inserted cake tester comes away clean. Allow the cake to rest for about ten minutes before turning it out onto a wire rack.

When it is cool, decorate the top of the cake with piped whipped cream, sweetened to taste. You could serve the cake with chocolate sauce (page 261).

Author's note: The cake can be made on February 13th.

ANYTIME

A buffet for a wedding, christening or birthday
West Country high tea
A vegetarian supper
A fish dinner in London

English cheeses
Store cupboard
Sauces
Basic recipes

A buffet for a wedding, christening or birthday

Stuffed vine leaves
Lobster patties
Crayfish

Hot or cold salmon
Salmon pasty

Cold chicken robed in lemon sauce with rice salad
Westmorland ham
Jellied brisket of beef

Strawberry and tomato salad
Potato salad
Macaroni salad
Prawn and grapefruit salad

Chartreuse of strawberries

English cheeses

Simnel cake
Celebration cake

Celebrations call for a feast, something a bit more splendid than mere Sunday dinner and for numbers sometimes greater than the house can hold. A marquee goes up in the garden, or the village hall is hired; for instance, you need space for bridesmaids and pages to scamper about, for babies to kick their legs, and perhaps for a knees-up for everyone else. And those long, long buffet tables have to be filled.

This lunch or supper menu offers a choice of dishes that can be cooked, with a bit of advance planning, in your own kitchen. The items can be made to look quite grand and festive and are big enough to feed plenty. They call for knives and forks, and tables to sit at, but most of them are cold: the hot things only need a little warming up. Suggestions for other salads can be found elsewhere in the book, but I have included two traditional celebration cakes in this menu to go with the coffee.

Stuffed vine leaves *(makes 20–30)*

This recipe comes from Pilton Manor in Somerset, where the vineyard's prunings provide young leaves for stuffing from June to September (they are best early on in the season). At the wine bar attached to the shop you can drink several different wines, all grown and made here – and eat locally made Cheddar cheese with Mrs Godden's stuffed vine leaves.

20–30	young vine leaves	20–30
100 g	minced cooked meat (preferably lamb)	4 oz
150 g	cold cooked rice	6 oz
	mixed fresh herbs (parsley, thyme, marjoram)	
	pinch of cumin or coriander powder	
	lemon juice	
	olive oil	
125–275 ml	finely sieved tomato sauce (page 257)	$\frac{1}{4}$–$\frac{1}{2}$ pt

Cut the stems of the vine leaves close to the leaf. Blanch them in boiling water (this softens them and makes them easier to fold). Refresh them in cold water and drain them.

Make a stuffing of the minced cooked meat (lamb is very good), cold cooked rice and a mixture of herbs such as parsley, thyme and marjoram. A pinch of cumin or coriander powder adds a slightly warm spicy flavour.

Roll each leaf round a small spoonful of the stuffing, and put them closely together in a flat, oiled, fire-proof dish.

If they are to be eaten in the fingers, poach them in salted water to which you have added lemon juice and a little olive oil. Otherwise, make a very finely sieved or liquidised tomato sauce (page 258). Add a squeeze of lemon. Pour over the sauce and simmer the vine leaves until they are well heated through – about half an hour. Serve them warm or cold.

Lobster patties *(makes 8)*

These can be made either in vol-au-vent cases, or in open patty cases. Use puff pastry for the vol-au-vent and shortcrust for the patties. To make patty cases, use plain shortcrust pastry (page 264) and proceed as for the fruit tartlets on page 69, baking them blind.

vol-au-vent cases

500 g	puff pastry (page 266)	1 lb
1	beaten egg	1

Preheat the oven to 230°C/450°F/gas 8.

Roll out the pastry to 1 cm/½ inch thick. Using a hot, wet cutter 6.5 cm/2½ inches in diameter, cut out eight or nine rounds. Brush them over with the egg, then using a cutter of 4 cm/1½ inches diameter, press an inner circle halfway through each of the rounds.

Bake them on a greased baking-sheet for about ten minutes. They will rise considerably and the inner circle can now be prised off with a pointed knife; this forms the lid. Scoop out any soft pastry from inside the vol-au-vents. Let them cool on a wire rack. The cases can be frozen until you need them.

lobster filling

250 g	cooked lobster meat (page 79)	8 oz
40 g	butter	1½ oz
15 g	flour	½ oz
125 ml	fish stock (page 263) or milk	¼ pt
two or three 15 ml sp	double cream	2–3 tbsp
3	egg yolks	3
	squeeze of lemon	
	anchovy essence	
	salt, cayenne	
	sprigs of parsley	

Cut the lobster meat into small pieces. If it has any coral, reserve it for decoration.

Make a béchamel (page 254) with the butter, flour and stock or milk. Simmer it for 5 or 10 minutes, then add the cream, egg yolks, lemon juice and seasonings. Let it cook a little longer until it has thickened slightly. Add the lobster meat and fill the warmed cases. Decorate them with sprigs of parsley and lobster coral.

AUTHOR'S NOTE: The same weight of cooked chicken breast, salmon or crabmeat may be used instead of lobster. Make the patties and vol-au-vents smaller if they are not to be eaten with knives and forks.

Crayfish

Crayfish (*Astacus astacus*) are native to Britain and may be found in many fast-flowing chalk streams, ponds or rivers. They can be caught, like eels, by dangling a bait of meat in the water (ox liver, chicken giblets or a horse's head are traditionally the best baits).

However, this species is vulnerable to a plague causing many rivers to lose all their native crayfish. The recent introduction of the American signal crayfish which is resistant to the European crayfish plague, and which can be successfully reared here, is proving to be a solution to the problem. They are sold for eating between August and October by the few fish farms that have enough stocks of them. Baskets of live, imported crayfish (from Turkey) may sometimes be found in good fish shops.

The English way of cooking them is to boil them in salted water until they turn pink. They are then eaten cold with salad or hot and peeled with an anchovy-flavoured béchamel sauce (page 254).

The Swedes, who are mad about them, eat them this way. This makes enough court-bouillon for 50 crayfish.

5 litres	water	10 pt
30 g	salt	$1\frac{1}{2}$ oz
1	lump of sugar	1
500 ml	lager	1 pt (scant)
	large bunch of dill weed	

Bring all the ingredients to the boil. Drop the crayfish in this court-bouillon and cook them for 10–12 minutes. Allow the court-bouillon to cool with the fish in it.

When they are cooked pile the crays (which are by now bright red) into a great conical heap, with a dill weed flower like a pompom at the top. Serve them cold.

Eat them by pulling them apart and sucking the meat from the heads as well as from the peeled bodies, with tasty Cheddar cut into thin slices (use a cheese slicer) and crusty bread. Most important, drink lots of lager with them. The Swedes have schnapps on the table as well.

Author's note: Cooked Dublin Bay prawns or small crawfish would also make a fine dish. Serve them with mayonnaise (page 254).

Salmon

Izaak Walton called salmon the king of fish, and although its true habitat and feeding grounds are far away and deep in the Northern seas it is in freshwater that it is born, spends it youth and will return to breed in its turn. What is more, it returns to the same river as the one it was born in. The fishing of salmon and the stocking of these rivers is therefore closely controlled. They are in season at various times in English rivers between February and mid-September, but imports, farming and freezing have made salmon available all the year round. There is nothing to beat freshly caught salmon, eaten the same day and at its peak (in July and August) and nothing looks more magnificent on a buffet table.

Salmon reach weights of over 18 kg/40 lb, but those weighing over 6 kg/12 lb are considered rather too rich and oily to eat cooked; however they are superb smoked – another British delicacy (page 177). The best weight for a cooked salmon is between 3–6 kg/6–12 lb. Calculate 100 g/4 oz per head for a first course and 200 g/8 oz per head for a main course.

To cook a salmon for eating hot: The salmon should be whole, or in a piece, weighing about 5 kg/10 lb. Put the cleaned, scaled fish into cold, salted water – salt it at the rate of one large spoonful of salt per litre/quart of water. Bring it *very slowly* to simmering point and leave it just simmering for about 15 minutes. Adjust the timing slightly according to the weight and thickness of the cut. Drain it and serve it with a little of its cooking liquid. It needs nothing else with it but melted butter or a hollandaise sauce (page 256), and plain, boiled new potatoes, and there is no better way to cook it. Serve a salad beside it, or hot cucumber (page 239).

To cook a salmon of the same weight for eating cold: Bring the cleaned, scaled fish to simmering point, in salted water as above. Let it boil for one minute only, then turn off the heat and leave the fish to become quite cold in the liquor. Serve it, drained, skinned, and decorated with aspic if you like, with mayonnaise (page 254), potato salad (page 206) and crisp cucumber salad.

AUTHOR'S NOTE: An old-fashioned way of serving salmon is to 'crimp' it. This is best done with freshly caught fish cooked whole. It is supposed to improve the flavour and it certainly makes it easier to serve. To crimp a fish, have it cleaned but left whole. Make deep cuts on both sides at 2.5 cm/1 inch intervals, right through to the bone. Cook it as above in a fish kettle with a tray so that it can be served whole. Salmon trout can be cooked in the same way.

Salmon pasty *(for 6)*

100 g	mussels in their shells	4 oz
300 g	salmon tail	10 oz
500 g	prawns	1 lb
2	sliced, hard-boiled eggs	2
100 g	chopped, cooked bacon rashers	4 oz
two 15 ml sp	finely chopped capers or gherkins	2 tbsp
	béchamel made with 575 ml/1 pt of milk (page 254)	
	salt, cayenne pepper	
	chopped parsley	
	puff pastry made with 250 g/8 oz of flour (page 266)	
1	beaten egg	1
	cream (optional)	

Cook the mussels (page 100), and poach and flake the salmon, reserving the cooking liquors from each. Shell the mussels and the prawns.

Preheat the oven to 200°C/400°F/gas 6. Cut a salmon shape from a piece of thick paper about 38 cm/15 inches long and 18 cm/7 inches wide, and use it as a template.

In a large bowl, combine the salmon, hard-boiled eggs, bacon and capers or gherkins. Add about half the quantity of the béchamel to the mixture and some of the reserved cooking liquor from either the salmon or mussels to make a smooth mixture. Season with salt, cayenne and chopped parsley.

Roll the puff pastry out to a thickness of 0.5 cm/¼ inch. Cut a base for the pasty using the fish template and cut a top that is 1 cm/½ inch larger all round than the template. Put the salmon filling on the base, leaving a 1 cm/½ inch border. Brush the border with the beaten egg, and place the top over the filling. Lightly press the sides together.

Decorate the top of the fish with the remaining bits of pastry, fixing them with beaten egg. Brush the fish, twice, with more beaten egg. If you like, make shallow snips at regular intervals with a pair of scissors to give the fish scales.

Bake the fish for 45 minutes or until it has risen and is golden-brown, especially along the sides.

For the sauce, reheat the remaining quantity of béchamel and add enough of either (or both) of the reserved cooking liquors to make a sauce of medium thickness. A little cream may be added for extra richness. If you like, liquidise the prawn shells, pass them through a sieve and add the resulting puree to the sauce.

AUTHOR'S NOTE: This filling could also be used for small patties (see the lobster ones on page 200).

Cold chicken robed in lemon sauce *(for 10–12)*

This is a slightly updated version of Hindle Wakes which was a handsome-looking dish: a boiling-fowl was cooked whole with a stuffing of prunes and almonds, then cooled, skinned and coated with a lemon sauce. The whole thing was decorated in black, yellow and green with whole prunes, slices of lemon and parsley. It is an English version of the French chaudfroid, but the stuffing is somewhat heavy for modern tastes.

If the name of the dish sounds familiar, it was used as the title of a play written in 1912 about Lancashire life during Wakes Week. The play is set in an imaginary town called Hindle but, in fact, has nothing to do with this way of eating a chicken, which derives its name more likely from a corruption of Hen de la Wake, a dish that was possibly brought here by the Flemish spinners who settled near Bolton in the 12th century. Wakes Week is an annual holiday in the North; other festivities include well-dressing, when holy wells are decorated with flowers, the holding of fairs and the making of all sorts of cakes – Eccles cakes, gingerbread and Wilfra tarts among them. Here the chicken is already cut into pieces and is served without the rather filling stuffing. Leave the chicken whole if you want a spectacular dish, but you will then have the business of carving it to serve it.

2	medium-sized roasting chickens	2
1	blanched, split pig's trotter	1
	bunch of herbs	
	salt	
1	carrot	1
1	unpeeled onion	1
250 ml	white wine	½ pt (scant)

Skin the chickens and cut each one into eight pieces. Make a well-flavoured and gelatinous stock with the chicken skins, backs and giblets, adding the pig's trotter, the herbs, salt, vegetables and wine. Strain it and poach the chicken pieces in it until they are tender (about ½–¾ of an hour). Strain the stock again and leave it to set so that you can remove the fat from the top and also make sure that it has formed a strong jelly. If you are leaving the chickens whole, follow the basic chicken stock recipe (page 263) and poach them in it without cutting them up.

for the sauce

25 g	butter	1 oz
25 g	flour	1 oz
275 ml	firmly jellied stock (see below)	½ pt
	juice of half a lemon	
2	large egg yolks	2
125 ml	double or soured cream	¼ pt

Make the sauce with a roux of the butter and flour, adding the melted stock and the lemon juice. Put the egg yolks in a bowl and pour the hot sauce on them, beating them with a fork as you do so. Return the sauce to the pan and stir in the cream. Add salt and more lemon juice if necessary. Pour it into a jug and chill it until it is very nearly set, but still pourable. Put the chicken pieces on a wire rack and give them one coat of sauce, returning the drippings to the jug. Leave the first coat to set and then give them a second coat, slightly warming the sauce in a bain-marie if necessary.

When the coating is well set arrange the pieces around a pile of watercress or a heaped-up rice salad (see below). If you like, intersperse them with slices of ham or tongue and quarters of hard-boiled egg.

AUTHOR'S NOTE: Make a *rice salad* by cooking 500 g/1 lb of long-grained rice with a sautéed onion and 1 litre/2 pt of the chicken stock, diluted with water if you haven't got enough. Allow it to cool, then mix in a vinaigrette (page 255) and decorate it with strips of red or green pepper.

To cook a ham the Westmorland way

This very old recipe calls for new, sweet hay, which gives a delicious flavour to any meat, whether pot-roasted or, as in this case, boiled. The ham should be soaked the night before.

'Line a large pan with sweet hay, and put in one of every kind of root vegetable such as celery, carrot, onion, etc., the greater the variety the better. Put in the ham and cover it with cold water, adding two bottles of beer. Add a large tablespoon of syrup. Allow 20 minutes for each 1 lb weight of the ham and simmer it very gently. When the ham is cooked let it remain standing in the liquor in which it has boiled, for twelve hours. This allows it to retain the full flavour.' (From Orton W. I., Cumbria)

Jellied brisket of beef *(for 10–12)*

This cut, from the breast bone of the animal, is an economical yet well-flavoured piece of meat, and as it is excellent cold and cooks best in large pieces it is ideal for big parties. The important thing is to cook it slowly and sympathetically, paying attention to its flavour, texture and tenderness. The recipe given here is for ten to twelve people; briskets can be larger, but are not easy to accommodate in the average-sized casserole. On the other hand, it is not worth cooking a piece of meat much smaller than 2.5 kg/5 lb. Brisket can be bought fresh or salted. If you get it fresh, ask for the bones as well.

3–3.5 kg	fresh brisket of beef	6–7 lb
	finely chopped marjoram	
	salt, pepper, crushed garlic	
	good dripping for frying	
1–2	pig's trotters, split in half and blanched	1–2
	the bones from the brisket (if available)	
250–500 ml	white wine	½–1 pt
500–750 ml	water	1–1½ pt
	bunch of herbs	

Preheat the oven to 160°C/325°F/gas 3.

Ask for the brisket to be boned, but not rolled up. Spread the inside with a mixture of finely chopped marjoram, salt, pepper and crushed garlic. Roll it up and tie it firmly.

Melt the dripping in a heavy, oval, iron casserole which is big enough to hold all the ingredients, and brown the brisket on all sides. Add the rest of the ingredients.

Cover the pot with several sheets of grease-proof paper or foil before putting on the lid, and cook the meat for 4–5 hours.

When the time is up, put the meat aside and strain its liquor into a bowl. Leave it to set so that you can remove all the fat. There should be a good, deliciously flavoured jelly beneath, strong enough to chop up. Arrange it along either side of the brisket which should be served in neat slices, each with a helping of the jelly.

Strawberry and tomato salad *(for 8)*

This unlikely combination is surprisingly good with cold roast duck or cold meat; its garnish of cucumber slices ensures that people will take it as a salad and not as a pudding.

500 g	large, firm strawberries	1 lb
1.5 kg	large, ripe tomatoes	3 lb
	salt	
	paprika	
	lemon juice	
	freshly ground black pepper	
	shredded lettuce heart and thin slices of cucumber	
225 ml	sour cream	8 fl oz

Hull the strawberries and cut each berry in four. Put them aside and keep them covered. Skin the tomatoes, halve them, scoop out their seeds and cut them into fine strips. Season them with salt, paprika and lemon juice.

Just before serving, mix the strawberries with the tomatoes and sprinkle them with the black pepper. Arrange the shredded lettuce in a white bowl, and pile the strawberries and tomatoes in a mound on top. Encircle it with the sliced cucumbers and put the sour cream as a border between the two.

Potato salad *(for 12)*

1.5 kg	waxy potatoes	3 lb
1	clove of garlic	1
125 ml	well-seasoned vinaigrette (page 255)	¼ pt
three 15 ml sp	mixed, chopped fresh green herbs (chives, mint, parsley, chervil)	3 tbsp
half 5 ml sp	curry powder	½ tsp
275 ml	mayonnaise (page 254)	½ pt
	a little creamy milk	

Cook the potatoes in their skins until they are just tender, then peel them, if you like, and either slice them or cube them.

Rub a china bowl with a cut clove of garlic and put the potatoes in it while they are still warm. Turn them about in the vinaigrette and sprinkle them with half the herbs. Add the curry powder to the mayonnaise and make it fairly runny with a little milk. Mix the mayonnaise into the potatoes and heap them up in the bowl, scattering the rest of the herbs on top.

Prawn and grapefruit salad *(for 6)*

Shell and chop 1½ kg/3 lb of cooked prawns. In a bowl, combine the prawns with chopped celery, onion and parsley, a little lemon juice, capers, and salt and pepper to taste. Bind all the ingredients with mayonnaise (page 254) and toss well. Divide the salad among plates lined with lettuce; arrange the flesh from three grapefruit on top with a few very small tomatoes, and sprinkle with chopped parsley. Serve the salad with triangles of cold brown toast.

Macaroni salad

Cook as much macaroni as you need and drain it. Toss it with just enough vinaigrette (page 255) to coat all the pieces and chill it for several hours. Just before serving, add finely chopped onion, celery, parsley and hard-boiled eggs. Bind the mixture with sour cream and season it. Serve the salad on a bed of lettuce and decorate it with tomato slices.

Chartreuse of strawberries *(for 10–12)*

six 5 ml sp	powdered gelatine	6 tsp
575 ml	red wine	1 pt
125 g	sugar	4 oz
1	orange	1
1	lemon	1
15 g	coriander seeds	½ oz
100 ml	kirsch	4 fl oz
500 g	strawberries	1 lb
	little angelica strips	
275 ml	lightly whipped double cream	½ pt

Dissolve the gelatine in a little of the red wine. Combine the sugar, the rest of the wine, and the rinds of the thinly peeled orange and lemon in a large enamelled saucepan. Slowly bring the liquid to the boil and remove the pan from the heat. Add the juice from the fruit, the coriander, and the kirsch and stir in the gelatine. As soon as the mixture starts to cool, but not to solidify, strain it into a large bowl. Mask a 1 litre/2 pt mould with the jelly, working over a bowl of crushed ice, so that the jelly will set quickly.

Pick out some of the best-looking strawberries. Remove their calixes and replace them with the angelica strips. Dip them in jelly and line the bottom and sides of the mould with them, the calixes pointing downwards. Chill the mould.

Slice the remaining strawberries and add them to the jelly. Fold in the whipped cream. Stir the mixture over ice until it starts to set, then pour it into the mould.

Refrigerate it for at least six hours or overnight before unmoulding it.

AUTHOR'S NOTE: Make this in the most elaborate mould you can find. Sliced fresh peaches, apricots, stoned cherries, raspberries or blackberries could also be used.

English cheeses

Include a fine array of traditionally made English cheeses as part of the buffet (page 241).

Simnel cake

These cakes were originally made for the fourth Sunday in Lent, Mothering Sunday, when gifts were brought home by sons and daughters away at work, not only to their actual mothers but also to their Mother Church. The origins of the custom are obviously connected with rites concerning Mother Earth and springtime fertility, but the origins of the name of the cake are not so clear. Scholars point out that 'simnel' is derived from the Latin word for fine flour *simila*; others connect it with the baker who was Lambert Simnel's father, but these cakes were known of long before the reign of Henry VII. The most popular, but least likely attribution to the name is a couple called Simon and Nelly who couldn't agree whether the cake should be boiled or baked, so compromised by doing both and called it a Sim-Nel. In fact a most laborious recipe does exist, in which the cake mixture is first boiled for hours, in a pastry case enclosed by a cloth, then baked without the pastry; this lends a little strength to the story, but today the cake is just baked.

It has also moved to Easter, and in place of the saffron which made the much plainer, earlier cake yellow, it has a disc of marzipan baked in it across the centre, with another disc on top, encircled by eleven little marzipan balls to represent the faithful Apostles.

Although it is richly egged and fruited, it is still not as dark and rum-soaked as a traditional wedding cake. In fact it comes in very useful as a Golden Wedding cake; the marzipan can be moulded to suit that occasion, and a gold ribbon tied round it gives the proper finishing touch.

for the marzipan

375 g	ground almonds	12 oz
	few drops of almond essence	
375 g	caster sugar	12 oz
1	egg	1
2	egg yolks	2
	icing sugar	

Preheat the oven to 150°C/300°F/gas 2.

To make the marzipan, mix together the ground almonds, almond essence and caster sugar in a large bowl. Combine the whole egg with the yolks and lightly beat them with a fork.

Stir enough beaten egg into the almond and sugar mixture to make a stiff paste. Sprinkle a work surface with a little icing sugar and knead the paste until it is smooth and pliable. Wrap it in plastic film until you are ready to use it.

	for the cake	
250 g	butter	8 oz
250 g	caster sugar	8 oz
5	eggs	5
375 g	plain flour	12 oz
one 5 ml sp	baking powder	1 tsp
100 g	ground almonds	4 oz
500 g	currants	1 lb
500 g	sultanas	1 lb
100 g	mixed peel	4 oz
one 15 ml sp	finely chopped crystallised ginger	1 tbsp
	milk	
	apricot jam	
	beaten egg	

To make the cake, cream the butter and sugar together and add the eggs, one at a time. Fold in the dry ingredients and the fruit and add a little milk if the batter seems very stiff. Transfer half the mixture to a well-greased and lined tin (20 cm/8 inches).

Roll out half the quantity of marzipan to a thickness of 0.5 cm/$\frac{1}{4}$ inch and cut a round to fit inside the tin, using the base as a template.

Place the round on top of the cake mixture and cover it with the remaining mixture. Cook the cake for three hours or until a skewer inserted in the centre comes out clean. Cover the top with a piece of grease-proof paper if it starts to brown too much. Cool the cake in its tin for about two hours, then turn it out onto a rack.

When the cake is completely cool, roll out the remaining marzipan to a thickness of 0.5 cm/$\frac{1}{4}$ inch, and from it cut out another round to fit the cake, leaving enough to make eleven little balls (see below). Brush the surface with a little apricot jam (to help it stick to the cake) and place the brushed side down onto the smoothest side of the cake.

Place the eleven small balls all round the edge of the cake, dipping the bottoms in jam before positioning them. Beat an egg and glaze the top of the cake with it, and put the cake into a moderately hot oven (160°C/325°F/gas 3) for ten minutes to give it a sheen. Slivers of glacé cherries or angelica can be additional decorations. Tie a gold band or ribbon round the cake.

Celebration cake

A Daleswoman farmer makes this dark, moist and very rich cake for all local birthdays, weddings and christenings, as well as for Christmas. It makes one enormous cake (using all the mixture, 6 kg/13 lb of it) or it can be divided into smaller ones, for tiers. She bakes hers in a square tin which was specially made for her. It is about the size and shape of a biscuit tin – 25 cm/10 inches square and 12 cm/5 inches deep. If you want to use a round tin it should be the same depth, with a diameter of 30 cm/12 inches.

750 g	softened, salted Wensleydale butter	1½ lb
750 g	soft brown sugar	1½ lb
150 g	finely chopped candied peel	6 oz
150 g	glacé cherries	6 oz
500 g	raisins	1 lb
1.75 kg	currants	3½ lb
850 g	plain flour	1 lb 11 oz
13	eggs	13
two 5 ml sp	milk	2 tsp
275 ml	rum or brandy	½ pt
one 5 ml sp	mixed spice	1 tsp
one 5 ml sp	nutmeg	1 tsp
half 5 ml sp	baking powder	½ tsp
150 g	ground almonds	6 oz

Preheat the oven to 140°C/275°F/gas 1. Butter and line the tin.

Beat the butter into the sugar until it is light and fluffy. Mix the fruit with a few spoonfuls of the flour, then, using your hands, combine the fruit with the sugar and butter mixture. Beat the eggs and milk with the rum or brandy and add this to the fruit mixture. Sift the remaining flour, spices and baking powder onto the mixture and fold them in with your hands. Lastly, incorporate the almonds.

Put the mixture into the tin and smooth the top. Leave it to settle for about ten minutes, then put it into the oven. Cook the cake for 6½ hours (a little less for smaller cakes); then turn off the oven and leave the cake in it until it is quite cold.

My friend arranges to start baking the cake at 5 p.m. so that she can turn the oven off just before going to bed. Then the cake cools off in the oven all night.

It is then covered with marzipan (see page 208) and icing (see below) and decorated.

Royal icing

The quantities given below make enough icing for a 25 cm/10 inch cake.

1.25 kg	icing sugar	2½ lb
5	egg whites	5
	juice of half a lemon	
one 5 ml sp	glycerine (optional)	1 tsp

Sift the icing sugar twice. Break up the egg whites with a fork, then beat the sugar into them a little at a time. Add the lemon juice. Beat for about 15 minutes by hand, or eight minutes with a mixer, until the mixture is satiny, smooth and light. Leave it to rest for an hour or two. This quantity is enough to coat the top and sides of the cake.

Incorporate glycerine and more sugar for decorative piping. Keep the icing soft until you use it by covering the bowl with a damp cloth.

A West Country high tea

Marinated mackerel
Chipple (or spring onion) pie

Chipple salad or green salad

Cornish and Devon splits with strawberry jam and clotted cream

Cornish seedy cake
Heavy cake
Saffron cake

Cornish fairings

Apples in cider syrup

Cream teas begin somewhere in Dorset and continue down through Somerset and Devon, then on through Cornwall until you reach Land's End. To the summer visitor this rich form of afternoon tea may look like a treat laid on by teashops, guesthouses and hotels, especially for the holiday trade. But it isn't. Clotted cream, the tea and traditional delicacies that go with it are enjoyed by the locals not just in summer, but in winter too, in village and town alike, all over the West Country.

Marinated mackerel *(for 4)*

Mackerel, sardines and pilchards are found in abundance off the South-Western shores; mackerel are by far the most usual fish to be caught by anyone trailing spinners or feathers from a small boat in summer. Pilchards, alas, are rarely seen outside Cornwall, as once landed they go straight to the canning factories. Sardines (fresh, not frozen) are sometimes landed at Brixham by French boats which usually call at this port when the price of our Dover sole is attractive to them. They catch the sardines off the far West of France.

This is a useful way of cooking and keeping (for a few days at least) fish that seem never to be caught in ones and twos but always in shoals.

4	small mackerel or 2 large ones	4
1 or 2	bay leaves	1 or 2
1	finely sliced small onion	1
one 15 ml sp	salt	1 tsp
one 15 ml sp	brown sugar	1 tbsp
6	peppercorns	6
two 5 ml sp	pickling spices	2 tsp
275 ml	malt, wine or cider vinegar	½ pt
275 ml	cold tea	½ pt

Cut off the heads and tails of the fish and remove the guts. Split the fish open and remove the spines, so that each fish forms two fillets.

Pack them with the rest of the ingredients into a deep, straight-sided oven-proof dish (an oval earthenware casserole is suitable).

Cover the dish with two or three sheets of brown paper. (If you dampen it first it can be more easily crimped to fit the pot.)

Cook the mackerel in a very low oven overnight at 120°C/250°F/gas ½. If you use fish as small as sardines you can leave them unfilleted but they must cook long enough for the bones to be quite soft by the end.

Although this may all seem somewhat vinegary, Cornish people eat them cold with chipple salad, or a green salad, and plenty of brown bread (page 230) and West Country butter.

AUTHOR'S NOTE: The cold tea dilutes the rather overpowering taste of vinegar and adds a little tannic acid of its own.

Chipple (or spring onion) pie *(for 4–6)*

This pie is cousin to the quiche and provides another link between the West Country and the other side of the Channel. Cooks in Devon and Cornwall – more than cooks in other parts of the country – like baking pies or tarts with egg (or cream) as part of the filling.

Cornish people call spring onions chipples or chivvels, and in Devon they call them chibbles. Speakers of French, Spanish or Italian will recognise the similarity to 'ciboule', 'cebolla' and 'cipolla'.

For this recipe use fat chipples, like Welsh onions.

375 g	shortcrust pastry (page 264)	12 oz
2 or 3	rashers of bacon, rind removed	2 or 3
5	fat chipples (or 1 bunch)	5
3	beaten eggs	3
two 15 ml sp	milk	2 tbsp
	salt and pepper	
25 g	butter	1 oz
	more beaten egg (optional)	

Preheat the oven to 200°C/400°F/gas 6.

Line a 20 cm/8 inch pie dish or tart tin with half the pastry, covering the bottom with the bacon cut into pieces. Split the chipples in two, then cut them into short lengths and arrange them over the bacon. Mix the eggs with the milk, salt and pepper and pour this over the chipples. Dot with butter.

Cover the filling with the rest of the pastry, cutting a hole in the centre for the steam to escape. Brush with beaten egg if you want to glaze the pie.

Bake it for 45 minutes, reducing the heat to 190°C/375°F/gas 5 halfway through. Eat the pie hot or cold.

Chipple salad

In Cornwall 'chipples' are eaten cut up into short strips. They are then left to marinate overnight in a bowl with cider vinegar, salt and pepper. Cooked, cubed beetroot is sometimes added.

Cornish and Devon splits

These are small, soft rolls, made expressly for splitting open and filling with clotted cream and strawberry jam (page 251). The addition of fat and milk to the dough helps to make them soft: you don't want to have to bite so hard that all the filling squidges out. As an added precaution against the formation of a hard, crisp crust, wrap them in a tea towel as soon as they come out of the oven.

Devon splits are a little smaller than Cornish ones and are sometimes called 'cutrounds' or 'Chudleighs' after the place of that name, though a girl in a baker's shop in the neighbouring town of Bovey Tracey called them 'tuffs' (a corruption of turf-cakes, as they were once cooked on griddles over peat; see also page 116).

This recipe makes 12 Cornish splits or 18 Devon splits.

50 g	butter, margarine or lard	2 oz
250 ml	tepid milk, or milk and water mixed	½ pt
one 5 ml sp	sugar	1 tsp
25 g	fresh yeast (or half quantity of dried)	1 oz
500 g	white or wholemeal flour	1 lb
one 5 ml sp	salt	1 tsp
	oil	
	butter	

Melt the fat and stir it into the warm milk or milk and water. Cream the sugar and yeast together in a teacup. Stir in a little of the liquid and a sprinkling of the flour.

Mix the flour and salt in a bowl and put it in a warm place. When the yeast has started to froth, pour it into a well in the centre of the flour. Add the rest of the liquid, mix well by hand and then knead the dough on a table top until it feels smooth and springy.

Put the dough back in the bowl, with a smearing of oil to prevent a skin forming. Lay a damp cloth over it and leave it in a warm place until the dough has doubled in size. Punch it down and knead it briefly again before forming it into twelve or eighteen rolls.

Put them on a floured baking-sheet (or sheath, as the Cornish call it), flattening them slightly to about 1 cm/½ inch thick. Leave them to prove for about 20 minutes while the oven heats up to 220°C/425°F/gas 7.

Bake the splits for 20 minutes. Brush the tops with a little butter to make them shine, and keep them warm and soft in a tea towel.

AUTHOR'S NOTE: Instead of strawberry jam and cream you can eat the splits with treacle and clotted cream which is always called thunder and lightning.

Clotted cream

Clotted cream is made mostly in Cornwall and Devon, and to a lesser extent in Somerset and Dorset. Until you actually taste it, freshly made and served straight from the huge bowls in which it has been scalded, the addictive nature of this exquisite stuff may never become apparent to you.

I don't think clotted cream travels well, but if you do decide to send it by post, it should be eaten as soon as it arrives, before it has a chance to lose its fine flavour and creamy texture. If it has become solid, tasteless and grainy, the best way to rescue it is to mix it with a little creamy milk.

At its best, it has a bright yellow 'crust' on top. Below this, the cream is thick, pale and sticky, with a consistency like honey. The remains of skim milk lie under and around it.

Clotted cream can be eaten in pies and pasties, with puddings, cakes and pastries, sauces, soups and purees; it also goes with eggs, fish, poultry, vegetables, and with fruit. Best and most gluttonous of all is the West Country habit of eating it with scones or splits and strawberry jam.

Clotted cream is made by putting the fresh milk or cream (from any sort of cow, not necessarily from a Channel Island breed) into a shallow earthenware, enamelled or copper pan. It takes the cream 12 hours in summer and 24 in winter to rise to the top. The pan is then put over a very low heat, usually in a bain-marie. Very slowly the cream begins to 'clout' or clot, the edge forming a ridge round the rim and the middle wrinkling, but it must never boil, otherwise the top breaks. When the cream is sufficiently well clotted, the bowl is carefully moved and left to cool and set for 12 to 24 hours.

The cream is then lifted off, so that the crust remains on top. The delicious skimmed milk left behind tastes slightly nutty.

Cornish seedy cake

Almost every county in England has a recipe for seed cake with minor variations; the one constant factor is caraway seed. This plant once grew wild in many places and is easy to grow in the herb garden.

250 g	butter	8 oz
250 g	caster sugar	8 oz
one 15 ml sp	caraway seeds	1 tbsp
two 15 ml sp	candied lemon peel	2 tbsp
2	separated eggs	2
	pinch of salt	
250 g	plain flour	8 oz

Preheat the oven to 180°C/350°F/gas 4. Butter and flour a 25 × 10 cm/10 × 4 inch loaf tin.

Cream the butter and sugar together, beating until the mixture is light and fluffy. Add the seeds and peel. Add the egg yolks, one at a time, beating after each addition.

Beat the egg whites with the salt until they are stiff, then fold them alternately with the flour into the egg and butter mixture.

Turn the mixture into the prepared loaf tin. Bake the cake for about an hour, or until a cake tester comes out clean.

Heavy cake

Heavy cakes are not so called because they are 'heavy', but because the word is a corruption of 'hevva', according to a Cornish cookery book: 'The huer looking out for the pilchard shoals from his hut on the cliffs would give the signal and shout "Hevva!" The fishermen would pull in the catch in their nets and their wives would make "Hevva" cake to serve to them hot with a "dish of tay" on their return.'

The recipes for this slab-shaped, fruited, pastry-like cake are many and varied. Some have flour and fat in proportions similar to a shortcrust, others are more like flaky pastry. Some include eggs, others cream, some have both. The only things common to all recipes are the inclusion of currants, the flat rectangular shape and the criss-cross cuts on top.

The recipe given here tries to recreate the first heavy cake I ever tasted, in Helston. It was soggy inside, and thick and crumbly. We ate it warm, sliced open and buttered.

300 g	plain flour	12 oz
	pinch of salt	
one 5 ml sp	baking powder	1 tsp
150 g	butter or margarine	6 oz
100 g	mixed currants and sultanas	4 oz
100 g	granulated sugar	4 oz
	milk to mix	

Preheat the oven to 200°C/400°F/gas 6.

Mix the flour, salt and baking powder. Rub in the fat as if you were making pastry. Mix in the fruit and sugar, then add enough milk to the mixture to make a firm dough.

Press it into a flat shape about 2.5 cm/1 inch thick. Put it onto a greased baking-sheet. Cut diamond-shaped criss-crosses on top and bake it for 30 minutes or until it is brown on top.

Saffron cake *(makes 1 large cake or 12 buns)*

The tradition of eating saffron cakes and buns at 'times and tides' is still going strong. It is said to date back to the days when Phoenician traders exchanged it and other spices for Cornish tin. All over Cornwall bakers display trays of bright yellow loaves and buns labelled 'Saffron Cakes', but, in fact, unless they are labelled 'Genuine Saffron' their colour is usually a dye, and of the true warm saffron flavour they will have nothing.

As real saffron (stigmas of the *Crocus sativus*) costs £500–£550 a kilo, which represents the harvest of half a million flowers, it is hardly surprising that bakers don't use it every day. But you can buy it more easily in Cornwall than anywhere else in the land – even the humblest grocer sells it.

To obtain the maximum flavour and colour from saffron, crumble the strands between two sheets of grease-proof paper and steep them overnight in a cupful of water.

This cake is based on a Women's Institute recipe. The lady who gave it to me drinks ginger wine (non-alcoholic) with it.

1	small packet of saffron	1
125 ml	water	¼ pt
15 g	fresh yeast (or half quantity of dried)	½ oz
100 g	sugar	4 oz
500 g	flour	1 lb
	pinch of salt	
75 g	butter	3 oz
75 g	lard	3 oz
100 g	currants	4 oz
100 g	sultanas	4 oz
25 g	mixed peel	1 oz
	pinch of nutmeg	
	pinch of cinnamon	
60 ml	milk	2½ fl oz

Steep the saffron overnight in a little of the measured water.

Next day cream the yeast with a small spoonful of the sugar, 50 g/2 oz of the flour, and the remaining water, which should be warmed to a little over blood heat. Leave it, covered, to double in size, which will take about 30 minutes.

Sieve the remaining flour with the salt into a large bowl. Rub in the fats until the mixture is very crumbly. Add the currants, sultanas, peel, spices and the rest of the sugar. Mix well.

Add the saffron water to the yeast sponge, wiping out every drop with a handful of the dry ingredients, and add it to the mixture with the milk. Mix everything well and knead it until it is smooth. Cover it, and leave it to rise until it has doubled in bulk – this will be quite slow, even in a warm place (at least 1½ hours). Knead it again and put it into a large, well-greased cake tin, either loaf-shaped or round, so that the mixture comes about halfway up; or divide the mixture between twelve bun tins. Leave it to rise again.

Heat the oven to 190°C/375°F/gas 5. When the dough is almost at the top of the tin, bake it for 30 minutes, then reduce the heat to 180°C/350°F/gas 4 for another 30 minutes at least if it is a large cake; less for smaller cakes and still less for buns.

Cornish fairings *(makes 16)*

These crisp, flat, ginger biscuits are traditionally sold at fairs.

125 g	butter or margarine	4 oz
two 15 ml sp	golden syrup	2 tsp
250 g	self-raising flour	8 oz
	pinch of bicarbonate of soda	
	pinch of salt	
one 5 ml sp	mixed spice	1 tsp
one 5 ml sp	ground ginger	1 tsp

Preheat the oven to 200°C/400°F/gas 6. Warm the butter and the syrup and mix them into the dry ingredients. Shape the mixture into walnut-sized balls. Put them on a greased baking-sheet and flatten them with a damp cloth wrapped round the bottom of a glass, to a thickness of 0.5 cm/¼ inch.

Bake them for about 15 minutes. They will keep crisp if you store them in an airtight tin.

Apples in cider syrup *(for 4)*

There are many West Country legends about Hardyesque characters having 'the legs taken from them' by a seemingly harmless kind of cider called 'scrumpy'. It certainly has a higher alcoholic content than ordinary beer. It is also very good to cook with, especially if it is reduced by as much as half – this concentrates the flavour and all the alcohol evaporates. It is as good an ingredient as wine in both savoury and sweet dishes, and is cheaper too.

This recipe comes from Taunton in Somerset, which is surrounded by cider apple orchards.

250 g	soft brown sugar	8 oz
275 ml	medium dry strong cider	½ pt
8	small Cox's Orange Pippin apples	8

Put the sugar with the cider in a pan and boil it till the volume is reduced by half.

Peel and core the apples and put them in a single layer in a large pan. Cover them with the cider syrup and weight them down with a plate. Bring them slowly to the boil, then take them off the heat and allow them to cool. Do this several times. The apples will shrink quite a bit and eventually become tender and translucent. When this occurs let them cool, then drain them and pile them into a pyramid.

Pour what remains of the syrup over them and serve them cold with thin cream or, if you can't resist it, clotted cream.

AUTHOR'S NOTE: The apples must be Cox's because they are nice and firm. The stop-start method of cooking is necessary to keep the apples whole. If you simmer them continuously they break up.

A vegetarian supper

Nettle and sorrel soup
Sorrel omelette with sorrel sauce
Winter vegetable terrine

Spinach loaf with walnuts
Vegetarian curry pasty
Summer vegetable stew

Swiss chard fritters
Stuffed fennel

Various salads

Stir-fried rice
Wholewheat noodles

Frumenty
Dried fruit tart with wheatmeal pastry

The Grant loaf

I will not go into the pros and cons of a vegetarian diet here, but I am including a vegetarian menu in this book because I think that many of the ideas and principles espoused by vegetarians have had an interesting, as well as a beneficial, influence on the food we eat. In any case, it is impossible, if you write about food, not to be aware of the wholefood movement in England today.

Of course wholefood principles and vegetarianism are not the same, but they complement one another, and this menu is designed to please those who follow or are interested in either of those ways of life. Their continual and watchful enthusiasm for healthy eating ensures that things like wholemeal bread, natural sea salt, herb teas, all sorts of unusual vegetables, useful herbs and spices, all the many different grains, peas, beans and dried fruits and various sorts of oil, dried seaweed, honey and nuts are increasingly obtainable in most English towns and villages today; such things would otherwise have been made almost extinct by the overwhelming demand for crisps, chips, sweeties and things from the freezer. If you totally disapprove of sugar, leave it out of all the following recipes, and if you don't eat butter, substitute margarine instead.

Nettle and sorrel soup *(for 4)*

This springtime soup is supposed to revitalise you and cleanse the blood.

150 g	fresh young nettle tops	6 oz
250 g	fresh sorrel	8 oz
two 15 ml sp	butter	2 tbsp
50 g	minced spring onions	2 oz
	salt	
575 ml	stock, water, or half and half	1 pt
150 ml	double cream	6 fl oz
	pepper	
	chopped parsley	
2	finely chopped hard-boiled eggs *or* croûtons	2

Blanch the nettles in boiling water for two minutes, drain them and refresh them under cold water. Squeeze out as much moisture as possible. Stem the sorrel and coarsely chop it with the nettles.

Melt the butter in a medium-sized saucepan and stir in the spring onions. When the onions are soft, add the nettles and sorrel to the pan. As soon as the vegetables are soft (after about five minutes), season them with salt, add the water or stock, and simmer the soup for ten minutes.

Puree the vegetables either by passing them through a sieve, or by putting them in a liquidiser or food processor. Return the puree to the pan, stir in the cream and cook the soup just long enough to heat it through. Taste for seasonings and add some chopped parsley. Pass around a bowl of chopped hard-boiled eggs or croûtons when you serve the soup.

Sorrel omelette *(for 2)*

50 g	trimmed, washed and dried sorrel	2 oz
25 g	butter	1 oz
5	eggs	5
	salt and pepper	
	butter for cooking	
250 ml	sorrel sauce (page 257)	½ pt

Shred the sorrel and sauté it in the weighed butter for a few minutes, stirring all the time. It will go to a mush. Put it aside to cool. Beat the eggs with salt and pepper. Mix in the sorrel.

Make two omelettes, cooking them in more butter and tipping them from the pan to the plate so that they form nice rolls. Make a slit down the centre of each and pour a helping of sorrel sauce over each one.

Winter vegetable terrine *(for 8–12)*

1	Savoy cabbage, leaves separated, and ribs removed	1
250 g	thinly sliced rounds of turnip	8 oz
250 g	thinly sliced strips of carrot	8 oz
150–250 g	broccoli heads	6–8 oz
225 ml	milk	8 fl oz
2	whole eggs	2
2	egg yolks	2
	chopped parsley	
	chopped tarragon or chives	
	salt, pepper	

Preheat the oven to 180°C/350°F/gas 4. Parboil the Savoy cabbage for four minutes and the other vegetables for two minutes. Generously butter the sides and bottom of a 1 litre/2 pt terrine or loaf tin. Line the tin with the softened cabbage leaves, making sure you do not leave any gaps for the custard to leak through. Let enough of each leaf hang over the edge of the tin to fold over the assembled terrine.

Put half the turnips on the bottom of the terrine. Cover them with a layer of cabbage leaves. Neatly arrange half the carrot strips, lengthwise, on top of the cabbage. Put all the broccoli, heads upright, on top of the carrots.

Repeat the layering process with the remaining carrots, cabbage (reserving a few leaves) and turnips – in that order.

For the custard, mix the milk with the eggs, yolks, herbs and seasoning. Spoon it over the whole terrine, inserting a knife in a few places to allow the custard to seep through. Fold the cabbage leaves over the terrine and cover it with the remaining leaves and a piece of foil.

Put the terrine on a rack in a bain-marie and cook it for about one hour or until it seems firm when pressed. Take it out of the oven and let it stand for about 15 minutes. Remove the foil and turn the terrine out onto a plate.

The terrine can be served hot with tomato sauce (see page 257), or cold with a fresh tomato sauce (page 255) or mayonnaise (page 254).

AUTHOR'S NOTE: This recipe can be adapted to suit summer vegetables too. French beans left whole, asparagus, peas, courgettes, wild mushrooms and so on, could all be used.

Spinach loaf with walnuts *(for 6–8)*

As this is a very satisfying dish, you only need small slices if it is being served as a first course. Be careful if you cook this in a tin – the walnuts may turn purple.

750 g	spinach	1½ lb
2	eggs	2
125 ml	cream	¼ pt
100 g	grated cheese	4 oz
25 g	chopped walnuts	1 oz
	salt, pepper	
	nutmeg	
	grated cheese for the top	

Preheat the oven to 180°C/350°F/gas 4. Strip the stems from the spinach and cook it in boiling salted water. Drain it well and chop it finely. Beat the eggs and cream together. Add the weighed cheese, the spinach and the walnuts. Season it all well with the salt, pepper and nutmeg.

Fill a buttered ½ litre/1 pt terrine or non-stick loaf tin with the mixture and bake it in a bain-marie for an hour. Allow it to cool before turning it out. Cover the top with very finely grated cheese. Serve it cold, garnished with small lettuce leaves.

AUTHOR'S NOTE: The texture I like best is rather coarse, but if you prefer it fine, sieve or liquidise the spinach instead of chopping it. On the other hand, the nuts should not be chopped too small.

Vegetarian curry pasty *(makes 6)*

This is the filling made by a Somerset friend for her vegetarian daughter's pasties. The rest of the family has meat pasties, and they are marked accordingly on the crust.

1	small chopped onion	1
1	small chopped apple	1
	a little butter	
1	small chopped green or red pepper	1
one 5 ml sp	mixed curry,	1 tsp
	coriander and ginger powders	
	chilli pepper	
	salt	
	a little vegetable stock	
one 15 ml sp	chutney	1 tbsp
250 g	cooked red kidney beans	8 oz
1	small tin of mushy peas	1

Sauté the onion and apple in a little butter until they are soft, and add the red or green pepper. Stir in the curry powder mixture and add chilli and salt to taste. Make a fairly runny sauce by adding the stock and the chutney, then stir in the beans. Sieve or liquidize the peas, and add them to the mixture. Cook it all for about five minutes to let the flavours amalgamate. Allow it to cool before using it as a pasty filling. For the pasty recipe, see page 39.

Summer vegetable stew *(for 4–6)*

1	sliced onion	1
one 15 ml sp	butter	1 tbsp
150 g	green peas	6 oz
150 g	sliced courgettes	6 oz
2	sliced tomatoes	2
8	small new potatoes	8
8	small new carrots	8
150 g	broad beans	6 oz
	salt	

Brown the onion in the butter in a heavy saucepan. Add the rest of the vegetables, with water almost to cover them, and a little salt. Cover the pan and let the contents cook very gently for two or more hours. It should be a very thick stew, but it may need more water halfway through.

AUTHOR'S NOTE: The vegetables may be altered to make a winter stew.

Swiss chard fritters *(for 4–5)*

These are made with the green parts of that handsome and useful spinach-like vegetable which is also known as seakale beet or blette. The white stems, separately cooked, can be served in a cheese sauce.

1	finely chopped medium-sized onion	1
	oil or butter for frying	
250 g	green parts only of Swiss chard leaves	8 oz
2	large beaten eggs	2
one or two 15 ml sp	flour	1–2 tbsp
75 ml	milk	3 fl oz
two 15 ml sp	finely grated cheese	2 tbsp
	salt, pepper	
	melted butter	
	grated cheese (optional)	

Sauté the onion until it softens but does not colour. Wash, then roughly chop the chard leaves. Put them with the onion, eggs, flour, milk, cheese and seasoning into a food processor or liquidiser and let the machine work until you have a slightly rough, bright green batter. Pour the mixture into a jug. Heat the oil or butter in a large frying-pan and gently fry ladlefuls of the batter, a few at a time. (Stir the mixture in the jug from time to time as the leaves tend to float to the top.) Turn the fritters over as soon as the underneath sets. Serve them arranged in a tile pattern, on a flat dish, sprinkled with melted butter and more grated cheese if you like.

Author's note: Children who loathe spinach cooked as a puree will quite probably like these fritters; they look rather like waterlily leaves, especially if you put a vandyked tomato-half for a lily flower on each serving.

Stuffed fennel *(for 4)*

1 kg	fennel	2 lb
100 g	stemmed and blanched spinach (raw weight)	4 oz
2	finely chopped shallots	2
	olive oil for frying	
375 g	sieved cottage cheese	12 oz
1	crushed clove of garlic	1
50 g	dried breadcrumbs	2 oz
2	eggs	2
	thyme	
	nutmeg	
	cayenne	
	chopped parsley	
575 ml	tomato sauce (page 257)	1 pt
	grated cheese or sautéed breadcrumbs	

Preheat the oven to 180°C/350°F/gas 4.

Cut the round green stems and feathery leaves from the fennel bulbs. Cut a thin slice off the root end of each bulb to release the curved, spoon-shaped white stalks. Pull off the stalks, one at a time. If they don't come away easily, cut another slice off the bottom. Rinse the stalks in cold water. Reserve the hearts of the bulbs and some of the feathery leaves for the stuffing.

Boil the fennel stalks in salted water for five to ten minutes to soften them. Drain them and leave them on a kitchen towel. Finely chop the blanched, drained spinach. Sauté the shallots in a little olive oil until they are soft, and add the spinach. Set it aside to cool. Combine the cottage cheese with the garlic, breadcrumbs, eggs, finely chopped fennel hearts and leaves, spinach, and the remaining seasonings. Taste it for seasoning. Put a spoonful of filling inside each fennel stalk and press the edges together to keep the filling in. Arrange them 'seam' side down in rows in a buttered gratin dish.

Coat the stuffed fennel with the tomato sauce; if you like, sprinkle the top with grated Cheddar cheese, or sautéed breadcrumbs. Bake them for 45 minutes to one hour, until the sauce has reduced and the fennel has heated through.

Various salads

Hop-shoot salad: This is a springtime salad. If you live in a hop-growing area you may find hops growing wild. Blanch the hop-shoots in salted water, drain them and allow them to cool; then dress them in a vinaigrette and serve with slices of hard-boiled egg.

A winter salad: This can be composed of the following vegetables. Have them in whatever proportion you like but put them in the bowl in this order:

Potatoes, boiled in their skins, then peeled and sliced or diced fairly finely.

Onions, baked in their skins till they are tender, then peeled and broken into segments.

Sweet peppers, grilled until their skins turn black. (To remove the skin put them at once in a paper bag, tightly shut. After five minutes the steam will have softened the skin and it will come off easily. De-seed them and cut them into wide strips.)

Beetroots, cooked, then cubed and added at the last minute, with a vinaigrette dressing (see page 255).

Optional additions: hard-boiled eggs, olives, cooked green beans, lightly cooked cauliflower, cooked haricot (dried) beans, chicory.

Cucumber salad with yoghourt: This is excellent with curries. Follow the instructions on page 83, or mix in a small spoonful of paprika and a little sugar instead of garlic. Sprinkle this one with chopped parsley.

Orange and watercress salad: This is a favourite with non-vegetarians as well, to go with roast duck or pork. Peel two or three oranges, removing all the pith as well as the skin. Take out the segments of fruit, leaving the membrane behind (use a sharp, pointed knife for this).

Arrange a bed of lettuce hearts, or shredded lettuce, put the orange pieces on it, and add some well picked-over sprigs of watercress. Pour a vinaigrette over it (page 255) to which a little sugar has been added.

See also other salads in the book – for example the chicory one on page 193, the bulgar salad (page 128), and the spring salad (page 31).

Stir-fried rice *(for 4)*

This is Chinese in origin, but it makes a wonderful, quick vegetarian meal. It is also a good excuse to use a wok, that extraordinarily useful and foreign-looking basin-shaped pan that can be employed as a steamer and braiser as well as a frying-pan. The main ingredient of this dish is left-over rice. Other ingredients depend on what you have to hand. The main thing is, don't overcook anything, so cut firm vegetables small enough to cook fast and yet retain their 'bite'.

Metric	Ingredient	Imperial
four 15 ml sp	cooking oil	4 tbsp
1	chopped medium-sized onion	1
3	beaten eggs	3
	salt, pepper	
four 15 ml sp	chopped celery or cubed cucumber	4 tbsp
four 15 ml sp	fresh or frozen peas	4 tbsp
50 g	beansprouts	2 oz
350 g	cold, cooked rice (white or brown)	12 oz
one 15 ml sp	soya sauce	1 tbsp
	a few chopped spring onions	

Heat the oil in a wok or large frying-pan. Sauté the onion and stir as it cooks (using chopsticks) for about one minute. Reduce the heat and pour in the eggs, seasoned with a little salt and pepper; stir them as they cook so that they become scrambled. Add the celery or cucumber, then the peas and then the beansprouts. Keep stirring, and add the rice (break it up first if it is in a solid mass). Cook it well for two minutes, still stirring. Add the soya sauce and the spring onions, mix them in thoroughly and serve the rice at once.

Wholewheat noodles *(for 4)*

The making of fresh noodles is no problem at home if you have a food processor to mix the dough and a pasta machine to roll it out. If you have neither of these machines it takes a little more time and energy but it is worth it as these noodles are delicious, and so light that they hardly need cooking.

Although this might be thought of as exclusively Continental, I include the recipe since the English have always loved pasta, especially at its extremes of size; in particular they like vermicelli soup and macaroni cheese. For vegetarians these noodles should be served with any nutty, mushroom or tomato sauce.

	for the noodles	
250 g	wholewheat flour	8 oz
3	medium-sized eggs	3
half 5 ml sp	salt	½ tsp
one 15 ml sp	oil	1 tbsp

	for serving	
750 ml	tomato sauce (page 257)	1–1½ pt
	grated cheese	

Mix the flour, eggs, salt and oil together, in a food processor, or in a dough mixer or a bowl. Process or knead the mixture as if you were making bread dough, adding more flour if it seems very sticky, and more oil if it seems very dry; it will be crumbly at first but it should become a soft pliable dough in due course. Leave it to rest for 30 minutes, covered, while you prepare the tomato sauce.

Make the noodles as fine as you can, according to the instructions if you have a pasta machine. If not, divide the dough into two. Roll each half on a floured board, as thinly as you can. Keep rolling from the centre outwards, flouring the pasta a little if it seems likely to stick and tear. When both pieces are as thin as you can make them, leave them to dry a little on cloths over the table, then roll them up lightly and cut the dough into strips about 0.5 cm/¼ inch wide. Keep them spread out until you are ready to cook them.

Cook them in a large pan of boiling salted water for about five minutes, drain them well, then serve them with the sauce and grated cheese.

AUTHOR'S NOTE: These noodles are also good with brown or green lentils. Sauté an onion with a little garlic, add a pinch of cumin and coriander, and 500 g/ 1 lb of cooked, seasoned lentils. Heat them through and mix them with the cooked noodles. Left-over noodles can also be deep-fried and mixed with lightly fried vegetables (use beansprouts, sliced courgettes, mushrooms, onion, shredded cabbage, and so on).

Frumenty *(for 4–6)*

Some Northern mills still prepare whole wheat grains especially for the traditional Christmas dish of frumenty (furmenty, fromity, and so on). This 'frumenty wheat' is wheat that has been 'husked', 'hulled' or 'pearled'. It is polished in a special drum so that one layer of the outer skin is rubbed away and the ends of the 'berry' are nipped off. When it is cooked each grain swells into a deliciously soft little ball suspended in a creamy jelly, but it is still contained in enough of the skin to make it chewy. Wholewheat grains and cracked, crushed or 'kibbled wheat' (as sold in wholefood shops) will also do.

Frumenty appears to be one of the oldest dishes known to man. Until very recently it was served not only at Christmas and the twelve days thereafter, but also during Lent and at other religious occasions. A dairy farmer of Chipping Sodbury in Gloucestershire served his frumenty on 'Bristol china'. They were sent to the best customers filled with a frumenty enriched with eggs, fruit and cream as a cold dinner sweet for mid-Lent or Mothering Sunday. 'The bowl was returned.' In the colliery district between Durham and Stockton-on-Tees it was served sweet, fruity and spicy with a blob of butter on each bowl (a teacupful of frumenty was considered about the right amount) with the idea that 'the magic properties will cure a nagging wife or grumpy husband'.

It is certainly a very soothing, sustaining and nourishing dish and makes a good alternative to porridge if served plain; unsweetened it would make a nice accompaniment to meat or game instead of potatoes.

The Yorkshire recipe given here is enriched with ingredients similar to those used in a modern Christmas pudding or cake; frumenty is, in fact, the ancestor of both.

750 ml	water, or half milk, half water	1½ pt
250 g	'pearled' wheat (see introduction)	8 oz
100 g	currants	4 oz
50 g	sultanas	2 oz
two or three 15 ml sp	rum or brandy	2 or 3 tbsp
1 litre	milk	2 pt
3	beaten eggs	3
three or four 15 ml sp	honey	3 or 4 tbsp
	lemon peel or bay leaf	
	cinnamon and grated nutmeg	

The day before, bring the water or milk and water to the boil, then pour it over the well-washed wheat.

Put the wheat and liquid into a pot or stoneware jar, with a lid on, and leave it in a warm place such as a low oven, or airing cupboard, to 'cree'. After 24 hours the wheat should have swollen and burst, taking up most of the liquid and turning the rest to a very thick jelly. If it hasn't, cook it gently till it does and allow it to cool again. This is now 'cree'd' wheat, and ready to make into frumenty.

Soak the fruit in the rum or brandy for an hour or so. Add all the ingredients to the wheat in a saucepan. Stir well and cook gently. The frumenty will soon become softer, thicker and creamier. Add extra honey and spice if you like.

Serve it either hot or cold, in little bowls, with cream on top.

Dried fruit tart with wheatmeal pastry *(for 4–6)*

The way to make the delicious, light and crisp wheatmeal pastry for this tart was demonstrated to me by a follower of macrobiological eating named Jordan. Until I ate his wheatmeal pastry I had never really enjoyed the stuff. If you try to make it by conventional methods it not only looks like heavy cardboard but tastes like it as well. Make the filling of the tart first as it needs to cool down before you bake it.

for the filling

50 g	dried apple rings (page 252)	2 oz
50 g	dried apricots	2 oz
50 g	currants	2 oz
350 ml	boiling water	12 fl oz
50 g	brown sugar	2 oz
	nutmeg, cinnamon	
	grated rind of one lemon	

Put all the fruit in a large saucepan. Pour the boiling water over it and cook the fruit over a medium heat for about 15 minutes, or until it is tender. Add the sugar and spices to taste, and the lemon rind, and cook the fruit for another five minutes, by which time all the water should be absorbed. Allow the filling to cool completely before using it.

for the pastry

200 g	wholewheat flour *and*	7 oz
35 g	plain flour *or*	1 oz
250 g	85% wheatmeal flour	8 oz
one 5 ml sp	salt	1 tsp
90 ml	corn oil	$3\frac{1}{2}$ fl oz
160 ml	water	$5\frac{1}{2}$ fl oz

Mix the flours and the salt in a large bowl. Make a well in the centre and add the oil and water. Combine the ingredients (Jordan used three chopsticks but your hands would do) until you have a nice dough. Form it into a ball. Take two sheets of waxed or grease-proof paper and put the pastry between them. Roll it out very gently between the papers until it is as thin as you can manage. Remove the top piece of paper and flip the pastry into an ungreased tart tin measuring 20 cm/8 inches across. Remove the second sheet of paper from the surface of the pastry and trim the edges around the tin. Keep the spare bits for a lattice top to the tart.

Preheat the oven to 190°C/375°F/gas 5. Put the filling into the pastry and decorate the top with a pastry lattice. Bake the tart for 40–45 minutes. Serve it warm with double cream.

The Grant loaf

Doris Grant is one of the sturdiest supporters of the 'Real Bread' Campaign and has for years done all she can to encourage people to make their own health-giving and tasty wholemeal bread.

This recipe is quick to make – the mixing, proving and baking can all be done within an hour and is, as she says, as easy as making a mud pie. The dough requires no kneading and it is only proved (that is, left to rise) once. This makes one loaf weighing just under 1 kg/2 lb.

500 g	wholemeal flour	1 lb
one 5 ml sp	sea salt	1 tsp
15 g	fresh yeast (or half quantity of dried)	½ oz
one 5 ml sp	Barbados sugar, honey or molasses	1 tsp
350 ml	lukewarm water	12 fl oz

Put the flour in a warm bowl (just enough to take off the chill) and add the salt.

Mix the yeast and sugar in a cup with about 75 ml/3 fl oz of the warmed water. In about ten minutes there should be a thick, creamy froth on top. Add this to the flour, then add the rest of the warmed water.

Mix well, either by hand, or with an electric mixer, until the dough leaves the sides of the bowl. It should be sufficiently moist to drop slowly from your hand or from the beater.

No kneading is required after this; merely put the dough straight into a warmed and greased 1 litre/2 pt tin, pressing it well into the corners. Sprinkle the top with some of the flour for decoration. Cover the tin with a cloth or put the tin into a large polythene bag to prove in a warm place while the oven heats up. Set the oven to 200°C/400°F/gas 6.

When the dough has risen to within 1 cm/½ inch of the top of the tin (around the edges), put it in the oven. Bake it for 35 to 40 minutes. Don't let the dough rise too high, or the loaf will be too 'open' and crumbly. If it doesn't rise enough, on the other hand, it will be too 'close' and heavy.

AUTHOR'S NOTE: Some flours absorb more water than others – be prepared to add a little more or less.

A fish dinner in London

Fried whitebait
Mussels in lemon sauce
Scallops and bacon
Poached cod's roes
Crab thermidor

Collared whiting
Jellied eels
Stewed eels and liquor
Sea-bass stuffed with spinach

Buttered spinach
Mushrooms with cream
Hot cucumber

Sylvabella
Fruit salad of preserved figs

Fish from every port in the country is sent to London; Londoners can therefore enjoy an enormous variety of first-class fish. Oyster bars and fish restaurants flourished here until very recently, as popular with people with weak digestions as with businessmen or theatre-goers in a hurry. They were smarter than fish-and-chip bars by a long way, but perhaps because we are so conditioned to meat-eating nowadays, these places have almost all disappeared, or taken to serving meat as well.

I would like to see a revival of fish dinners – the following menu offers some ideas and there are other recipes for fish elsewhere in the book. If you start with a grilled or fried first course, follow it with a poached one, or vice versa, and do likewise if you start with something cold – follow it with a hot dish.

Fried whitebait

Although the Thames is said to be getting cleaner every year you would be amazed if the stretch below Greenwich that traditionally yielded the best catches of whitebait in the 17th century were to do so today. The whitebait dinners given there in July and August were a regular event until early this century. Now, if these tiny little silver fish do reach the shops, they are not from the Thames but from further afield and most often they are frozen. They are, incidentally, a species in their own right, and not, as is often thought, the fry of a larger species.

They make a nice start to a fish dinner: 500 g/ 1 lb is enough for four people. Flour them first, then fry them in deep fat. They only take a couple of minutes to cook, but they should be well drained so that they can be dished up in a rustling heap and served with brown bread and butter and lemon wedges.

Mussels in lemon sauce *(for 4)*

500 g	mussels	1 lb
25 g	butter	1 oz
25 g	flour	1 oz
	juice of a lemon	
one or two 15 ml sp	cream	1–2 tbsp
	cayenne, salt, pepper	
	chopped parsley	
	bread, butter and oil for croûtons	

Clean the mussels (page 100) and put them in a large pan with about 0.5 cm/ ¼ inch of water in it. Cover the pan and cook the mussels over a high heat until they are all open – this takes 3–4 minutes (discard any that don't open). Take each mussel out of its shell and strain the liquor through muslin into a basin.

Make the sauce by melting the butter in a small pan. Stir in the flour and slowly add some of the mussel liquor, stirring all the time until you have a thick creamy sauce. Add the lemon juice and then the cream. Taste for seasoning, adding cayenne and more salt and pepper, if necessary. Add the parsley and let the sauce simmer while you make some finger-sized croûtons. At the last moment, heat the mussels in the sauce, but don't let it boil or they will toughen. Serve the mussels in their sauce in four small bowls, with the croûtons strewn on top.

Scallops and bacon *(for 4)*

This can be made with the large scallops that now seem to be in season all the year round, except for mid-winter, or with the small, sweet queenies from the Isle of Man (and elsewhere), if you are lucky enough to find any that have come to London instead of going to Europe or the USA.

Allow two small scallops or one large one, or three or four queenies, per person. Have them removed from their shells and trimmed, leaving the corals attached.

	scallops (see introduction)	
two or three 15 ml sp	olive oil	2 or 3 tbsp
	juice of a lemon	
	salt, pepper	
	seasoned flour	
1	beaten egg	1
50 g	breadcrumbs	2 oz
2 or 3	finely sliced small bacon rashers	2 or 3
	butter	
1	clove of garlic	1
	finely chopped parsley	
	lemon wedges	

Marinate the scallops for half an hour in a mixture of olive oil, lemon juice, salt and pepper, turning them over from time to time. Drain them, roll them in the seasoned flour, then dip them first in the beaten egg, and then in the breadcrumbs. Leave the coating to set a little while you fry the finely sliced rashers of streaky bacon, cut into strips, in a little butter. Put them aside to keep them warm and sauté a few slivers of garlic in the same fat until they are golden. Add them to the bacon.

Put a little more butter and some olive oil into the frying-pan and cook the scallops gently, until both sides are crisp and golden (about three or four minutes). Put them with the garlic and bacon. Put another little knob of butter into the pan and scatter parsley over the scallops. Give the whole dish a squeeze of lemon and serve it at once, with more lemon cut in wedges and brown bread and butter.

Poached cod's roes

These are usually sold already cooked, or smoked, but they can sometimes be bought uncooked. If so, you can cook them yourself and eat them hot. The already cooked variety are meant to be cut into slices, floured, egged and breadcrumbed, or battered, and fried, which I find rather dry and unappetising. This way is far better – rich, succulent and buttery.

Each roe comes in two lobes, weighing anything from 750 g/1½ lb to 1 kg/2 lb (this is ample for eight people). They are covered in veined skin. Wrap one or both of the lobes in grease-proof paper or foil and simmer the roe gently in salted water for 25–30 minutes (start in cold water and time it from when it boils). It will turn pinkish grey.

As soon as it is cooked take the roe out, remove its skin and cut it into 1 cm/½ inch slices. Serve it at once with melted butter to which you have added a squeeze of lemon juice.

Crab

Crab is one of our most under-esteemed foods. I suspect that the trouble is that it is rather bothersome to prepare – all that fiddly picking away at the shell to get at the meat is more than most people's patience will run to, even if they do know how to go about it. Ready-dressed crab is fine, as long as it has not had time to dry out in the shop, which it does very quickly, and has not been bulked out with breadcrumbs.

Crabs are usually sold ready-cooked, but to cook live ones, see page 79. If you buy a freshly boiled crab it should be heavy and moist (but not watery). Females, with more orange speckling on their broader tails, sometimes contain coral, but males have bigger claws and so more meat.

Crab is in season all the year round. They are at their least good in midsummer when they become less meaty and rather watery.

The simplest way to eat crab is as a salad with lettuce, hard-boiled eggs and a vinaigrette (page 255).

Crab thermidor *(for 6)*

This recipe treats crab like lobster; it would therefore suit lobster just as well. Serve it if you can in small individual crab shells, or in scallop shells, or in individual ramekins. Two crabs weighing 875 g/ 1¾ lb each, in their shells, should be enough.

one 15 ml sp	butter	1 tbsp
one 15 ml sp	finely chopped shallot or onion	1 tbsp
1	small glass of white wine or sherry	1
275 ml	béchamel sauce (page 254), made with half cream and half milk	½ pt
two 15 ml sp	chopped parsley	2 tbsp
	salt, pepper, cayenne	
750 g	fresh crabmeat	1½ lb
50 g	grated cheese	2 oz

Melt the butter in a small pan and sauté the onion. When it softens add the wine and let it reduce to half the quantity by boiling it fast. Stir this reduction into the béchamel sauce. Add the parsley, seasoning and crabmeat and heat it through, but don't let it cook. Add half the grated cheese and stir it in until it melts.

Put the mixture into individual serving dishes, and sprinkle the tops with the remaining cheese. Either put them in an oven (180°C/350°F/gas 4) for 20 minutes, until they are brown on top, or brown them under the grill.

Serve them with sippets of fried bread, toast, or fresh, crisp rolls.

Collared whiting

Whiting were once very much in favour for their delicate flavour and light, digestible flesh. Now this fish has gone out of fashion, possibly because it looks dull; but more likely because few fishmongers can be bothered to enhance its appearance by skinning it for the customer. If you are lucky enough to have a fishmonger who knows how and is willing to skin a whiting, ask him to do it; if not, you will have to do it yourself. The fish is fixed in a collar shape by making it bite its own tail. Serve one small whiting per person as a first course; serve larger ones for a main course.

To skin and collar a whiting, clean out the fish, scraping the inside with the point of a knife but leaving the head on. Scoop out the eyes and cut off the pectoral fins, the bones behind the jaw and the floppy skin under the lower jaw, but leave the lower jaw attached.

Slit the skin on either side of the dorsal fin, from head to tail. Cut through the skin behind the head and gently peel it away, working towards the tail. Be careful not to tear the soft flesh beneath. Skin the head as well. Remove the dorsal and anal fins. Press any ragged bits back into the fish.

Flour it all over and curl it round so that you can put the tail into the mouth; the fish's sharp little teeth will hold it quite firmly.

Dip the floured, collared fish into slightly salted beaten egg, then into fine dry breadcrumbs. Either fry it in lard or butter, turning it over halfway through, or pour melted butter on it and grill it slowly, or 'oven-fry' it – that is to say, bake it with butter in an oven heated to 190°C/375°F/gas 5 for 30 minutes. Serve it with lemon wedges, fried parsley and anchovy sauce (anchovies and butter pounded to a paste with mace and cayenne, and served hot).

AUTHOR'S NOTE: You may find it easier to flour, egg and breadcrumb the fish before curling it up.

Jellied eels *(for 4)*

Eel, pie and mash shops were once common in every working-class part of London. Here, in rather spartan surroundings (oak, pew-like benches and chilly marble-topped tables with thick china plates), hot stewed eels and liquor (parsley sauce) would be dispensed from deep stainless-steel cauldrons at the counter, with small steak pies and mashed potatoes; or you could have jellied eels, served from enamelled basins. All this was to be eaten there or taken home, as were the live eels on show in shallow tanks by the door.

Other attractions in the take-away and convenience-food lines, plus an astounding increase in the price of eels, has meant that there are now hardly any of these eating places left, but good London fishmongers still sell live eels, and most old Cockneys still eat them whenever they can.

The pie shops' jellied eels are rather bland. This recipe makes them a bit more interesting. You have to be nimble with your teeth to get rid of the bones if you eat them the Cockney way. Otherwise, have the eel boned as well as skinned before you cook it.

750 g–1 kg	small, skinned eels (boned, if you prefer)	1½–2 lb
	coarse salt	
275 ml	fish stock (made from the heads and bones; see page 263)	½ pt
1	large glass of white wine or cider	1
	chopped parsley	

Leave the eels in cold salted water for half and hour. Chop them into 2.5 cm/1 inch pieces. Cook them in the wine, a little salt and enough water to cover them for one hour, not above a simmer. Leave them to cool in the liquid, which should set to a jelly (test a little on a plate in the refrigerator). If it does not, drain it off and add a little gelatine. Stir in plenty of chopped parsley, and pour it over the eels. Serve them cold in bowls with the jelly roughly broken up.

AUTHOR'S NOTE: Boned eel, if left in 12 cm/5 inch lengths, can be spread with chopped parsley and a little lemon, then rolled, tied and cooked. Remove the ties before serving.

Stewed eels and liquor *(for 4)*

This is a comforting dish, always accompanied by mashed potatoes, and often served with a steak pie.

750 g–1 kg	skinned and boned eels cut into 5 cm/2 inch pieces	$1\frac{1}{2}$–2 lb
50 g	butter	2 oz
1	chopped medium-sized onion	1
	salt, pepper	
	bay leaf	

for the sauce

25 g	butter	1 oz
25 g	flour	1 oz
275 ml	eel liquor made up to the right quantity with milk (see method)	$\frac{1}{2}$ pt
	plenty of chopped parsley	

Put the pieces of eel into a basin or a stoneware jar, such as you would use for a jugged hare or soused herrings, with the butter, onion, salt, pepper and bay leaf. Stand the container in a pan of deep water and cover it and the pan individually. Cook the eels for $1\frac{1}{2}$ hours from when the water boils, or until the eels are tender. Keep them warm and strain off the liquor that will have formed to make the sauce.

Make a béchamel using the sauce ingredients (page 254), stirring in the parsley at the end. Serve the eels in this sauce.

Sea-bass stuffed with spinach *(for 4)*

As 75 per cent of the sea-bass sold in London are bought by the Chinese, search for this delicious, firm-fleshed fish in areas where the Chinese do their shopping if you can't find it anywhere else. Sea-bass are not allowed to be sold under a weight of 750 g/$1\frac{1}{2}$ lb. Choose the smallest fish you can get for this recipe, allowing one fish for two people. Buy them whole and uncleaned.

2	sea-bass (see introduction)	2
1	finely chopped large onion	1
750 g	finely shredded spinach	1½ lb
	sorrel (optional)	
	salt, pepper	
1	finely sliced large onion	1
1	glass of white wine	1
	butter	
	cream	

Preheat the oven to 200°C/400°F/gas 6. Split the sea-bass down the back, leaving the head and tail on. Take out the spine and clean out the guts. Trim the red parts away from behind the gills. Wash the fish well and stuff it with a cooled mixture of finely chopped sautéed onion and finely shredded sautéed spinach, to which you could add sorrel and should add seasoning. Put the stuffed fish in a buttered gratin dish, belly down, so that it looks like a little canoe, on a bed of finely sliced onion, seasoned and moistened with the wine. Cover the fish with buttered foil.

Bake it for 20 minutes (give larger fish longer). Put the fish onto a serving dish and liquidise or sieve the sliced onion with the cooking juices. Heat it up and add a dash of cream. Pour this sauce over the fish and serve it with boiled new potatoes.

AUTHOR'S NOTE: Salmon trout and grey mullet may also be cooked this way.

Accompaniments for fish

Nearly all vegetables go well with meat but fewer go well with fish.

French beans and peas suit hot fish, and most green salads or plain watercress go with cold fish. See also sorrel sauce (page 257), and watercress puree (page 192). Remember that mayonnaise (page 254) is a good accompaniment to cold poached fish (such as salmon, turbot, sea-bass). If you serve the same fish hot, pass hollandaise (page 256) with them. Other suggestions for vegetables to accompany fish follow.

Buttered spinach

Wash the spinach leaves well and strip out their stems. Cut the leaves across in broad shreds, then cook them gently in a little salted water. Drain them as soon as they are tender, refresh them under the cold tap and press the water out through a colander. Melt plenty of butter in the same pan and heat the spinach in it, making sure the butter is well incorporated.

Mushrooms in cream

Slice the mushrooms and sauté them in plenty of butter with a slice of lemon. As soon as they look darker in colour (after three or four minutes) add salt and pepper. This will make them give out their juice. Sprinkle them with a little flour and stir it in, to absorb the juice. Remove the slice of lemon and pour enough cream over the mushrooms to make plenty of sauce. Heat it through and serve them at once.

Hot cucumber

Cut a good, firm and not too coarsely seeded cucumber into three or four lengths. Peel and quarter them lengthways, then shape each quarter into 'olives' (put the waste pieces into a stock or soup). Par-boil them in salted water for four or five minutes, then cook them very gently with a generous amount of butter and a little chicken stock (page 263). Season, and finish the cucumber with enough spoonfuls of thick cream to make a white coating. Serve it sprinkled with chopped parsley.

A hot puree of shredded, cooked cucumber with a little mint and cream stirred in is also good, as is a plain cucumber salad (see page 255 for a vinaigrette and page 83 for cucumber with yoghourt).

Sylvabella *(for 8)*

This is one of those chocolatey-eggy mousses so much liked at dinner parties in London. It must be prepared the day before the dinner party.

125 g	sugar	5 oz
50 ml	rum	2 fl oz
125 ml	water	$\frac{1}{4}$ pt
12–16	boudoir biscuits	12–16
100 g	chocolate	4 oz
150 g	unsalted butter	6 oz
4	separated eggs	4
	whipped cream (optional)	
	candied violets (optional)	

Line the bottom of a 600 ml/$1\frac{1}{4}$ pt charlotte mould or soufflé dish with a buttered piece of grease-proof paper or foil. Dissolve a little of the sugar in the rum and all but two spoonfuls of the water. Dip the biscuits in it and place them round the sides of the mould – rounded side outwards. Melt the chocolate in the rest of the water and set it aside to cool.

Cream the butter and the rest of the

sugar (reserving a few spoonfuls of sugar for the egg whites) until light and fluffy. Beat in the egg yolks, one at a time. Stir in the chocolate.

Beat the egg whites with the reserved sugar until they are light and fluffy (add the sugar when the whites are nearly stiff). Fold the whites into the chocolate mixture and spoon it into the lined mould. Cut the biscuits level with the top of the mousse.

Cover the mould with foil and set a weight on top of it. (A near-equal sized mould or a flat-bottomed basin filled with water makes a good weight.) Refrigerate it overnight before unmoulding it.

The top of the sylvabella could be decorated with rosettes of whipped cream and candied violets.

Fruit salad of preserved figs

Serve two preserved figs (page 252) per person with peeled and skinned orange segments. Use the juice of another orange to thin down a little the syrup from the figs. You could also add a few slivered almonds.

Preserved figs can also be sliced up and added to fruit salads.

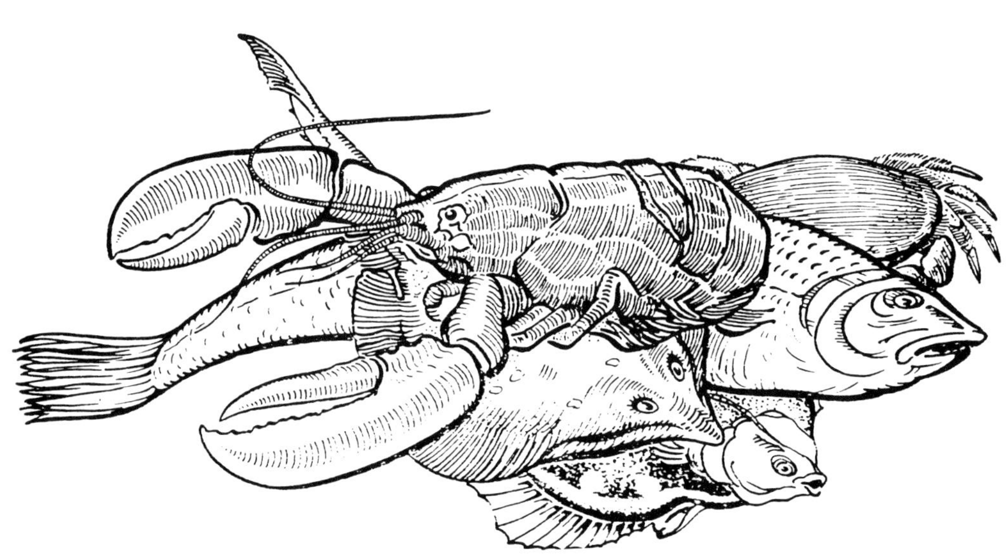

English cheeses

A cheese board with a choice of traditionally made English cheeses is a rare but cheering sight. Cheese-making in the old style all but died out after the war, strangled by rules and regulations governing the selling of milk, the applications of subsidies and the difficulties faced by small farmers in reaching the right markets. Efforts are now made by the Milk Marketing Board to encourage the making of traditional cheeses in large creameries and approved farm dairies, but they don't always compare too well with the originals, some of which are still made in old-fashioned farms for family use. Time, skill and constant attention are the important factors in cheese-making, plus scrupulous attention to where and when the raw material – the milk – is obtained. The main cheeses are described in this section; see also curd cheese on page 113.

Gloucestershire cheese This is a hard cheese with a close, silky texture and a creamy, mellow flavour. It is the colour of pale straw in its natural state, but some dairies like to give it a golden colour with anatto. Double Gloucester resembles a millstone in shape and is about 38 cm/15 inches across and 15 cm/6 inches high. It weighs 12–14 kg/28–30 lb; this is the most usual and best-liked kind. Single Gloucester, rarely made today, is so called because it is half as thick and half as heavy. It is also much whiter, more open in texture, milder, less creamy and takes half as long to mature (only two months). Both have a natural crust or rind, with no wax or cloth coverings. Traditionally, they were made with the milk of Gloucester cows, which has particularly fine fat globules. The cheese used to be made only in the summer. Today, with the exception of Mrs Martell's (page 28), the two cheeses are made anywhere *but* in Gloucestershire and with the milk of every other breed of cow. A local springtime custom, still observed, is 'cheese-rolling'. At some places they roll the cheeses downhill and at others three times round the church. Some say it is simply a ceremony to celebrate the beginning of the cheese-making season, others that it is a relic of a pagan festival worshipping the return of the sun. Either way the cheese needs to be very well matured to withstand the buffeting.

Leicestershire cheese This is the largest English cheese to be made in a wheel shape; it weighs 20 kg/45 lb. It is dyed deep red with anatto and is cloth-covered. When the cloth is removed the rind goes blue; this is done just before the cheese reaches maturity, which is at around three months. It is considered better for eating at six months however, and best at nine. The flavour is similar to Double Gloucester – mellow, clean, nutty and mild; the texture (because the curds are shredded twice) is slightly flaky, close and fine. This cheese sometimes develops blue veins. The rind, which also tastes nutty, can be eaten as well. It is good for toasting.

Cheddar cheese Although cheese called Cheddar is made not only all over England, but also in Ireland, Australia, Canada and New Zealand, it is still made according to traditional methods in Somerset, and several farms will allow visitors to watch the process. Buy it here if you can, for on a small scale the producers can afford to let it mature as it should. The flavour can vary with age, from deep, sweet, mild and 'dewy' to 'mouth-burning', sharp and tangy. Some mature in a few months; others may take a year. It is firm; it should not be crumbly or too dry, and is pale straw in colour, with a pale hard rind. It is made in cylinders which are cloth-wrapped and weigh anything from 2–27 kg/4½–60 lb, though they used to be bigger (the Mendip farmers made a cheese for Queen Victoria's wedding weighing 11 hundred-weight and measuring nine feet across). Cheddar cheese is ideal for a hefty sandwich, with a slice of raw onion and a smidgin of pickle.

Lancashire cheese In Lancashire itself the cheese sold as 'mild' is rather fragile and crumbly, creamy yellow, buttery-tasting and about two months old – it is sold as 'tasty' when it becomes firmer in texture, white, sharper-tasting and is about three to four months old. It is rarely sold older than that. Its fragility may be one reason why it is not popular with cheesemongers further south: they hold that it doesn't travel well. A pity, because it is an excellent cheese. One of the characteristics that sets it apart from other English cheeses is that it is made with day-old as well as new curds. It is only lightly pressed for a day or so at the beginning of its making. It is sold to the shops as 18–20 kg/ 40–45 lb tub-shaped cheeses, with a wrapping of waxed cloth. The rind is a pale, beigy yellow. Lancashire people like to eat their cheese with apple pie and also with blackcurrant jam. There are some farms who add sage to the cheese at Christmas, and some who add walnuts, mustard or pickles. But traditionalists like it plain. It is also excellent for toasting and indeed for all cooking as it doesn't separate.

Cheshire cheese This is another great English cheese and is probably the oldest. It is traditionally made in Cheshire and Shropshire and there are three varieties. *Red Cheshire* is dyed a warm apricot-yellow and is moist, crumbly and salty, but not unlike Cheddar in flavour (this is at its best between one and two months old). *Blue Cheshire* sometimes has the same body colour as Red Cheshire, but with blue veins running through it; this is between two and three months old, is fat and moist and has a creamy, tangy flavour. Lastly, there is *White Cheshire,* which is the natural undyed colour of the cheese; this is also sold at one to two months old. At five months and over it becomes rich and strong. These cheeses are prepared in a similar way to Cheddars, except that they are not hard-pressed and are therefore moister and more crumbly; they also ripen faster and do not keep so long. They are made in 8 and 12 kg/18 and 28 lb waxed cloth-covered cylinders. The great Dr Johnson is said to have loved this cheese – there is a pub round the corner from his house in Fleet Street named the Cheshire Cheese, after either him or it. *Shropshire cheese* is similar to Blue Cheshire, but it is dyed a darker orange.

Stilton cheese Stilton, as is well known, is the name of the town in Huntingdonshire in which a certain Mrs Paulet sold her cheese at the Bell Inn some 300 years ago. This Inn was on the Great North Road and thus the fame of 'Stilton' cheese spread up and down the country, though, in fact, the cheese was made in Melton Mowbray. It is still made there, and at seven nearby dairies. It is the only English cheese to have a trademark and a trade copyright. It is sold subject to strict regulations and can be sold as first grade Stilton only if it has been passed as such by the makers. The cheeses are cylindrical but the crust – which looks like the bark of a tree, tough, wrinkled and hard – is not wrapped once the cheese has matured. It should not be cracked. The colour and texture varies from dairy to dairy. It should not be powdery; this is a sign that the cheese mite is at work. Inside, the cheese is creamy-yellow (not white) and the greeny-blue mould which is injected in the 'blueing' room should be well spread throughout. The texture of the cheese varies from smooth, moist and soft, to firm. The taste is velvety, tangy, unforgettable and it is judged by most cheese-lovers to be the best of all English cheeses. Stilton cheese is not pressed, and is ready to eat at ten weeks old, though it is at its best at 13–14 weeks old. If it is kept cool it can even be eaten at 20 weeks. Good grocers, with an eye on the Christmas trade (which accounts for the greater part of Stilton sales) should manage to do this without spoiling the cheese. The cheeses are made in the traditional weight of 7 kg/16 lb and also as babies of 2.5 kg/5 lb. If the large ones are cut across into halves or thirds they make a handsome sight for the sideboard at Christmas, but arguments often arise as to how they should be cut. The answer is not with a scoop (as in Victorian times) because this exposes too much of the surface to the air, but across, with the aim always to keep the cheese level as it gets lower and lower. To keep it at its best, cover the cut surface with a muslin cloth dampened in brine, and keep it in a cool place.

White Stilton is young, immature and unblued Stilton. It is very damp and soft, white and rather crumbly. It has a delightful, fresh, tangy 'dairy' taste. It is eaten at two to three weeks old and is not often found, or appreciated, outside the area in which it is made. Like Lancashire cheese it is not thought to travel well.

Wensleydale cheese Like Stilton, Wensleydale can be a white or a blue cheese. The difference lies in the shape and wrapping (Wensleydale is a taller, thinner, cloth-wrapped cylinder), the pattern of its blue mould (Wensleydale, because it is pressed, has a 'sunburst' pattern), and its flavour, which is milder and sweeter than Stilton. It also keeps longer. The flavour is largely due to the sweet, herby, high limestone pastures where the cows graze. The art of making cheese was originally brought to Yorkshire by the Norman monks whose ruined abbeys can be seen at several places in this area. They used sheep's milk, but the methods are the same. Today the milk is pooled and the dairies use bacterial starters to obtain the proper fermentation, but there are one or two farmers' wives who still make cheese with unpasteurised milk from their own cows. The white cheese is ready a week to a fortnight from the couple of days it takes to press it. The blue cheese must be kept in a cellar with appropriate moulds, turned daily at first and then every other day until it is ready. Old-fashioned methods included leaving the pressed cheese in brine for three days. The habit of eating cheese with spice cake or apple pie is widespread in the North. There is a cheese-rolling custom here too: 'on Christmas Eve the cheese is taken outside by the youngest person there, and rolled up the front doorstep into the house and right up to the table, where it is placed on a dish and cut.'

Cotherstone cheese This cheese is sold in the village of Cotherstone itself and in the nearby town of Barnard Castle and in Darlington market. It is similar in character to Wensleydale cheese, though it is made only in 1 kg/2 lb or 2.5 kg/5 lb truckles and is usually sold when it is two or three weeks old. It is therefore soft, white, fresh and cream-cheesy tasting, with a soft, pale yellow crust or rind. It is made only between May and the first frosts of winter. Some late spring cheeses are kept until Christmas, when they may develop a blue mould inside; the rind turns pinkish. This matured cheese is much sharper, with more 'snap' than the young cheese. It was once made quite widely in the Border country.

Dorset cheeses In passing, some mention should be made of a cheese that is no longer made in Dorset (except for the farmer's family and friends). This is *Blue Vinney*. It was rather a strange cheese, delicious, but owing its blue mould to the proximity of mouldy harness, old boots and strawy stables. Harness was even put into the milk to infect it with the right moulds. *Dorset Blue* is not the same as Blue Vinney and is not in fact made in Dorset. It is usually a rejected cheese from elsewhere which has been allowed to go blue in Dorset.

Derby cheese is also made in a wheel shape, covered in waxed cloth. It is whiter, moister and smoother than Cheddar, but is similar in character, being hard and mild. It is honey-coloured, ready for eating at six months and maturing to a rich and tangy cheese by nine months. It tends to become over acid with age. It is made in 10, 13 and 15 kg/20, 30 and 35 lb wheels. *Derby Sage* is smaller, between 6 and 8 kg/14 and 18 lb, and made at harvest-time for Christmas. The curd is marbled at an early stage in the cheese's making with the juice of sage leaves mixed with chlorophyll to keep them bright green. The sage is very strongly flavoured. If you are eating a selection of cheeses leave this one till last.

Other flavoured cheeses are made in the same way as Derby Sage, that is to say the curds are mixed with the flavours or other ingredients before the cheese is pressed. One of the most familiar is *Windsor Red*, which is actually made in the Midlands, from Cheddar curds mixed with Sussex elderberry wine – it is sweet and fruity. *Walton cheese* is Cheddar or Stilton curds mixed with walnuts. The outside is coated with chopped walnuts as well. It is moist and crumbly. *Ilchester cheese* is Cheddar curds mixed with beer, chives and sometimes pickle. *Rutland cheese* (made in Nottinghamshire) is Cheddar curds mixed with beer, garlic and parsley. *Sherwood cheese* is Double Gloucester curds mixed with beer and pickle. *Applewood cheese* is Cheddar curds with paprika, and it is also smoked. *Charnwood* is similar. *Cotswold cheese* is Double Gloucester curds mixed with chives and onion.

Store cupboard (preserves and pickles)

Pickles
Pickling vinegar
Eggs
Onions
Red cabbage
Samphire
Walnuts
Piccalilli
Apple chutney

Jellies
Crab-apple
Mint
Sage
Redcurrant
Rowan
Sloe

Other preserves
Lemon curd
Uncooked raspberry preserve
Strawberry jam
Marmalade
Preserved green figs
Dried apple rings

Pickling vinegar

You can make up a good pickling vinegar with any or all of the following spices. It can be used in various ways (see below).

1	seeded, dried chilli	1
one 15 ml sp	black peppercorns	1 tbsp
one 15 ml sp	allspice berries	1 tbsp
1	thick slice of fresh ginger root	1
1	bay leaf	1
1	blade of mace	1
15 g	mustard seeds	$\frac{1}{2}$ oz
	cloves to taste	
	garlic to taste	
1 litre	malt, red or white wine vinegar	2 pt

Bruise the spices and tie them in a muslin bag. Boil them in the vinegar for ten minutes. Allow the vinegar to cool completely, with the bag still in it, before you use it for pickling.

Pickled eggs

Boil a dozen eggs for ten minutes, then leave them to cool in cold water. Shell them when they are cool enough to handle. Pack them in an attractive wide-mouthed glass jar and pour over the pickling vinegar (see previous recipe) to cover them. Seal the jar and store it for at least two weeks before eating the eggs.

Pickled onions

Add 1 kg/2 lb small pickling onions to a large pan of boiling water and let them sit for ten minutes. Drain them, refresh them, and drain again. Peel them and put them into a large bowl.

Dissolve 125 g/4 oz salt in 1 litre/2 pt water and pour the solution over the onions. Weight them down with a large plate and leave them to soften for two days; then rinse them and leave them to drain.

Dissolve 75 g/3 oz sugar in the pickling vinegar (see above). Allow it to cool. Pack the onions in sterilised jars with enough vinegar to cover them. Seal the jars immediately, and store them for at least a week.

Pickled red cabbage

Take a red cabbage, cut off the coarse outer leaves and shred it finely, leaving out the core. Spread it on a large meat dish and salt it well. Leave it for 24 hours.

Next day wash it and put it in jars. Cover it with pickling vinegar (see previous page). Leave it for at least one week before eating it.

Pickled samphire

This goes well with sandwiches and cold meats.

Soak 500 g/1 lb washed samphire sprigs in brine for 24 hours (use 50 g/2 oz salt to 600 ml/1 pt water).

Rinse them well and boil them in pickling vinegar (see previous page) for seven to ten minutes. Keep the samphire tightly sealed with the vinegar for three weeks before eating it.

Pickled walnuts

Walnuts for pickling must be gathered while they are still under-ripe (from about the end of June to mid-July). They must be soft enough for the eye of a needle to pierce them all the way through.

Put 1 kg/2 lb fully grown green walnuts in a large enamel or glass bowl and cover them with brine. Change the brine every two days for ten days (use 150 g/6 oz salt to 1 litre/2 pt water).

Drain the walnuts, rinse them under cold water and place them on a tray in a sunny place, turning them occasionally. When after a day or so the walnuts are dry and black, pack them in sterilised jars, cover with spiced vinegar, and seal them. The walnuts are ready to eat after about two months.

Piccalilli (mustard pickle)

500 g	green tomatoes	1 lb
500 g	green beans	1 lb
500 g	carrots	1 lb
500 g	cauliflower	1 lb
500 g	small pickling onions	1 lb
250 g	salt	8 oz
3 litres	water	6 pt

for the sauce

one 15 ml sp	turmeric	1 tbsp
three 15 ml sp	dry mustard	3 tbsp
three 15 ml sp	dry ginger	3 tbsp
one 5 ml sp	celery seed	1 tsp
100 g	sugar	4 oz
1 litre	malt vinegar	2 pt
25 g	cornflour	1 oz

Wash all the vegetables and peel the onions. Cut the green tomatoes, beans and carrots into bite-sized pieces. Separate the cauliflower into individual florets.

Put the vegetables in a large bowl and add the salt and measured water. Stir the mixture well so that all the vegetables are thoroughly moistened. Weight them down with a large plate and leave them in a cool place (not the refrigerator) overnight. Rinse them thoroughly in cold water and leave them to drain.

Put the spices, sugar and all but a few spoonfuls of vinegar into a large saucepan and mix well. Add the vegetables, bring the mixture to the boil, and simmer it for about 15 minutes or so, just long enough to soften the vegetables without overcooking them. Transfer the vegetables, with a slotted spoon, to warmed, sterilised jars. Dissolve the cornflour in the reserved vinegar and stir it into the cooking liquid. Bring the mixture to the boil and boil it for a few minutes, stirring constantly, until it has thickened.

Pour the sauce over the vegetables and seal the jars immediately.

Store them for at least eight weeks before eating the pickle.

Apple chutney

1 kg	chopped green tomatoes	2 lb
four 15 ml sp	salt	4 tbsp
855 ml	cider vinegar	1½ pt
500 g	soft dark brown sugar	1 lb
2 kg	peeled and chopped cooking apples	4 lb
2	peeled and chopped large onions	2
500 g	sultanas	1 lb
two 15 ml sp	ground ginger	2 tbsp
	large bunch of finely chopped mint	
two 15 ml sp	flour	2 tbsp
two 15 ml sp	water	2 tbsp

Mix the tomatoes with half the salt and leave them for two hours to drain in a colander, then mix them with the vinegar, the rest of the salt, and the sugar.

Put all the ingredients (except the flour and water) in a saucepan and cook over a low heat until the apples and onions are tender – about an hour.

Mix the flour and water to a paste and add it to the chutney, mixing well.

Simmer it for 15 minutes more, then put it into sterilised, warm jars and seal.

Keep this chutney for at least four months before eating it.

Crab-apple jelly

3 kg	crab-apples	6 lb
	preserving sugar (see method)	
	rose geranium leaves (optional)	

Wash and quarter the apples, and cut out any bad bits. Put the fruit in a preserving pan and add just enough water to cover it.

Cook it, uncovered, until the fruit is soft (about an hour).

Pour the apples and the juice into a jelly bag hung over a bowl and allow the juices to drip overnight.

Measure the juice and return it to the preserving pan. Add 500 g/1 lb of sugar for every 575 ml/1 pt of liquid. Bring the mixture to the boil, stirring constantly to dissolve the sugar. Allow the mixture to boil, without stirring, until it reaches the setting point. Remove the pan from the heat and skim off any scum before potting it in sterilised jars.

AUTHOR'S NOTE: If you like, you can put a geranium leaf on the bottom of very small pots before adding the jelly. This improves the flavour and makes an attractive-looking jar for sales at fêtes. Crab-apple jelly can be eaten as a sweet, with cream or curd cheese (page 113). This recipe will also work for ordinary apples and quinces.

Mint jelly

Proceed as for the crab-apple jelly (with either cooking or crab-apples), adding a large bunch of fresh mint while cooking the apples.

Once the jelly has reached the setting point and has been skimmed, add finely chopped fresh mint and a dash of green colouring before putting it into pots. Mint jelly is a good alternative to mint sauce. Eat it with roast lamb.

For a natural green dye, finely chop a handful of fresh spinach. Put the spinach in a piece of muslin and wring the juices out into a small saucepan. Set the pan over a moderate heat and cook until all the juices evaporate. This leaves a green residue which can be used as a colouring agent. (It really works!)

Sage jelly

Follow the recipe for mint jelly, substituting sage for mint. Leave out the green colouring. Sage jelly is good with duck, goose and roast pork.

Redcurrant jelly

This jelly accompanies roast lamb or game. It is also useful in pâtisserie.

3 kg	redcurrants	5 lb
	preserving sugar (see method)	

Put the redcurrants as they are (with stalks and leaves) into a preserving pan, with enough water to cover the base. Bring the fruit to the boil, crushing it with the back of a wooden spoon. Reduce the heat and simmer the fruit until it is soft and the currants have rendered their juice (about ten minutes).

Tip the fruit and juices into a jelly bag hung over a bowl. Allow the juice to drip overnight.

Measure the amount of liquid, and pour it back into the preserving pan. For every 575 ml/1 pt of juice, add 500 g/1 lb of sugar. Bring the mixture to the boil, stirring to dissolve the sugar. Allow the mixture to boil, without stirring, until it reaches the setting point (about five minutes).

Remove the pan from the heat and skim off any scum before potting the jelly in sterilised pots. Seal immediately and store when cool.

AUTHOR'S NOTE: For a spiced version of this jelly, add four cloves and a 5 cm/2 inch cinnamon stick to the redcurrants for the initial cooking, and add approximately 450 ml/16 fl oz of malt vinegar to the juice of every 3 kg/6 lb of redcurrants at the final cooking stage with the sugar.

Rowan jelly

This jelly has a lovely orangey-red colour and an astringent taste that makes it particularly good with sweet, gamey meat, as well as with roast lamb. Rowans grow on hilly moorland in their natural state, but because of their pretty clusters of berries they are also grown in suburban streets, parks and gardens, as ornamental trees.

To make rowan jelly, gather equal quantities of rowanberries and crab-apples, boil them together till both are tender, then strain the juice and proceed as for crab-apple jelly (page 248).

AUTHOR'S NOTE: *Sloe jelly* can be made in exactly the same way (sloes are the small purple-blue fruits that grow on blackthorn bushes in the autumn). This jelly is even more astringent than rowan jelly and a beautiful dark red.

Lemon curd

4	egg yolks	4
100 g	caster sugar	4 oz
	grated rind and juice of 2 lemons	
50 g	cubed, unsalted butter	2 oz

In the top of a double-boiler (or in a bowl in a bain-marie) mix the egg yolks and sugar. Beat the mixture over simmering water until it is light and airy. Add the lemon juice, rind and butter and stir continuously, until the butter has melted and the mixture is thick enough to coat the back of a wooden spoon; do not let it boil or the eggs will curdle. Transfer the curd to clean jars and seal them if it is not to be used immediately.

An uncooked raspberry preserve

This is a marvellous preserve: because it is not cooked it tastes exactly like fresh raspberries; it even 'sets' to a fairly solid consistency, but it keeps for at least a month or two in the refrigerator. A better plan is to put some in small quantities in the freezer. It is a delicious filling for sponge cakes.

To make the preserve, choose ripe, dry raspberries. Pick them over, weigh them and put them in a china bowl in a very low oven (about 110°C/225°F/gas $\frac{1}{4}$). Put an equal weight of sugar in another bowl in the oven. After about half an hour the raspberries should be oozing a little juice. Take them and the sugar out of the oven and mash the two together with a wooden spoon, until all the sugar is dissolved (about five minutes). Put the preserve into small clean jars and seal them as usual.

Strawberry jam

Strawberries make one of the best jams in the world, but are low in pectin, which is what makes jam set. Gooseberries and redcurrants which ripen at the same time are high in pectin, so instead of putting commercial pectin in my strawberry jam, I use the juice from these fruits.

2.5 kg	small, clean, ripe strawberries	5 lb
3 kg	preserving sugar	6 lb
575 ml	strained juice from 750 g/ 1½ lb cooked redcurrants or gooseberries	1 pt

Put the strawberries and sugar in a preserving pan (a copper one will keep the colour of the fruit best).

Stir until the sugar is dissolved, then add the juice. Boil until setting point is reached.

Allow to cool a little, then stir before putting the jam into clean, hot jars. This should ensure that the fruit is evenly distributed in the jelly. Seal when the pots are cold.

Seville orange marmalade

The making of this marmalade is spread over three days, which sounds like a long time, but it is worth doing as the fruit is softened by soaking, rather than by cooking, and this produces a higher yield than a more conventionally made marmalade.

2.5 kg	Seville oranges	5 lb
2	lemons	2
4.5 litres	water	9 pt
5 kg	sugar	10 lb

First day: wash and halve the oranges and lemons. Squeeze the juice from the fruit and put the pips in a muslin bag to soak in ½ litre/ 1 pt of the water. Cut the rinds into shreds, coarse or fine as you like. Put them to soak in the rest of the water and leave them until the next day.

Second day: put the soaked pips, still in their bag, to cook with their soaking water, with the rest of the peel and water. Use a deep pan with a lid to cook the pips and peel (not a preserving pan, as you wish to conserve the liquid at this stage). Simmer the pan for about 1–1½ hours, or until the peel is tender. Leave the cooked peel and the pips to soak in their liquid for another 24 hours.

Third day: put the peel and liquid into a large preserving pan, but throw away the pips after straining the juice from them. Bring the pan to the boil and then add the sugar, stirring until it is all dissolved. Cook the marmalade fast until it sets, then pot and seal it in the usual way.

AUTHOR'S NOTE: This marmalade can be made with ordinary oranges as well, in which case raise the proportion of lemons to oranges, or it will be too sweet.

Preserved green figs

Figs grow well in the South of England and ripen too, but there are always a few unripe ones left at the end of the season, almost fully grown, but hard and green. These can be preserved in syrup and used whenever you want them for a delicious fruit salad. (The lime referred to in the ingredients is the same as garden lime.)

3 kg	unripe figs	6 lb
	lime water made from 2 cups of slaked lime to 4 litres/1 gallon of water	
3 kg	sugar	6 lb
3 litres	water	6 pt
2	unpeeled, sliced lemons	2
	slices of preserved ginger	

Wipe the figs with a damp cloth and make a small criss-cross cut at the fat end of the fruit (wear gloves as the juice is like latex and is painful if you get it in a cut). Steep the figs in the lime water for 18–24 hours. Wash them in several rinses of water and drain them well.

Make a syrup with the sugar and water and when it is boiling fast add the figs. Boil them gently until the fruit is transparent. The syrup will foam less at this point and become a little thicker. This stage will take 3–4 hours.

Add the lemon slices about halfway through the cooking, and add the ginger slices half an hour before the end.

Pack the preserve into wide-necked jars and seal them.

AUTHOR'S NOTE: To make crystallised figs, prolong the cooking after the stage when the syrup is fairly thick and the figs are still resistant. You can dry them at room temperature on paper-covered trays.

Dried apple rings

If you have a glut of apples this is a very simple way to preserve them.

Peel the apples and remove the cores. Slice them into rings about 0.5 cm/¼ inch thick and drop them into water which has been very lightly brined (about 15 g/½ oz salt per 575 ml/1 pt water) – this will keep them white while they dry. Leave them in the water for about 15 minutes, then take them out, pat them dry on a towel and spread them out on wire racks. Put them in a very low oven (110°C/225°F/gas ¼) or over a radiator to dry. After about 24 hours they should be dry enough to store. They will shrink considerably.

To reconstitute them, simmer them in a little water for a few minutes; you can also eat them as they are.

Sauces

Mayonnaise
Béchamel
Vinaigrette
Uncooked tomato

Hollandaise
Maltese
Béarnaise
Sorrel
Hot tomato

Horseradish
Hot chilli mint

Apple
Laver
Bread
Onion
Sharp

Cream sauce for fish

Camperdown
Chocolate
Orange or lemon
Egg custard

Mayonnaise

An egg yolk can only emulsify with a certain amount of oil; for this reason I give the following chart:

yolks	olive or sunflower oil	wine vinegar or lemon juice	yield
2	225 ml/8 fl oz	two 15 ml sp/2 tbsp	350 ml/12 fl oz
3	350 ml/12 fl oz	three 15 ml sp/3 tbsp	450 ml/16 fl oz
4	450 ml/16 fl oz	four 15 ml sp/4 tbsp	575 ml/1 pt
6	675 ml/1¼ pt	six 15 ml sp/6 tbsp	850 ml/1½ pt

Beat the egg yolks together using a balloon whisk rather than a wooden spoon. Add the vinegar or lemon juice, a little salt and, if you like, a little prepared mustard (this is an excellent emulsifying agent). Whisk in the oil, a few drops at a time, and continue until all the oil is used up. The mixture should be very thick and creamy. Check the seasoning. If it curdles you have probably added the oil too fast. Start again in a new bowl with another egg yolk, and add the curdled mixture to it *very slowly.*

AUTHOR'S NOTE: This makes a thick sauce. To make a thinner mayonnaise (e.g. for egg mayonnaise), dilute it by whisking in a little milk.

Béchamel sauce (white sauce)

There should be no lumps in a béchamel sauce if the flour and butter are well amalgamated first, and if the liquid is added really slowly; it helps if the liquid is warm. Whisking brings a gloss to the sauce. As long as the roux is properly cooked the sauce will not taste floury. This recipe makes 275 ml/½ pt of medium-thick sauce. Use more liquid for a runnier sauce. Use half cream and half milk for a richer sauce. The cooking liquids from fish, meat or vegetables may also be used.

	bay leaf (optional)	
275 ml	milk	½ pt
25 g	butter	1 oz
25 g	flour	1 oz
	salt, pepper	

Steep the milk with a bay leaf if you have time. Heat the milk to just below boiling point. Melt the butter in another pan; stir in the flour and let both cook together gently for a minute or two. Add the milk, a little at a time, beating it in vigorously with a wooden spoon or small wire whisk. When all the milk is incorporated you should have a smooth, thickish sauce. Let it cook for at least five minutes, and stir it occasionally; to stop a skin forming on top cover it with a butter paper.

Vinaigrette or French dressing

This is the simplest dressing for salads. Use the best olive oil if you can; otherwise sunflower oil or walnut oil are very good. Use wine vinegar or lemon juice, and season it with a little salt, freshly ground black pepper, and sugar and French mustard, if you like. I also add chopped fresh green herbs to a tomato salad or a green salad.

Mix the seasonings with the vinegar first, then beat in the oil – the proportion of oil to vinegar is usually three to one.

Uncooked tomato sauce *(makes about 275 ml / 1/2 pt)*

The tomatoes for this sauce need to be sweet, richly red, ripe and meaty, as close as possible to the kind grown in the Mediterranean (Marmande or Italian plum are good in England: I have had fine crops, in a fine summer, from plants growing out of doors). The kind to avoid are the pale, tasteless, watery tomatoes grown commercially in hot-houses.

Use this sauce for cold vegetable or fish terrines or the cheese pudding on page 111.

500 g	ripe tomatoes	1 lb
	salt, pepper	
	a little sugar	
one 15 ml sp	wine or cider vinegar	1 tbsp
three 15 ml sp	olive oil	3 tbsp
	chopped parsley	
	chopped chervil or tarragon (optional)	
	garlic (optional)	

Loosen the skins of the tomatoes by covering them with boiling water for a minute or two, then refreshing them under a tap. Peel them. Cut them in half and scoop out all the pips with a teaspoon.

Chop them quite finely but be sure you don't make a mush.

Put the tomatoes in a bowl and add salt, pepper and sugar, then with either a wooden spoon or a balloon whisk carefully incorporate the oil and vinegar as if you were making mayonnaise.

Check the seasoning.

AUTHOR'S NOTE: If you want to increase the strength of this sauce you can blend in a little tinned tomato puree.

Hollandaise sauce *(makes about 225 ml/8 fl oz)*

3	egg yolks	3
one 15 ml sp	cold water	1 tbsp
250 g	cold, cubed unsalted butter	8 oz
	salt, white pepper	
	cayenne pepper	
one 5 ml sp	strained lemon juice	1 tsp

Put the egg yolks and cold water into the top half of a double-boiler and beat them over simmering water until they are smooth. Whisk a few cubes of butter into the yolks and when the butter has been absorbed, continue adding more, whisking until all the butter has been used. Beat the sauce until it becomes thick and creamy. Season it with the peppers and salt to taste, and add the lemon juice.

AUTHOR'S NOTE: To avoid curdling, cook this sauce more off the heat than over it. For a *Maltese sauce*, pare the rind from half an orange. Cut it into julienne strips, blanch them in boiling water for 1–2 minutes, and drain them. Squeeze the juice from the half-orange. Add the strips and juice to 225 ml/8 fl oz of hollandaise sauce. Check the seasonings.

Béarnaise sauce *(makes about 225 ml/8 fl oz)*

This goes with barbecued or grilled meat or fish.

three 15 ml sp	white wine vinegar	3 tbsp
three 15 ml sp	white wine	3 tbsp
3	finely chopped shallots	3
two 15 ml sp	chopped fresh tarragon	2 tbsp
3	egg yolks	3
175 g	melted butter	6 oz
	salt, white pepper, cayenne pepper	

Boil the vinegar, wine, shallots, and half the chopped tarragon until it has reduced to two 15 ml sp/2 tbsp. Allow it to cool, and add the egg yolks. Whisk the yolks and liquid together until light and well blended. Set the pan over a low heat or over a double-boiler, and whisk constantly until the mixture is creamy.

Take the pan off the heat, and whisk in the tepid melted butter, a little at a time. When all the butter has been added, strain the sauce, pressing well to extract the flavours from the shallots and tarragon. Add the rest of the tarragon leaves and season the sauce with the salt, white and cayenne peppers.

Sorrel sauce *(makes 275 ml / ½ pt)*

This is a creamy sauce with a lemony tang; it is beautiful for fish or with an omelette (see page 221).

1	finely chopped shallot	1
	butter	
100 g	trimmed, shredded sorrel	4 oz
225 ml	double cream	8 fl oz
	salt, pepper	

Sauté the shallot in a little butter until it is soft. Add the sorrel and cook it, stirring all the time, for a few minutes. It will soften completely. Add the cream and cook the mixture until the cream has thickened slightly (about ten minutes). Season the sauce to taste and serve it hot.

Hot tomato sauce *(makes about 275 ml / ½ pt)*

This is a suitable sauce for the hot cheese pudding on page 111, stuffed fennel bulbs (page 224), and many other dishes.

750 g	coarsely chopped ripe or tinned tomatoes	1½ lb
1	bay leaf	1
1	sprig of dried thyme	1
	salt	
1	sliced onion	1
1	crushed garlic clove	1
	pepper	
	sugar (see below)	
	finely chopped parsley	

Put the tomatoes, bay leaf, thyme and a pinch of salt in a saucepan. Add the onion and garlic. Bring the mixture to the boil, crushing the tomatoes with the back of a wooden spoon, and cook, uncovered, over a medium heat for about ten minutes or until the tomatoes have become a pulp. Strain the mixture into a bowl, to get rid of the skin, pips and herbs. Return the puree to the saucepan and continue to cook it, uncovered, over a low heat until the sauce is reduced to the desired consistency. Check the seasonings, and sweeten the sauce with a pinch of sugar if you are using tinned tomatoes, and add the parsley.

Horseradish sauces

For a mild horseradish sauce, grate into a quantity of whipped cream as much fresh horseradish as it will hold. Stir in a little salt and sugar and a little freshly made mustard to make it the palest yellow.

For a strong horseradish sauce, mix grated horseradish with white wine vinegar; add a little single cream and a crushed clove of garlic, with lots of freshly ground black pepper and a little salt.

Hot chilli mint sauce *(makes just over 125 ml / 1/4 pt)*

This goes well with grilled spiced chicken or lamb kebabs.

125 ml	plain yoghourt	¼ pt
1	crushed clove of garlic	1
one 15 ml sp	finely chopped green pepper	1 tbsp
1	finely chopped, de-seeded, fresh green chilli	1
one 5 ml sp	grated fresh ginger	1 tsp
2 or 3	finely chopped spring onions	2 or 3
	lime juice	
	sugar	
	salt	
	several finely chopped mint leaves	

Blend everything well, adding the chopped mint last.

Apple sauce *(makes about 275 ml / 1/2 pt)*

This is to accompany roast pork, duck and goose.

500 g	peeled and chopped cooking apples	1 lb
	a very little water	
40 g	sugar	1½ oz
25 g	butter	1 oz

Put all the ingredients in a saucepan and simmer them, covered, until the apples have become a mush. Beat it with a fork, taste for sweetness (but it should be quite sharp) and serve it hot.

Laver sauce

This is the traditional sauce to eat with roast Welsh or Devon lamb; it is made from the prepared seaweed known as laverbread (see page 17). Put 500 g/ 1 lb laverbread into a saucepan and with a wooden spoon stir 75 g/ 3 oz butter into it over a high heat. Add lemon or orange juice to taste. Seville oranges are particularly good with it; so, according to Florence White in *Good Things in England*, is tangerine juice. Serve it very hot.

Bread sauce *(makes 425 ml/¾ pt)*

1	large onion, stuck with cloves	1
275 ml	milk	½ pt
	salt, pepper	
	bay leaf	
2–3	crustless slices of stale bread	2–3
75 ml	cream	3 fl oz
	a pinch of nutmeg	

Simmer the onion with the milk, seasoning and bay leaf in a covered pan for about an hour, by which time it should be quite soft. Cut the bread into cubes. Remove the onion and bay leaf from the milk. Pick out the cloves and chop the onion. Put it, with the bread, back in the milk and roughly mash it up with a fork. Add the cream and nutmeg, taste the sauce for seasoning, heat it up gently and serve it hot. It goes with roast chicken, turkey, grouse or pheasant.

Onion sauce *(makes about 425 ml/¾ pt)*

This goes well with hot roast lamb, or boiled mutton. (It is also excellent on sliced hard-boiled eggs, for the dish known as oeufs à la tripe.)

4	peeled and roughly cut, medium-sized onions	4
275 ml	milk	½ pt
	(or half milk and half water)	
	salt, bay leaf	
15 g	butter	½ oz
15 g	flour	½ oz
	pepper	
	nutmeg	

Cook the onions in the milk, with salt to taste and a bay leaf, until the onions are tender. This can take as much as an hour. Strain off the liquid and reserve it, remove the bay leaf and chop the onions finely. Make a roux with the flour and butter, and add the liquid to make a thickish sauce. Stir in the chopped onions. Taste for seasoning adding pepper and nutmeg, if not more salt. Serve it hot.

Sharp sauce for boiled beef *(makes 575 ml/1 pt)*

425 ml	thin béchamel (page 254) made with milk and some of the liquid from the meat	¾ pt
one or two 15 ml sp	horseradish (freshly grated if possible)	1–2 tbsp
one 15 ml sp	chopped capers	1 tbsp
one 15 ml sp	freshly made mustard	1 tbsp
one 15 ml sp	chopped gherkins with a little of their pickle juice (see below)	1 tbsp
	lots of freshly ground black pepper	

Check that the pickle juice contains no acetic acid because this will spoil the flavour of the sauce. If it does, substitute ordinary wine vinegar instead. Mix all the ingredients together and heat the sauce through, but don't let it boil.

Cream sauce for fish *(makes 575 ml/1 pt)*

This sauce is for hot fish terrines or plainly poached white fish.

575 ml	fish fumet (fish stock, page 263)	1 pt
275 ml	double cream	½ pt
	cayenne pepper	
	salt, pepper	

Reduce the fumet by half, by boiling it over a high heat. Add the cream and continue to reduce the sauce, over a lower heat, until it is very thick. Add a touch of cayenne, taste for seasoning. Serve the sauce hot.

AUTHOR'S NOTE: Just before serving you can enrich the sauce by whisking in a couple of large spoonfuls of butter. Do this off the heat, or it will go oily.

Camperdown sauce

This is a featherlight, fudgy sauce, to serve with Christmas pudding and mince pies. It comes from Clare College, Cambridge.

250 g	caster sugar	8 oz
250 g	unsalted butter	8 oz
50 ml	dry sherry	2 fl oz
one 15 ml sp	brandy	1 tbsp
	a pinch of nutmeg	

Cream the butter and sugar together for far longer than it takes to make them fluffy – until the mixture is almost running. (This is not difficult if you have a food processor.) Add the sherry and brandy very carefully so that they are well incorporated. Add the nutmeg and there is your sauce. Serve it chilled.

Chocolate sauce *(makes about 425 ml/¾ pt)*

This is a sauce for vanilla ice-cream (page 268), poached pears, or chocolate cake when it is eaten as a pudding.

250 g	plain chocolate	8 oz
225 ml	water	8 fl oz
three 15 ml sp	double cream	3 tbsp
25 g	unsalted butter	1 oz

Melt the chocolate with the water in a heavy pan over a low heat. Stir continuously with a wooden spoon and when the mixture is smooth remove the pan from the heat. Beat in the cream and butter. Serve the sauce either hot or cold.

AUTHOR'S NOTE: The sauce can be flavoured to taste with vanilla, brandy or a liqueur.

Orange or lemon sauce *(makes 275 ml/½ pt)*

This is for serving with steamed or baked puddings.

100 g	sugar	4 oz
275 ml	water	½ pt
	pinch of salt	
four 5 ml sp	cornflour	4 tsp
	rind and juice of one lemon or orange	
25 g	diced butter	1 oz

Mix the sugar, water, salt and cornflour together and when the mixture is smooth add the finely grated rind. Cook it over a low heat, until the mixture thickens. Cook for a minute more, then, away from the heat, whisk in the juice and the butter, a piece at a time. Serve this hot or cold.

Egg custard *(makes just over 575 ml/1 pt)*

This makes a runny, pouring custard – for a custard to go solid it needs more eggs, and has to be baked.

2	eggs	2
one 15 ml sp	sugar (or vanilla sugar, page 268)	1 tbsp
575 ml	hot milk	1 pt

Beat the eggs and sugar together in a basin. Stir a little of the hot milk onto the mixture, then add the rest. Put the custard into the top half of a double-boiler and stir it with a wooden spoon until it is just thick enough for your finger to leave a track when drawn across the spoon. Don't cook it more or it may curdle (it will thicken a little as it cools). Serve it hot or cold.

Basic recipes

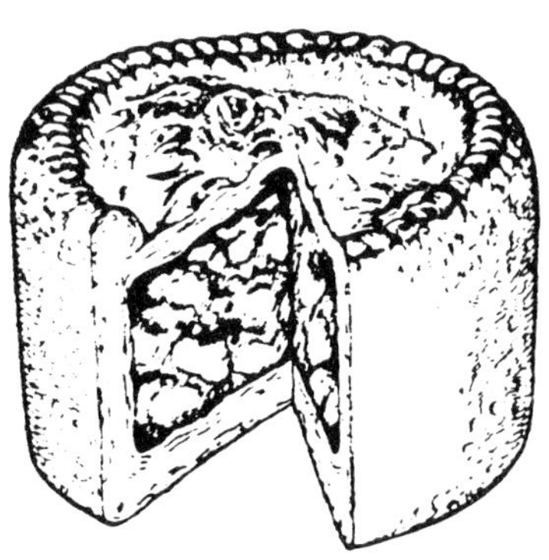

Chicken stock *(makes about 4 litres/8 pt)*

The best stock is made from uncooked bones, but the carcases of cooked birds are a good second best, and should never be thrown away before they have been made use of in stock. Vegetable trimmings, as long as they are not of a starchy or cabbagey nature, may also be used, for instance watercress stems, mushroom stems, celery leaves, tomato pips and skins. Onion skins give stock a good colour. A good chicken stock sets to a light jelly when it is cold.

1 kg	veal bones or pigs' trotters (optional)	2 lb
1.5 kg	chicken backs, pinions, necks, feet and giblets	3 lb
4 litres	water	8 pt
2	carrots	2
2	onions stuck with 1 or 2 cloves	2
1	clove of garlic (optional)	1
	bunch of parsley, thyme and bay leaf (bouquet garni)	

Put the bones in a large pan and cover them with the water. Bring them slowly to the boil and skim off the foam and scum that float to the top.

Add the vegetables and herbs. Partly cover the pan and let it simmer for at least two or three hours, skimming occasionally. Strain it into a bowl and when it is cool lift off any fat that may have set on the top. This stock will keep for two or three days in the fridge; it can also be frozen. To increase its flavour, reduce it by fast boiling – this also increases the strength of the jelly. Do not season it therefore until you want to use it.

Fish fumet (fish stock)

500 g (approx.)	fish heads, bones and trimmings, washed and broken up	1 lb (approx.)
1	onion, carrot and leek, all sliced thinly	1
1	thinly sliced lemon	1
	parsley sprigs	
	a very little salt	

Cover the ingredients with water and bring them to the boil, removing the scum as it rises to the top until there is no more. Simmer the fumet for about 30 minutes. Strain it through a damp cloth. This liquid can now be used as a base for a fish sauce, or as a poaching medium for fish. It can be kept for two days in the fridge; it can also be frozen.

Clarified butter

Use this to seal potted meats or fish, or as a sauce for asparagus.

When butter is heated until it liquefies, a milky residue sinks to the bottom of the pan. The clear, yellow liquid above it must be separated from it to become clarified butter. This burns less easily than unclarified butter, as it is the milky particles in ordinary butter which burn first.

To clarify butter, heat it in a saucepan over a low heat until it has just melted. Skim any froth from the surface. Pour the melted butter into a bowl, leaving the milky residue behind in the pan. The residue may be used to enrich soups or sauces.

Plain yoghourt *(makes about 1 litre/2 pt)*

1 litre	milk	2 pt
three 15 ml sp	plain commercial yoghourt	3 tbsp

Pour the milk into a heavy enamelled casserole with a tight-fitting lid. Heat the milk slowly until it reaches a temperature of 70°C/175°F on a sugar thermometer, or until small bubbles form around the edge. Stir constantly to prevent any skin forming on the top. Remove the casserole from the heat and, stirring occasionally, allow the milk to cool to 45°C/110°F. Stir in the commercial yoghourt and cover it. Place the casserole in a warm draught-free spot, and leave it undisturbed for about six hours. At this point the yoghourt should be set and fairly firm. Chill the yoghourt for about four hours before using it.

Note about types of milk: all types of milk can be used to make yoghourt – milk from sheep, goats, or cows – whether pasteurised, non-pasteurised, sterilised or homogenised, and even evaporated, powdered, or skimmed.

Shortcrust pastry

100 g	150 g	250 g	500 g	flour	4 oz	6 oz	8 oz	1 lb
½ sp*	¾ sp*	1 sp*	2 sp*	salt	½ tsp	¾ tsp	1 tsp	2 tsp
50 g	75 g	125 g	250 g	fat†	2 oz	3 oz	4 oz	8 oz
1–2 sp**	2–3 sp**	3–4 sp**	4–5 sp**	water	1–2 tbsp	2–3 tbsp	3–4 tbsp	4–5 tbsp
150 g	275 g	375 g	750 g	yield	6 oz	9 oz	12 oz	1½ lb

*5 ml spoons **15 ml spoons †'fat' means butter, margarine or lard

Sift the flour and salt together into a large mixing bowl. Cut the cold fat into small pieces and add them to the flour. Rub the fat and flour together using your fingers until all the fat is incorporated and the mixture resembles coarse breadcrumbs. Alternatively, cut the fat into the flour with two knives to achieve the same coarse texture.

Sprinkle the water over the dough and gather the mixture together with one hand; if the dough feels too crumbly add more water until the dough begins to cohere. Don't add too much or it will make the pastry tough. Press the dough into a ball. Wrap it in plastic film and chill it for at least 15 minutes. The resting makes the dough easier to work with.

AUTHOR'S NOTE: To make *suet pastry (suet crust)*, follow the method above, but use suet for the fat, and self-raising flour instead of plain flour.

Rich shortcrust pastry

100 g	150 g	250 g	500 g	flour	4 oz	6 oz	8 oz	1 lb
¼ sp*	¼ sp*	½ sp*	1 sp*	salt	¼ tsp	¼ tsp	½ tsp	1 tsp
50 g	75 g	125 g	250 g	sugar	2 oz	3 oz	4 oz	8 oz
50 g	75 g	125 g	250 g	butter	2 oz	3 oz	4 oz	8 oz
1	1	2	4	egg yolks	1	1	2	4
250 g	375 g	500 g	1 kg	yield	8 oz	12 oz	1 lb	2 lb

*5 ml spoons

Follow the method for making ordinary shortcrust pastry, adding the sugar to the flour at the beginning, and the egg yolks instead of the water.

Pre-baking pastry (baking blind)

Only shortcrust and rich shortcrust pastry can be baked blind.

Preheat the oven to 200°C/400°F/gas 6. Line each tin with a square of grease-proof paper or foil slightly larger than the area. Press the paper against the base and sides of the pastry. Pour enough uncooked rice or beans onto the paper lining to fill it to a depth of 1 cm/½ inch. Bake tartlet tins for 6–10 minutes, and a pie dish for about 15 minutes. Lift out the papers and rice/beans and continue baking for five minutes (tartlets) or 15 minutes (pie-dish) or until the pastry is lightly brown. Remove the cases from the oven and allow them to cool before filling them.

AUTHOR'S NOTE: The paper and rice or beans may be stored for subsequent use.

Rough-puff pastry

Make a basic shortcrust pastry (page 264) using half or up to the same weight of butter to flour (cut the butter in bigger pieces). The quantity of salt and water will be approximately the same as for shortcrust.

Lightly sprinkle the work surface with flour and roll the pastry into a rectangle three times as long as it is wide. Fold the pastry into three layers by bringing the bottom third up to the centre and the top layer down over the other two thicknesses. Seal the edge of the last flap with the rolling pin and give the pastry a quarter turn (90°), bringing the closed seam to your left side. Roll the pastry out again and repeat the folding and sealing process. Wrap the pastry and refrigerate it for 15–30 minutes. Roll, fold and chill twice more (a total of four times) before rolling it out for use.

Puff pastry

250 g	375 g	500 g	flour	8 oz	12 oz	1 lb
1 sp*	1½ sp*	2 sp*	salt	1 tsp	1½ tsp	2 tsp
250 g	375 g	500 g	butter	8 oz	12 oz	1 lb
125 ml	200 ml	275 ml	water	¼ pt	7 fl oz	½ pt
500 g	750 g	1 kg	yield	1 lb	1½ lb	2 lb

*5 ml spoons

Sift the flour and salt into a bowl. Rub a few spoonfuls of butter into the flour with your fingertips. Add just enough cold water to bind the ingredients, and work them into a ball. Wrap the dough in plastic film and chill it for 15 minutes.

Place the remaining butter between two sheets of grease-proof paper, and with a rolling pin, flatten it into a 15 cm/6 inch square. Refrigerate it until ready for use.

Place the pastry on a floured board and roll it into a 30 cm/12 inch square. Place the square of butter diagonally in the centre of the pastry and fold the corners of the pastry over the butter so that they meet in the centre. Turn the package over and flatten it slightly with the rolling pin. Roll the pastry out to a rectangle 18–20 cm/7–8 inches wide and 45–47 cm/18–20 inches long. Fold the pastry into three by bringing the bottom third up to the centre and the top layer down over the two thicknesses. Seal the edge of the last flap with the rolling pin and give the pastry a quarter turn (90°) bringing the closed seam to your left side. Roll the pastry again into a rectangle, and fold it again into thirds. Wrap the pastry in plastic film and chill it for 15–30 minutes. Roll and fold the pastry twice more, refrigerate and repeat, giving it six turns in all. After a final refrigeration it is ready for use.

Hot water crust

250 g	500 g	flour	8 oz	1 lb
½ sp*	1 sp*	salt	½ tsp	1 tsp
75 g	150 g	suet or lard	3 oz	6 oz
75 ml	175 ml	water	3 fl oz	6 fl oz
375 g	750 g	yield (approx.)	12 oz	1½ lb

*5 ml spoons

Because this pastry needs to be worked while it is still warm and pliable it is not advisable to make it with less than 250 g/ 8 oz of flour (or more than 500 g/1 lb). If you require a larger amount, make it in several batches.

Sift the flour and salt into a large bowl. Put the suet or lard and water in a saucepan and bring it to the boil. Pour this into the flour and mix the ingredients together quickly, kneading until a smooth dough is formed. Let the pastry rest in a warm place for about 30 minutes. While the pastry is still warm and easy to handle, roll it out on a floured board or shape it with your hands for a raised pie.

750 g/1½ lb pastry will be enough for one large raised pie mould (2–2½ litre/4 pt) or thirty 5–7.5 cm/2–3 inch individual pies.

Choux pastry

100 ml	125 ml	225 ml	water	4 fl oz	¼ pt	8 fl oz
50 g	75 g	100 g	butter	2 oz	3 oz	4 oz
65 g	80 g	100 g	flour	2½ oz	3¼ oz	4 oz
½ sp*	½ sp*	¾ sp*	salt	½ tsp	½ tsp	¾ tsp
2	3	4	eggs	2	3	4
(fifteen) 8 cm balls	(twenty) 8 cm balls	(twenty-five) 8 cm balls	yield (approx.)	(fifteen) 3 inch balls	(twenty) 3 inch balls	(twenty-five) 3 inch balls

*5 ml spoons

Heat the water and butter in a saucepan. Sieve the flour and salt onto a sheet of grease-proof paper.

When the butter has melted, bring the water to the boil. Turn off the heat, and slide all of the flour off the paper into the water. Beat the mixture vigorously for a few seconds, or until it is smooth and pulls away from the pan to form a ball. Beat the dough for about one minute over a low heat to dry the mixture.

With a wooden spoon, beat the eggs into the dough, one by one, beating thoroughly after each addition. The mixture should be very shiny and capable of sliding off a spoon.

For best results, use the dough immediately.

Pastry cream *(makes about 500 ml / 1 pt)*

This is a basic filling for fruit tarts (also known as crème pâtissière).

500 ml	milk	1 pt
5 cm	piece of vanilla pod	2 inch
125 g	sugar	4 oz
6	egg yolks	6
50 g	flour	2 oz

Heat the milk with the vanilla pod to boiling point, stirring frequently to prevent it sticking to the bottom of the pan. Remove the vanilla pod. (Dry it and keep it to use again.)

Meanwhile mix the sugar and egg yolks together with a whisk until the mixture is very thick and creamy in colour. Gradually whisk in the flour. Pour the hot milk in a thin stream into the egg mixture, stirring continuously.

Turn the pastry cream mixture into the pan and cook it over a medium heat until it comes to the boil, still stirring. Allow the mixture to boil for a few minutes before removing the pan from the heat.

The cream is ready as soon as it is cool; it may be refrigerated for a few days.

AUTHOR'S NOTE: You can also make *vanilla sugar* to use for recipes like this by storing the pod in sugar in a tightly stoppered jar; top up with fresh sugar as you use it.

Vanilla ice-cream *(makes about 850 ml / 1½ pt)*

575 ml	milk	1 pt
1	vanilla pod	1
6	egg yolks	6
150 g	sugar	6 oz
275 ml	lightly whipped double cream	½ pt

Put the milk and vanilla pod in a pan and bring it to the boil, stirring occasionally. When the milk reaches the boil, remove the pan from the heat and let the pod infuse in it for at least ten minutes.

Beat the egg yolks and sugar together until they are light and thick. Reheat the milk again until it reaches the boil, and gradually whisk it into the egg and sugar mixture. Pour the mixture into the pan and heat it, stirring constantly, until it thickens. Don't let it boil or it will curdle.

Strain the custard into a large bowl, remove the vanilla pod, and cool the custard. Pour the cooled custard into a churn freezer, sorbetière or ice-tray. When the ice-cream is partly set, add the whipped cream and continue freezing until it is set (about 20–30 minutes in all, or a little longer in an ice-tray).

AUTHOR'S NOTE: For fruit-flavoured ice-creams, blend in 850 ml / 1½ pt of sweetened fruit puree to the custard just before freezing.

Bibliography

Eliza Acton, *The People's Cookery Book* 35th edition (Simpkin, Marshall, Hamilton, Kent)
Elisabeth Ayrton, *The Cookery of England* (Andre Deutsch) 1974
Virginia Bath, *Lady Bath's Longleat Kitchen and Recipe Book* (Longleat House) 1980
Mrs Beeton, *Everyday Cookery* (Ward, Lock) 1859
Lizzie Boyd (editor), *British Cookery* (Croom Helm) 1976
Mary Chafin, *Original Country Recipes* (Macmillan) 1979
Elizabeth David, *English Bread and Yeast Cookery* (Allen Lane) 1977
Elizabeth David, *Spices, Salt and Aromatics in the English Kitchen* (Penguin) 1970
Alan Davidson, *North Atlantic Seafood* (Macmillan) 1979
All Hallows School Ditchingham, *Still in the Kitchen* 1980
Joyce Douglas, *Old Pendle Recipes, Old Derbyshire Recipes and Customs* (Hendon Publishing) 1976
Helen Edden, *County Recipes of Old England* (Country Life) 1929
Jane Grigson, *English Food* (Macmillan) 1974
Dorothy Hartley, *Food in England* (Macdonald) 1954
Marie Hartley and Joan Ingilby, *Life and Tradition in the Yorkshire Dales* (J. M. Dent & Sons) 1968
Peggy Howey, *The Geordie Cook Book* (Frank Graham) 1971
Peggy Hutchinson, *Old English Cookery Book* (W. Foulsham)
Law's *Grocer's Manual* 3rd edition (William Clowes & Son) 1930
Mrs C. F. Leyel and Miss Olga Hartley, *The Gentle Art of Cookery* (Chatto & Windus) 1925
Elizabeth Lothian (compiler), *Devonshire Flavour* (David & Charles) 1971
David Mabey, *In Search of Food* (Macdonald & Jane's) 1978
Pamela Michael, *All Good Things Around Us* (Benn) 1980
Countess Morphy, *English Recipes* (Herbert Joseph)
Pamela Pascoe, *Cousin Jennie's Cornish Cook Book* (Lovenek Press) 1976
Mary Ann Pike, *Town and Country Fare and Fable* (David & Charles) 1978
Joan Poulson, *Old Yorkshire Recipes, Old Cotswold Recipes, Old Thames Valley Recipes* (Hendon Publishing) 1977
Charles Herman Senn, *Senn's Century Cookery Book* (Ward, Lock) 1923
Margaret Slack, *Yorkshire Fare* (Dalesman Books) 1979
Dorothy Gladys Spicer, *From an English Oven* (The Women's Press, New York) 1948
Elizabeth Watts, *Fish and How to Cook it* (Fredrick Warne) 1866
Florence White, *Good Things in England* (Jonathan Cape) 1932
C. Anne Wilson, *Food and Drink in Britain* (Constable) 1973
Women's Institute Cookery Books from Devonshire, Hampshire, Cornwall, Cumberland, Westmorland, Herefordshire, Northumberland, Lancashire, Gloucestershire, Shropshire, Yorkshire, Lincolnshire & Northamptonshire, Somerset, Berkshire, Buckinghamshire
Marcus Woodward, *The Mistress of Stantons Farm* (Heath Cranton) 1938
Carol Wright, *Yorkshire, The Cotswolds, The West Country* (3 books) in the series *Cassell's Country Cookbooks* (Cassell) 1975

Index